D0915127

PRAISE FOR
INCONVENIENT MEMORIES

"The events of the June Fourth massacre in Beijing in 1989 were so extreme that descriptions of it tend to be emotional. Anna Wang's story of her decision to stay in China, hoping that economic development would bring democracy (while many of her friends were emigrating) helps us to understand what an ordinary Chinese citizen's life felt beneath all the sturm und drang of the times. The color of her descriptions brings to life a period of Chinese history that large forces seem to have pressed colorless."

Perry Link
University of California, Riverside

"Not only is this book extraordinarily entertaining and well written, it is likely to become a significant source of China's history and development as personally witnessed by an insightful participant. Highly recommended on many levels."

Grady Harp
Amazon Top 50 Hall of Fame Reviewer

"Anna Wang brings us a powerful and deeply personal story of China, human rights, and the progression of a people."

Pamela Gossiaux
Author and Speaker

"A deeply intimate and revealing portrait of 'real life' inside China before and after the climactic Tiananmen Square Incident. Writer Anna Wang confronts her own country's history with eyes wide open. Breathtaking!"

John J. Kelly
Detroit Free Press

"By just about any measure, author Anna Wang has crafted a remarkable and intense memoir that deftly blends her own personal life with pre- and post-events related to the 1989 Tiananmen Square protests led by students in Beijing, China. Wang also raises the question of whether citizenship in countries such as Canada and the USA will further immigrants' feeling of belonging to the host nation or will there always be a deep yearning for their motherland?"

Norm Goldman
Publisher & Editor
BookPleasures.com

"Wang's memoir artfully braids the personal and the political. This is an analytically rigorous and exceedingly thoughtful autobiography that intelligently chronicles the grand forces of history without ever forgetting about the lives caught up in them. A moving recollection of personal and national identity."

Kirkus Reviews

"In writing this fascinatingly informative book, the author Anna Wang has fulfilled a promise she made to herself long after the terrible massacre at Tiananmen Square, Beijing, a promise to tell her story about the events at that time."

Midwest Book Review

Inconvenient Memories

A Personal Account of the Tiananmen Square Incident
and China Before and After

Anna Wang

PURPLE PEGASUS
INCORPORATED

Published by Purple Pegasus Publishing Inc.,
26632 Towne Centre Drive, Suite 300.,
Foothill Ranch, CA 92610
USA

For more information about Purple Pegasus Publishing visit purple-pegasus.com

First published in 2019

Library of Congress Catalog Card Number: 2019901552
ISBN: 978-0-9966405-7-2
Editing by Paul Christian
Cover design by L1graphics

To those who do not want to forget

Peking University student on hunger strike, May 1989.

Photo by Yanguang He

CONTENTS

Inconvenient Memories

A Personal Account of the Tiananmen Square Incident
and China Before and After

Anna Wang

Prologue

An Unexamined Life

On October 20, 2014, around 9am, I drove Cambie Bridge over False Creek on my way to the Immigration, Refugees and Citizenship office at 1148 Hornby Street, Vancouver, Canada.

For years, I'd mistaken False Creek for an actual creek. The night before, while researching my route, I came to realize it was an inlet of salty water from the Pacific. I continued browsing and found that in 2010, a gray whale made a surprise visit to False Creek. For two days and nights, adults and children gathered at the inlet's banks, watching the whale lash the water back and forth. The audience cheered it on, thinking it was having fun. Marine biologists disagreed, and the lost creature was escorted back to the ocean by a police boat, a coast guard inflatable, and a small flotilla of kayaks.

I had been a Vancouver resident since 2007, and studied at Vancouver Film School in 2010. Every day on my way to school, I crossed False Creek. Why hadn't I really noticed the unusual agitation on its banks? It must've happened on a weekend, right? Then I came up with a better explanation. When homework piled up, I took the Canada Line to school so I could read. The train tunneled deep below the creek. I sat wrapped up in my reading while the gray whale floundered over my head.

The picture pained me. How many more things had I missed during those years?

I was born in China in 1966. From 1984 to 1988, I studied literature at Peking University. In 1999, I became a writer-in-residence at the Beijing Writers' Association. My husband Lao Xin was a literature student in college just as I was but in the '90s, he quit his job at a magazine and opened a fast food restaurant. After a while, he opened a second. By the time we first applied to immigrate to Canada in 2003, he and his partners had about 50 locations in northern China. Until then, his business seemed to me like a side job. I was certain that someday he would go back to his desk and get on with writing, but the company expanded effortlessly. By the time our immigration application was granted in 2006, my husband had become a full-fledged businessman. He could never go back to being a journalist.

In October, 2006, I, Lao Xin, our six-year-old daughter and our one-year-old son took a seven-day trip to Canada. At Vancouver International Airport, we had our immigration papers stamped, which meant we were qualified to become permanent residents of Canada. Our next step would be replanting ourselves in Canadian soil.

But we needed to figure out how to support ourselves in Canada before moving there. We spent the week visiting as many restaurants as possible, studying them for Lao Xin's next business adventure.

One day, on the edge of Stanley Park, we stumbled across Fish House. My guide-book said it was a difficult spot to get a reservation. I spoke to the hostess, showed her my *Lonely Planet*. It was a shameless card I'd learned to play during previous sojourns to Western countries, as if saying that "we're tourists. It's a one in a lifetime chance." She offered to add a table in the corner. The table faced the kitchen, so every plate of food coming out passed us. To Lao Xin, this was the best seat in the house. Each time that kitchen door swung open, he craned his neck to see everything he could before it shut again.

On the plane ride back to Beijing, Lao Xin told me that he was afraid he couldn't establish a successful business in Canada. China was still developing, and anyone with more than average talent or dedication could achieve unparalleled success. In Canada, with its long, stable, economic growth, even starting a single restaurant was a different story.

"I agree," I said. "So?"

So, Lao Xin became a "tai kong ren" to support our future lives as immigrants.

"Tai kong ren" means "astronaut" in English. It refers to a relationship in which the husband (occasionally the wife) splits their time between China and North America, while the spouse sets up in North America to look after the children and see them through school. The term "astronaut family" began appearing in conversation as early as the 1980s. Now it was our turn.

In March 2007, I moved to Canada with our daughter. Our son joined us in 2008. Lao Xin stayed in China, flying in to visit us once in a while. It wasn't an ideal arrangement, but countless families lived like that. If they all survived, so could we.

Five years went by. According to Canadian law, a permanent resident is obliged to live in Canada for two years out of a five-year period. Lao Xin stayed in Canada for only 250 days out of those first five years; 480 days short of keeping his permanent resident status.

In the interest of maintaining his "Maple Card"—the equivalent of the American "Green Card", the kids and I moved back to China at the end of 2011, three months after we became Canadian citizens. Canadian law allows the days a permanent resident spends living outside of Canada as physically present in Canada if they are accompanying a Canadian citizen. As long as we lived with Lao Xin, he could keep his permanent resident status. But even so, his Maple Card needed to be renewed, and on the morning of a fresh autumn day, we drove over False Creek on our way to the Immigration, Refugees and Citizenship office.

At the door of the office, Lao Xin handed his red notice to a security guard. Red meant final. Anyone with a red notice who didn't claim their Maple Card might as well never come back.

We waited under a giant red maple leaf painted on a snow-white wall. We were close to station one, where a female officer sat sorting papers. She called out a long name, and a heavily bearded man pushed an elderly Southeast Asian woman in a wheelchair toward the station. I overheard the officer tell the man, "You're so lucky!" The man mumbled something to his wife, presumably translating the officer's remark.

Part of my tension melted away. Glancing sideways, I noticed Lao Xin was busy with his iPhone. I nudged him and pointed to station one. "I hope we'll be interviewed by her," I said.

The old couple left, and another name was called. A middle-aged Asian man and his son came forward. The officer's tone and attitude changed dramatically, as if she expected the pair to pull some tricks.

The man was from mainland China and was a tai kong ren. Most "astronauts" have problems fulfilling their residency obligations. Some go as far as faking their records to renew their Maple Cards.

The officer asked the man why every time he went back to China, he went via the US. He replied that by flying from Seattle, he could shop at the Tulalip outlets on his way to the airport. His friends and relatives always gave him a long list of things to bring home.

"Home," the officer emphasized ominously. "You meant China is your home?"

"Yeah." The man nodded casually.

The officer asked for the man's passport, and carefully checked every page. Then she asked him to sign something. When he handed the document back, she coldly pushed an envelope across the desk and raised her voice. "If you really want to call Canada home…"

She's accusing them. I thought.

Lao Xin's application was all in order. All the officer needed to do was to verify my record. I reached into my bag to make sure I had my passport. It was there, with every page of it showing every time I entered and left China.

Still, I felt deeply uneasy.

If you guys really want to call Canada home...

The interviewee at station three got up and hastily left the hall. She looked Chinese. Her face was beet-red with a mix of dejection and anger. My heart was taut. I prayed Lao Xin wouldn't be called to station three but that's just what happened.

The officer at station three had an Asian face. In my experience, Asian officers, especially Chinese, were the hardest to deal with.

He pointed to the chair and asked Lao Xin to sit, before asking who I was. I stood there, replying that I was his wife. He responded that any questions he might ask needed to be directly translated to Lao Xin, and I was only to interpret his answers. At no time was I to answer for him.

"Sure," I said. It was a fair request, but I didn't remember these instructions being given to the old man pushing his wife's wheelchair.

The officer turned to his computer and typed a few commands before staring at the screen for what seemed an eternity. Then he turned to Lao Xin, and said angrily, "You think you're pretty smart, eh? You're using our system."

Lao Xin was dumbfounded. I was too shocked to translate.

He turned to me and repeated: "You're using our system."

"How?"

"Immigration law does allow for permanent residents living like this, but this law is intended for Canadian citizens who have no choice but to leave the country for work or other official reasons. In other words, of the two of you," he pointed to me, "you should be the party working in China." Then he pointed to Lao Xin, "He should be the one staying home to cook and watch the kids."

This was the law in Canada? How had I not paid closer attention when filling out the forms? Was it possible that there were tiny, light-colored letters printed in the corner that had escaped my attention?

Honestly, we never meant to use the system. We thought we'd followed an honest path to getting Lao Xin a new card. But now, I saw we weren't entirely innocent.

I fished around in my bag for a piece of paper on which was written: Alberta Slim / Beautiful British Columbia / Canada, My Homeland. I handed it to the confused interviewer.

"I've been searching for this song for years," I told him. "Today I got here too early and went to a second-hand bookstore to kill time. I asked the owner about the song. Based on the lyrics I remembered, he recognized it! He didn't have it in stock, but he wrote down all the information I'd need to find it online. The artist is Alberta Slim, the album is *Canada, My Homeland*, and the song is 'Beautiful British Columbia.'"

His glare softened. "I know you're a Canadian citizen. I don't have any doubts about you. But does your husband have any intention of actually living in Canada? What are you going to do if he can't live here for 730 days in the next five years?"

I hesitated.

He smiled. "Here's what I think he should do: He should give up his PR status right now and stop wasting his time."

I shook off my qualms and relayed the officer's question to Lao Xin. I watched him nervously. It was one of the most suspenseful moments of my life.

Without missing a beat, Lao Xin answered, "I want to live in Canada."

He sounded so convincing, even I believed him for a moment.

We left the building with Lao Xin's Maple Card in hand. We finally had it, but a sadness still lingered. For the past three years, I'd always claimed my move back to Beijing was just to help Lao Xin get his card renewed. Now he had it. Was I going to move back to Vancouver?

The whale knew the inlet wasn't its home. It was just lost. I thought of Beijing and Vancouver.

Sould I just keep wandering?

The middle-aged woman from station three was standing in the parking lot hungrily smoking a cigarette. On seeing us, she forced a smile.

"That's discrimination back there!" she shouted. "That's racism! Hostility against us Chinese is getting worse and worse!"

I faked a sympathetic smile before I hastily made my way to the car.

I'd also noticed that Chinese immigrants seemed to be targeted. Each time a Chinese person approached the counter, the officer's expression would turn suspicious.

I didn't entirely blame them. It was an undisputable fact that many Chinese immigrants took advantage of both countries. If the officer at station three was also Chinese, he'd have even more reason to be critical of us. He must feel that new immigrants like us averaged down the morality of all Chinese-Canadians, and made him look bad by proxy.

I may have done unethical things, but at least I had the hindsight guilt, feeling ashamed of myself. However, in the eyes of the immigration officer, that woman and I were the same. Perhaps my manipulation of the law had been cleverer, but I definitely wasn't a better person. We were both just suspicious Chinese immigrants.

A wave of depression settled over me.

In China, a person would never survive if they took the time to contemplate. People have to act on instinct and grab ahold of whatever they can. Otherwise they lose out. It was in this sense that I'd never thought of myself as a typical Chinese. My tendency to reflect both set me apart and put me at a disadvantage. That was my primary reason for emigrating. But now, it seemed I was no different from anyone else.

At what point did I start acting like this?

My memory carried me all the way back to 1989.

In 1989, I was working at a Japanese company, the camera manufacturer, Canon. Right after the crackdown on the Tiananmen Protests, in order to ensure the success of Canon's new Chinese manufacturing plant, my Japanese boss cozied up to a "princeling" by the last name of Yang. (A princeling is a decendant of a prominent and influential senior communist offical in the People's Republic of China.) When I found out Mr. Yang was the nephew of Yang Baibing: secretary-general of the Military Committee, and commander-in-chief of the Tiananmen massacre, I wanted to splash a cup of scalding tea in his face. But I also knew I shouldn't. After the Tiananmen massacre, the Western world imposed harsh economic sanctions on China. Japan was the only country that maintained its economic ties with us. As a result, Canon was one of the few foreign companies still hiring Chinese employees.

To make peace with myself, I worked hard to convince myself that I was unimportant. In the grand scheme of things, I was nothing. This was a role that didn't require a heart or soul to play. If I lost this job, there were a thousand people waiting to take my place. Why should I care?

In the end, I calmly brought Mr. Yang a cup of tea.

That incident was just the beginning. From then on, I made a habit of dissociating myself from what I did. Still, part of me longed to be an upright person. I told myself again and again that my character was seperate from my actions, but it wasn't always easy to tell them apart. I must have lost myself somewhere along the way.

I'd heard the old saying that "the unexamined life is not worth living," but I'd never truly wanted to examine my life until that moment.

On October 20, 2014, as I drove Cambie Bridge over False Creek once again, the clouds began to part. It was time to examine my life and my choices. Why did I immigrate in the first place? Why do I lack commitment to the places I choose to live?

It was time to reflect on my past.

I at least owe my children an explanation.

Chapter 1

Become Hundreds of Thousands of Words

My grandmother was born in 1920, my mother in 1941, and I, in 1966. Nine months after my birth, my mother left me with her mother until I was twelve. At the time, my grandmother was younger than I am now, but I always remember her as an old woman.

She had liberation-feet: bound feet that had been freed halfway through the process. China's brutal tradition of foot-binding goes back to around 1000 CE. After the last emperor's abdication in 1912, the New Culture Movement called for modern thinking based on Western standards. Even so, centuries of tradition didn't go away overnight.

My grandmother grew up in the countryside, where old habits die particularly hard. When she turned four, more than a decade after the collapse of the last dynasty, her parents decided to stick to the ways they knew well. Foot-binding was a notoriously long process. The big toe is left intact while the other four are broken and tied inward. It usually takes over two years to stall the growth of the broken toes. When girls with newly bound feet tried to walk, it was like stepping on needles.

Knowing that her bandages would only be wrapped tighter by the day, my grandmother cried her heart out every night, eventually crippling her parents' resolve. Plus, they'd caught wind of the New Culture Movement, so when my grandmother stealthily took her bandages off in the middle of the night, they pretended not to notice. Thus, my grandmother and countless others born in the '20s walked on liberation-feet. They were bigger than bound feet but smaller than if they'd been allowed to grow naturally.

By the time I was a child, fully bound feet were incredibly rare. Liberation-feet were as close I could get to seeing the inhumanity of the old society firsthand.

The official narrative of the Communist Party of China is that Chinese history is divided into two eras by the founding of the People's Republic in 1949. The two periods are referred to as the new society and the old society or heaven and hell. Each era had its own set of descriptors, totally opposite in meaning. For example, when looking at my grandmother's deformed feet, I thought of words like reactionary, oppressive, dark, ugly, and ignorant. That's probably why I always remember her as old.

However, even though we lived in a progressive, liberating, bright, beautiful, and ethical time, my grandmother had to make her own shoes. The new society and its planned economy didn't care about small minorities. Shoes on the market were either the wrong size or the wrong shape. Since the arches of the feet were broken, liberation-feet retained a pronounced curve when healed. As time went on, the number of living liberated women dwindled, making it harder for the centralized government to notice or care.

In my memory, my grandmother did needlework almost all day long, except when she cooked or did other chores. She not only made her own shoes, but made them for her friends in the same predicament. Demand was huge in this corner of the world, though not large enough in the eye of the State to have any resources allocated.

My grandmother usually did her needlework in bed. She'd sit surrounded by cloth, patterns, scissors, needles, thread, and a screwdriver.

Eighty percent of the work was making the soles. She'd glue three layers of cloth together with wheat paste, then cut the layered material the pattern required. Finally, she'd place three layers of cut material in a stack and sew them together. That's where the screwdriver came in. A needle can't penetrate nine layers of cloth and paste. She used the screwdriver to pierce a sole, then she'd pass the needle through after. Though she was an experienced hand, she'd occasionally stab her palm with the screwdriver, or prick her finger with the needle. The blood oozing from her wounds made me think shoemaking was incredibly dangerous.

My grandmother hurt herself usually while telling me about problems in her marriage.

My grandfather was an accountant at China's Ministry of Railways. There were thousands of positions for accountants at the ministry. Some pushed papers at the head office and went home each night to their families. My grandfather went out to the frontier, living side-by-side with the workers who laid the tracks. He visited his wife twice a year for two weeks each time.

One day, a man was seated at the table when I came home for dinner.

"Good evening, grandfather," I said politely. He nodded and mumbled a few syllables. I eyed him curiously. He didn't even look at me.

A few days later, that distant and fearsome man was gone.

I was relieved to be rid of the intruder, but my grandmother didn't feel the same.

"He never liked me. He only married me because I was delivered to his doorstep," she would say, totally out of blue.

"What are you talking about, grandma?" I asked absent-mindedly while playing with a broken paper clip I'd found in the garden outside our building.

"Never mind...Ouch!"

I raised my head and saw my grandmother's eyebrows furrowed in a painful frown. I knew she'd hurt herself again, but why?

In the 1960s in China, children were not allowed to ask questions. Parents trusted that everything would explain itself as kids grew up. They were right. I constructed the puzzle piece by piece without even knowing it.

My grandmother was born in a small village in Hebei province—a hundred kilometers (60 miles) from Beijing. She was engaged to my grandfather when she was seven and my grandfather was ten, as was common then. Three years later, my grandmother's mother passed away, and her father remarried. Soon after, her stepmother produced a son.

My grandmother had earned a living as a seamstress since the age of 13. Her clever hands led to word of mouth, which attracted orders from rich families. It was customary for young girls to make intricately embroidered quilts or pillowcases for matchmakers to bring to her future husband to showcase her ingenuity, talent and virtue. But not all girls had a knack for arts and crafts, so rich girls got away with purchasing ready-made dowry from poor but capable girls like my grandmother.

Since she contributed to household revenue, she lived peacefully, ignored by her stepmother. She came back into the picture in 1937 when Japan occupied northern China, terrorizing, murdering, and raping. The value of a seventeen-year-old girl from the countryside was at great risk of depreciation. Her father had decided to marry her off quickly.

Her arranged husband was from a neighboring village, from a family her parents knew, but weren't close with. He'd gone to Beijing to study at a school of railway management, and maybe he'd completely forgotten about his fiancée, or found himself a city girl with naturally developed feet. But as far as my great-grandfather was concerned, none of that was legitimate reason not to carry out the contract the two families signed ten years earlier.

He hired a horse-drawn cart, ordered his daughter to sit in it, and they hit the road, without even informing the poor boy beforehand.

Though shocked, the young man was faithful to his commitment, and they were married immediately. But their relationship didn't go well. After having two daughters, my grandfather, then in his late twenties, decided to seek solace out in the wide world.

He never liked me because I was delivered to his doorstep.

My little heart stirred, and my little brain went to work. Wasn't I delivered to her doorstep? While she rambled, my mind wandered out of the room and down the long, dark hallway.

She lived in a six-story apartment building above a convenience store. By the 1970s, a horse-drawn cart could still get all the way to the center of Beijing to deliver fresh produce before dawn. On hot summer nights, we slept with the windows open, and sometimes I could hear the clacking of hooves on the pavement directly below my window. The horse neighed softly as the driver threw melons to the shop owner. Occasionally we heard the crisp crack of splitting rinds, as melons missed their mark and smashed on the ground. My grandmother would go downstairs first thing in the morning to buy the cracked melons at a deep discount.

The words "delivered," "cracked," and "cheap" danced around in my mind. I wondered how I was delivered to my grandmother.

Was I a bundle left on her doorstep?

Was I driven by horse like the melons at the store?

I couldn't help but touch my head with my hand, feeling for that imaginary crack.

The six-story, gray apartment building my grandmother lived in had originally served as the offices of the Ministry of Machine Industry. It was designed and financed by a sister city in the Soviet Union back in the '50s. It looked magnificent from the outside. Each floor measured far higher than we normally saw in China. People often joked that Russians must be colossal compared to us Chinese.

For those of us living there, the lofty ceilings evoked the feeling of living in a well, making you wonder if you were the proverbial frog. (The "Frog in the Well" is a fable by ancient Chinese philosopher Zhuang Zi. When a frog lives in a well, it can only see a small hole far above. Metaphorically it portrays a person with no ambitions who is unfortunately satisfied with life.)

The building was a stack of L-shaped floors with rooms arranged along a hall running the length of its form. Each floor had a men's and women's restrooms, and a shared washroom. The restrooms were on the vertical part of the "L", and the shared washroom was on the horizontal. Those who lived next to the washroom had the advantage of setting up their portable stoves and utensils in it. Those who lived far from the washroom had to squeeze their mobile kitchens into their doorways. We didn't have gas lines back then and used portable stoves powered by propane tanks.

In theory, everyone had an equal right to use the washroom as their kitchen, but in China, "public" can be a very subjective term. In this case its limit was dictated by proximity. Those without eminent domain over the washroom chose to wash their vegetables, rinse their rice, and do any other prep in the nearest restroom. In our case, this was the men's room. Why not the women's? Our janitor was a woman, and the sink there had become her storage. It was always full of mops, sponges, and bottles of chemicals that shouldn't be anywhere near your dinner.

There were two stalls inside the men's room and a wash basin on the opposite side of the stalls. When the women entered the makeshift kitchen, they would first duck their heads to check for feet in either stall. If the stalls were occupied, the women would cough to let the men know they had company. The men would cough twice in reply. Despite the men granting their taciturn approval, women going in the men's room felt a bit wrong, and they would hurry to get their work done as quickly as possible. The whole operation was quiet and secretive. The public washroom was equally tight and unkempt, but at least let you feel honest doing your business there.

My grandmother's unit was right at the tip of the vertical part of the L shape. Therefore, of everyone on that floor, she had no claim to the public washroom. But I didn't care. I couldn't bear to be reduced to this vulgar way of life. Every time, I'd venture into the public washroom, navigate the whirlwind of pots and pans, steam and fire, and do my work with caution and pride.

So, from a very young age, I earned myself a reputation for thinking myself better than everyone else.

I started first grade in 1973 when I was seven. By second grade, I could recognize about five hundred characters, and started reading my first books. They were full of words I couldn't understand, but that did nothing to dissuade me.

There was a bookstore near my grandparents' house that would lend out novels for two pennies a day. Beginning in second grade, I tore through their inventory. I read one book a day, no matter the length, because I had to economize.

My grandmother wasn't one for reading. She didn't let me turn the lights on after dark. Every afternoon, I could be seen with a book virtually sewn to my hand, my eyes racing the sun across each page. As the room grew dark, I would unconsciously move to the stronger light by the window to squeeze out every last bit of daylight before I was finally defeated.

Out the window was a towering chimney rising to meet the sky. The chimney was in the courtyard of Beijing Children's Hospital. It was probably used by the kitchens, laundry, and to provide boiling water for drinking or sterilization. But if you asked the kids in my neighborhood, anyone would tell you, in a stage whisper, that it was a crematorium for dead children.

Childhood was a time of darkness. Children used ghost stories to fill the void and spice things up. Once I was able to read, I felt I was way above all that childish whispering and screaming, and ghost stories no longer had a hold on me. Still, that chimney worked on my nerves.

When it grew too dark to read, I'd rest my eyes on the chimney. I was so familiar with the different types of smoke that I could tell what kind of dead child was burning.

Everything had a personality. The dead children did, and so did the smoke. Sometimes, the smoke rose in mighty white pillars, and I pictured a strong child, almost a short adult, dead from an accident and bitterly protesting his or her unjust fate. Other times, thin white smoke softly rose up in a smoothing rhythm, merging seamlessly with the dark blue air, and I saw a vulnerable baby, heavily deformed since birth and finally granted escape.

In any case, I was living in two worlds from a very early age: One in real life, and the other in books. I didn't know which one I preferred, and honestly I didn't care to tell one from the other. It was convenient to live on the boundary.

Around 1976, I read Yang Mo's *Song of Youth*: a huge hit revolutionary romance. The protagonist is a girl named Lin Daojing. She was born in 1920 in a small village in Hebei. Lin had a stepmother, and faced mounting parental pressure to marry a man she hardly knew. She was almost like my grandmother, except that Lin fought back. She fled the emotional prison of her family and found solace and camaraderie in the Communist Party, intertwining her personal life with the earth-shaking changes of a nation.

The novel bolstered my disrespect for my grandmother. Next time she started running her mouth, I declared, "You could have chosen a life like Lin Daojing!"

"She's not real," grandma said casually.

"How about the author Yang Mo? She's real, isn't she?"

"She probably lives as a dull life as I do." Grandma returned to her needle work.

I stared at her for a while, thinking over what she'd said until I figured out a counter-argument:

It was true that the story of Lin Daojing was a made-up by Yang Mo. The author probably sat hunched over her desk, engrossed in writing from dawn to dusk, just like my grandmother with her scissors and needles. But suppose my grandmother was given all the ink and paper in the world. Could she ever produce a romance like that? Of course not. I'd already heard every sentence she could utter. Yang Mo's life had to be closer to Lin Daojing's than to my grandma's, and in this sense, Yang Mo could be quite similar to her character.

I love reading. When I read fiction, part of the enjoyment is trying to disentangle the autobiographical elements from the made-up parts. I'd like to think I do so with great dexterity. If I had met Gabriel Garcia Marquez in person, I would have expressed to him my sympathy for his long struggle with constipation. What other reason would he have to make it a recurring trait among his characters? Then maybe a handshake.

In 1988, I was studying literature at Peking University. The film *Red Sorghum*, based on one of Mo Yan's novellas, won the Golden Bear at the Berlin Film Festival. One afternoon, just after I'd finished reading *Red Sorghum*, I thought of my grandmother in a whole new light. In the story, a girl born in the 1920s was delivered to a man she hardly knew. How did she defy authority? Not by running to the Communist Party, but by seducing the man driving the cart. By perpetrating adultery, she claimed ownership of her body. The story represented a shocking departure from the accepted narrative of heroic revolutionary romance.

The second I turned that last page, I bolted out of school and went as fast as I could to my grandmother's house.

I pleaded with her to tell me her life story.

"What do you want to know?" her eyes gleamed softly with appreciation.

"When your dad brought you to Beijing..."

Her face fell. "What's there to talk about? If only he hadn't delivered me to his doorstep..." She raised her chin slightly and pointed to the next room. My grandfather had retired and was home that day.

I tried to breathe evenly and fumbled through the toolkit I'd acquired from journalism class.

I decided to cut to the details.

"How long was the trip? How was the weather? And the road conditions?"

"Two days." She answered the first question without any delay. She contemplated for a few seconds and answered the latter questions in as few words as possible: "Bad. It was terrible."

"How bad?" I pursued. "How terrible?"

"Oh," she shook her head, "you wouldn't want to know."

"You bet I would!" I cried like an overexcited child, startling her. I instantly regretted it and sweetened my tone: "Who was driving the cart? My great-grandfather? I mean, your father?"

She shook her head. "No, he hired a young man."

"A young man! How old was he? What did he look like? Where did your father find him? Did you know him before?"

She paused, before shaking her head, "There is really nothing to talk about. I only remember one thing."

After another painstakingly long pause, she came up with a single observation. "He had a big stomach."

"And?"

"And he caused disaster."

It seemed the topic of the young man's appetite had somewhat lifted a previously impenetrable haze.

A few more words emerged:

"Those times...they were horrible. Chaos everywhere. And bandits. My stepmother wouldn't let me bring any valuables with me, except for a gold wedding ring. She might have been right, but still...who would want a bride with nothing other than the clothes on her back? We took a basket of steamed buns. It should have been enough for a couple of days, but it turned out we'd underestimated that man's stomach. I had to sell my wedding ring for food. It was a shame. When we made it to Beijing, I didn't have a grain of rice to my name. Who would want such a thing dumped on their doorstep?"

I was dejected. My grandmother was dense beyond belief clinging to that narrative. I blurted, "You mean to tell me that not even one good thing came from your marriage?"

She paused, wandering through the years, and replied with a slight, wry smile: "There are good things, of course."

And she went on, giving me the flip side of the story.

China's system of residency was established around 1958, about nine years after the republic was first founded. In the new society, the most pressing task was to classify citizens. Which groups were desirable and which weren't? There were four classifications seen as undesirable by the state: landowners, rich peasants, counter-revolutionists and bad elements. Once you'd been labeled one of those four things, you lost your rights to almost everything. If you lived in the cities, you would be banished to the countryside immediately.

When screening began, people with jobs were to be screened by their employers. My grandfather had to recount his entire personal history to his supervisor at the Ministry of Railways. He was born to a family of rich peasants, but had left his father's home to study railway management on a scholarship at age 18. He graduated three years later and had worked for the ministry ever since. Even though he'd toiled for nine years under the reign of the old society, he remained an entry-level clerk who dealt only with numbers. My grandfather's story was easily verified. Almost every one of his classmates worked at the same ministry and testified for one another.

My grandmother was another story. As a housewife, she fell under the authority of the local registration office.

The first time the registration officer interviewed her, he eyed her suspiciously. "Where are you from?" he asked. "Who are your mother and father? Have you ever been a counter-revolutionary? A bad element?"

My grandmother's father was a land-owner. There was no denying it. Even though his land had been confiscated, he would forever be suspect in the eye of the new regime. In order to save herself, my grandmother just told the truth.

"I was driven out of my father's home when I was seventeen. Since then, not one grain of rice I've put in my mouth has come from him or his land," she claimed.

"Are you sure about that?" The registration officer wasn't easily convinced. "People usually have complicated relationships with their families. No matter how much you hate your father, you might miss him or sympathize with him. You might still have heirloom jewelry from your grandmother."

"Not me. My father and stepmother kicked me out for good when I was seventeen. I only had a gold ring with me when I left, and I didn't even get to keep that. I saved a peasant's life by trading it for food on my way to Beijing."

He didn't believe her, and she didn't have any local friends or acquaintances to speak on her behalf. The investigator had to travel to her father's village in the township of Anci in Hebei Province. Luckily, her story checked out. Her old neighbors still remembered how her stepmother mistreated her. People gossiped about that sort of thing all the time.

"Yes, I remember her. Her stepmother treated her pretty badly. She wouldn't even cough up any money for her dowry. I think it was around when the Japanese invaded. Pretty good excuse to get rid of a stepdaughter, hahaha. No idea where she is, though..."

In 1958, the local registration office finally determined that my grandmother was, in fact, on the right side. Still, it wouldn't be the last time her status was questioned. From 1958 up to the 1970s, the investigation process seemed to play on a loop every few years when the country found itself in the tumultuous throes of yet another political shift. With every movement came the ousting of those who had been in power, and the interrogations would start all over again. However, my grandmother always responded to the questioning with one simple narrative:

Since seventeen, not one grain of rice I've put in my mouth has come from my father or his land.

It had roughly the same meaning as her "I was delivered to my husband's door step" speech, though it emphasized the flip side of the fact. Her arranged marriage became somewhat of a blessing. That story protected her all the way through the 1970s.

That evening in 1988, even though I'd failed to extract a story from my grandmother, the gates to my own memory had blasted open. Just after New Year's, 1972, I heard a knock at the door in the middle of the afternoon. My grandmother opened the door and let in two people dressed in grey Mao Suits. They kept straight faces, no small talk. Immediately, they started questioning. My grandma gave her single solemn answer yet again.

"...not one grain of rice..."

I remember it all. I was six and I'd seen the question-and-answer routine play out a few times before. Somehow, this time was different. After seeing the men out, my grandmother sat in silence for what seemed an eternity. Lunchtime came and went without a hint of recognition. Starving, I went to the cupboard and stealthily nabbed a few cookies.

On any other day, if I even stepped a millimeter in the direction of the kitchen in search of a cookie, daggers would shoot from her eyes. But that day, I might as well have been invisible.

As I was wolfing down my ill-gotten gains, I suddenly heard her call out. I was sure I was in for the beating of my life, but instead, she wanted me to go mail a letter. Though she wasn't a woman of education, she had been to night school in the new society, and could read and write enough to get by. I wasn't even in elementary school yet, but I already had a writer's eye for detail. I saw a Chinese character sounding "Tian" on the envelope. My parents lived in Tian Jin. The letter had to be for them.

You may question the fact that a child barely old enough for school was sent out to run errands. There wasn't much child protection to speak of in China in the 1970s, but there were hardly any crimes around either. Pedophilia was virtually unheard of. Plus, there were barely any cars on streets. As a police state, the new society seemed sterile, as if there weren't even germs around to get us sick. The most heinous crime we could imagine back then was theft, and I was just about the only one I knew of who'd actually committed the act. There I went, brave and smart, bundled up in a heavy coat, scarf, hat, and mittens, all handmade by my grandma, tiptoeing high to stick a letter in the mouth of the big green mailbox.

It turned out I was right about Tian Jin. A few days later, my parents showed up at the front door. Like the investigators, they got straight to business. I didn't understand a thing, though I could hear every sound they uttered. The three of them were lost in conversation. It was a perfect chance to pull off the heist of the decade in the cookie cupboard.

My father wrote feverishly as he spoke, piling papers high on the desk. It wasn't until the sun went down that his pen rested with it and returned to his pocket. I instinctively knew it was the time to end my feast. I brushed all the evidence from my face and clothes.

After my parents had left, my grandmother tore up the papers my father had been writing on, and threw the tiny pieces into the garbage. I was confused. Wasn't that the point of my parents' visit? The outcome of my faithfully accomplished mission?

The next day, my grandmother paid a visit to the local registration office. She left me home alone and told me she'd be back by 11 am. I remember this crystal clear. It was precisely on that day that I started noticing a thing called time and learned that it was measured by a clock.

The clock in question sat on the bedside table. It was a round black box with a white dial and three red needles. There were no numbers on the white dial, just 12 dots, evenly distributed along the circumference. I'd seen it everyday, but I hadn't associated the movement of the red needles with time passing. My grandmother had never taught me how to read a clock, but that day, the knowledge of the dots just magically fell upon me. I used my finger to find the dot for when my grandmother was supposed to return, and I stared at it, watching the needle slowly close in.

It was my moment of enlightenment. From then on, every period of time I spent with myself wasn't as dark and endless.

My grandmother returned at 11 am as promised. The heavy, dark clouds across her face were gone. She went back to her old self: a woman occupied solely by house-running, penny-scrimping and shoe-making. The first thing she did was take stock of the pantry. Did we need any soap? Salt? Sugar? Cookies?

My fate was sealed. She punished me relentlessly with her fists. I screamed to no avail. What was next? Would she go on to bind my feet or hands? Thank god I was living in the new society, even if she was clearly more cold-hearted than her own parents. My imagination was running wild when my grandmother told me to wipe up my tears and finish my lunch. It was over.

Later, I decided to call the incident "cookiegate." After all, this round of investigations was brought on by Nixon's visit to Beijing.

From the founding of the People's Republic, right up to Nixon's visit, relations between China and the U.S. were cold, if not violent. We were taught that Americans were our worst enemies because they stood with Taiwan. If not for the support of the U.S., China would have liberated Taiwan long ago. Not only did America's military power doom Taiwan to suffer under capitalist rule, but the U.S. planned to invade our new society using Taiwan as a jumping off point.

In those days, propaganda posters were all over the place. They always depicted Americans as either monstrous or miserable. Monstrous, because they were threatening to destroy us; miserable because their invasion would doubtlessly be thwarted.

In early 1972, the local registration office delivered some shocking news: The president of the United States was coming to China.

"What? Is he coming to surrender?"

"No, just as a guest."

"What's his name again?"

"Richard Nixon."

"I thought it was Harry Truman."

"Well, you know, Americans change their presidents every few years."

The very idea was radical to us. We'd never thought that leadership of a country could simply change hands. Today, you play the president. Tomorrow, it'll be his turn. It was ridiculous. In our country, Chairman Mao would hold his position forever. What would we do if he died? Impossible. Long live Chairman Mao!

We knew who Truman was, but we hadn't heard anything about America since the Korean War. There was a children's rhyme that had become popular back then that had hung around ever since. We chanted it when we were jumping rope, or whenever we felt the need for a rhythm. It went like this:

"Tigers, tigers, tigers,
they don't eat human.
They only have eyes,
for Truman, Truman, Truman."

So, are we going to change to a whole new rhyme now?

Nevertheless, that kind of shock and confusion in children's mind was negligible. The greatest need for authorities was to check every household along Nixon's possible route for security threats. That was why registration officers visited again. Luckily, we passed the security check by a narrow margin. As a result, I was qualified to attend briefings with the rest of the Little Red Guard members in our neighborhood. We were too young for school, but old enough to be lectured. Our leader was a pretty young woman from the local auxiliary police. She told us: If the president of the worlds' largest capitalist empire was coming to China, he was sure to bring an army of spies with him. True to Chinese tradition, we were to appear welcoming, polite, and open, no matter how much our hearts burned with distaste or alarm. We could smile, but were never to reveal any precious state secrets.

My chest was puffed with excitement, pride, and a new sense of duty. I promised solemnly to a picture of Mao Zedong that I would meet the challenge. I would do my best to practice that mysterious smile, warm on the outside, but icy cold inside. I would remember the name of our guest/enemy. It was Richard Nixon, not Harry Truman.

There was a police box directly below our apartment on a half-meter platform. The purpose of the box had long remained unclear.

By the '70s, traffic control signals had been installed at intersections, and unfortunately outnumbered the automobiles. As a result, traffic lights merely lived out their days as silent sentries protecting no one. When people wanted to cross the street, they just looked both ways. Anyone who subjected themselves to the authority of traffic signals was instantly mocked by everyone on the street.

A few days before the big event, the police box below our apartment suddenly had a policeman in it. A small concrete island had also been added in the intersection, on which another officer stood. We swarmed onto the street to watch this strange development. Everyone wanted to know if their signaling contradicted the automatic signals. If they did conflict, which should drivers listen to? If they didn't, what the hell were they doing?

To our astonishment, they appeared motionless. One stood lifelessly on the island, like a toy that had run out of battery. The other sat frozen in the box, like a mannequin in a shop window.

They looked like they were daydreaming on duty.

As the big event closed in, tension was in the air. Three days before the arrival of the Americans, we were asked to stay inside and leave the streets empty. For all four days the Americans were in Beijing, workers were required to get to work by 7 in the morning, and couldn't return until 8 at night. Those without jobs (housewives and children) were all to stay in the house. No exceptions.

Late at night, two days before the big event, several horse-drawn carts pulled up to the small shop downstairs and the policeman shouted orders to stop it. Silence blanketed the street. The carts and drivers were likely being searched until the horses sighed and neighed as if in relief. A few minutes later, I could hear the sound of freight being unloaded came through the window. What on earth did they get in? It had to be something good.

We'd heard that stores were being stocked up in case the Americans wanted to see how well-to-do we were, but nobody was allowed to go to the store to buy anything. I could imagine how excruciating it must have been for my grandmother. Our nights were long, tense and silent. We could occasionally hear glass bottles shattering. What wonders did the store now contain? And how much cheaper were the wonders slightly damaged?

Early on the day that Nixon arrived, people dressed in grey Mao suits knocked at our door again. They warned us to stay away from the windows. If we tried to peek out, we might be met with bullets. Of course we obeyed. My grandmother and I took refuge in separate corners of the house. She was busy darning a pair of socks. I stared at the winter sky through the window. It was barren and pale. It would be occasionally interrupted by a column of smoke which would rise up, spread out, and disappear.

Every now and then, my eyes searched for the clock. My grandmother thought I was sulking because I couldn't run wild outside. "It will be over soon," she said, sounding hollow.

I was unhappy not just because I couldn't play outside. I

was indignant because all my effort had been wasted, and all my enthusiasm had been trumped. I was prepared. I'd done my homework, and practiced the complicated smile. But it turned out I was not considered trustworthy even to play backdrop for the president's visit.

The situation puzzled me. If the Americans were still our enemy, why would we welcome them with a smile, even if it was fake? If our lives really were nothing but happy, healthy and prosperous, why were stores stocked to the gills with fancy goods that weren't sold to any one? Things were no longer clearly divided into underdevelopment and progress, oppression and liberation, darkness and light, ugliness and beauty.

I had no idea about how to find the truth of everything, and how to know about the world at large. I painfully felt my own powerlessness. I studied the smoke from the chimneys at Beijing Children's Hospital. Decades later, while researching for this book, I discovered that Pat Nixon visited Beijing Children's Hospital on one afternoon. She was only yards away, and I stayed in solitary confinement, staring at the smoke pouring out of the hospital's chimney.

My grandmother looked at me from time to time, worried. "You need to learn to be grateful," she said. "I am thrilled that we could stay home." She meant she was glad that we had passed the security check and weren't sent to a remote camp.

"My one sentence got us through." She smiled complacently, bringing me back to the afternoon when I'd begged her for stories. Her face was completely bathed in crimson twilight from the window.

Another question arose. "When my father came that day to help you write your account of things, how come it looked like a novel? Did you memorize all of it? I remember seeing you tearing it into pieces."

She shook her head, eyes glowing with smugness. "I'm going to tell you something, and you'd better listen. I tore it up because it was too long. It might well have overwhelmed my simple sentence, and ruined us."

I savored that magic sentence. "Since I was seventeen, not one grain of rice I've put in my mouth has come from him or his land." It was concise and powerful. I would give her that. Still, something wasn't adding up, but I couldn't get anything further from her. She had simply given all she had. I quietly evaluated my options, and decided to bow out.

My grandmother passed away in 1997. After she was gone, I brought up cookiegate when chatting with my father. I told him how closely my grandmother held on to that magic sentence of hers, to which he replied, "If it weren't for me, you think she really could have gotten through that mess in '72? You really think one sentence was enough back then? If it was, why did she ask me to come all the way from Tianjin?"

According to my father, just before Nixon's visit, the Party brought on another round of intense scrutiny from the very top all the way down to local neighborhood registry offices. As a result, the office's new leadership had to investigate everyone starting from scratch. This time, they couldn't find my grandmother's old village on the map. It was the first time this had happened since the investigations began in 1958. My grandmother was terrified and asked for my parents' help. As an educated person, my father guessed that her village had possibly been incorporated to a different county. His theory proved true.

While my father's words weren't as succinct or powerful as my grandmother's one-line testimony, he played a major role in getting her out of what could have been a terrible situation. She should have been thankful. Instead, she attributed her survival wholly to her one terse sentence.

In retrospect, Grandma was my first narrative coach. She taught me the essence of a compelling narrative: to associate two things that might seem irrelevant and give the story meaning. But she only ever used two sentences to describe her whole life, and they were basically the same thing. I felt sorry for her. I solemnly promised myself that I'd live a fuller life than her. I would become hundreds of thousands of words.

A stamp printed in China with a face value of 1.5 cent
shows image of Tiananmen, circa 1966.

Photo by Tristan Tan

Chapter 2

A Tale of Two Cities

China resembles a rooster. Beijing is at its neck and Shanghai is on its chest. My father was born in 1941 in a small fishing village on the Shandong Peninsula, where the neck meets the chest. It was always a difficult place to live. From the 1880s to the 1950s, whenever there was famine or war, a great number of people would migrate to Manchuria in the rooster's comb, where vast virgin land waited to be cultivated.

My father's parents brought him to Manchuria when he turned seven. It was one year before the establishment of the new society. He grew up there and graduated from high school in 1959. He wasn't a top student but wanted to go to Beijing. He discovered that the Beijing Institute of Iron and Steel Engineering (BIISE) had a slightly lower bar for acceptance than other schools of its caliber. Its five-year bachelor's degree was one year longer than most in China, and dissuaded many who wanted or needed to join the workforce sooner. My father's father, a peddler who had just managed to buy a tiny shop, assured his son that he would support him as long as needed.

Going to Beijing was one of two crucial decisions in my father's life. He'd wanted to go to the capital because that's where Chairman Mao lived, but it turned out it saved his life. The years he spent in college were coincided with the Three Years of Great Famine, a disaster directly caused by the failure of the Great Leap Forward. Deaths from starvation reached 30 million, mostly in the countryside. Beijing residents fared slightly better, and college students better still. Campus cafeterias offered as much as cooked rice, steamed buns, or noodles as students needed, though vegetables were rationed, and eggs or meat were provided only on weekends.

My parents were students at BIISE but didn't meet until 1961. Shortly after they began seeing each other, my mother went back home every Saturday night, and left her meal tickets to her boyfriend, so that he could enjoy an extra egg at Sunday breakfast and one more cube of stewed meat at lunch. My mother would have given her Sunday dinner to him too, had my grandmother's patience not run thin before sunset each Sunday. Every week, my grandmother went on the same tirade about how she hadn't eaten one grain of rice from her father or his land since she was seventeen.

My mother's love for my father stood the test during those trying years. Before graduation, their relationship was met with an even more severe challenge. My mother easily landed a job in Beijing since she was a resident. Thanks to my grandmother being left on someone's doorstep in 1937, both her daughters were Beijingers through and through. It was a blessing people would have given anything for.

The lovebirds had two options: either my father found a job in Beijing, or my mother followed him where he landed. My mother kept her mouth shut, waiting to see what this young fellow from the rooster's comb could pull off.

The household registration system in China was similar to India's caste system, but with a lot more paperwork. In a Chinese person's adult life, one had only a few precious chances to climb the social ladder. Going away to college was one of them. A student from the countryside or a small city could enter a public university in Beijing and effectively reinvent themselves. In theory, my father could have applied for jobs in Beijing, but he would've been one of many hungry hands clamoring for the same few grains of rice. After meticulous research, he applied for a position in Tianjin. About sixty miles from Beijing, Tianjin is the fourth largest municipality in China. It's less attractive to college grads than Beijing, and thus a less competitive job market. Moving to Tianjin was my father's other crucial decision in his life.

He and my mother married right after they graduated, and I came into the world two years later. They lived separately untill I was nine months' old, because my mother hadn't made up her mind to give up her Beijing residency yet. It was a chilly morning after the Spring Festival in 1967 when she finally decided.

My mother never expressed any regret over forfeiting her coveted spot in Beijing, but in 2000 when my daughter was born, she cuddled her granddaughter, and chanted softly: "What a lucky girl, born a Beijinger."

My mother had fifty-six days of maternity leave, after which I was entrusted to a daycare center run by the factory where she worked. I remember the towering ceiling of the daycare facility which was partitioned off from the enormous foundry. I lay in a crib near a window, as a wind moved the curtain back and forth. When the curtain rose, half a woman's face was revealed, eyes darting left and right, before settling on mine. Her terrifying gaze scared me to tears. The second I cried out, she disappeared. The wind stopped. The curtain hung peacefully in place and a hush fell over the world. My mother always said I was just imagining things. After all, six-month-olds have a memory span of no more than 24 hours, which expands to a month at nine months old. It should be impossible for me to recall this scene today.

I conceded it could have been the product of my copious reading. I'd read memoirs by people who'd grown up in collective care. It was popular in the '50s and '60s, when the whole country was feeling a little idealistic. A true communist society would happen any minute.

Private property would be discarded and children impounded. Wang Shuo, a writer born in 1957, wrote that he spent his entire childhood in boarding schools, raised by a legion of nannies and teachers. Every year on picture day, a woman would burst out of nowhere, hug him, demand to be called "mother," and pose with him for the camera. At first he felt embarrassed, but after seeing that every one of his classmates was also harassed by a crazy woman, he felt relieved. Maybe I'd combined several these accounts into one of my own.

When my mother moved to Tianjin, I wasn't eligible for the Beijing factory's daycare, so I was left in my grandmother's care. But surely there was daycare in Tianjin too. My parents never explained why they left me in Beijing, though they recalled a failed attempt to move me to Tianjin when I was three. They'd somehow found me a spot at the best preschool in the city, but once I was there, I missed my grandmother and hated the school. After a couple days, I announced I would not return to school, which my father responded to with the back of his hand and I began to cry without stopping. We were crammed in a room of 150 square feet, and my wailing made the whole building lose sleep. By daybreak, my parents were exhausted. My mother took me to the train station, and we boarded the first train back to Beijing.

My parents' interpretation of the event was that I was an eccentric child who insisted on living in Beijing, and they were overly indulgent in appeasing me. But it still didn't explain why they left me at my grandmother's doorstep in the first place.

I lived with my grandmother in Beijing as an unofficial resident. There supposed to be a severe limit to what the city could offer me, but my father convinced a neighborhood elementary school to let me register. He told the principal that "the entire country is one chess board, and we are all pawns of the socialist order." It was another motto during the Mao Era.

One spring day in 1973, I sauntered in the front gate of Yuetan

Number One Elementary School, grinning ear-to-ear, with my backpack over my shoulders. Another saying popular in those days was "two-thirds of the world lives in misery, and us Chinese are the lucky other third." The saying made me feel lucky and chosen. My good fortune was destined.

My fate changed in 1978, two years after the death of Mao Zedong and the end of the Cultural Revolution. The page of the Mao Era had finally turned. At the start of the Cultural Revolution in 1966, universities ceased normal operations. In 1977, colleges began accepting students again. That winter, nearly six hundred million hopefuls flooded the nation's testing centers. About 4.8 percent were accepted.

Talk of education swept the nation. If you wanted to get into a good college, you needed to excel at a top high school, and to get into a top high school, you needed to do well in both middle school and elementary school. Overnight, teachers at my elementary school rolled up their sleeves. Homework and tests began eating up our leisure time. Good students were entered in contests, sometimes without notice.

Fierce competition among students ensued. In 1978, Beijing restructured its school districts, distinguishing schools as key or non-key schools. The city would put the best resources at key schools, and logically, any student who wasn't a Beijing resident was barred from key schools.

One afternoon in June, 1978, my father suddenly came to Beijing, announcing that he would take me to Tianjin immediately.

I was shocked and furious. I protested by hiding in the public restroom. I was determined to hold my post. No one could drag me away!

Shared by all the female residents on the third floor, our restroom was occupied almost all day long. I howled and choked, pouring out all my energy. After a while, I started to wonder when and who would come to rescue me. I felt ashamed, and didn't know how to get out of it. I saw a bottle of detergent under the wash basin. Not the mild, neutral household kind we use nowadays, but an acidic industrial cleanser. I opened the cap and poured some into the basin. The fumes made me tear up and cough. Just at that moment, a neighbor pushed the door open. She immediately took it upon herself to keep me out of the harm's way. I let her lecture me for a while before leading me back to my grandma. I felt like a suspect being handed to a prosecutor by a police officer.

My grandmother didn't say anything. She just handed me a backpack and my father whisked me off to the railway station.

The second the train lurched forward, tears welled up again. My father responded coldly: "You're going back to Tianjin. You have to face reality."

Those were his exact words, "face reality." Before then, I'd only heard the phrase in movies. It was usually said by a communist interrogator to a freshly caught Kuomintang spy: "You're in our hands now. Just face reality."

I returned to Tianjin in May 1978. The teachers at Chen Tang Zhuang Elementary School were less than thrilled to have me. With middle school entrance exams right around the corner, they didn't need a wild card bringing down the school's average. My father begged them to at least test me, and they finally relented. A teacher took me to an empty classroom and handed me two sheets of paper. When I was done, he took them and left without a word.

I looked out the window and saw row after row of gray, plain, single story buildings. There were cracks on the window sills. Desks and chairs were ugly. This place seemed twenty years behind my Beijing school. I also saw my father standing under a tree wearing a dress shirt as white as a sheet of paper, with a pen sticking out of his pocket. It was the standard outfit of every engineer or technician at the time.

I looked at him as if looking at a stranger. I thought, "Who is this guy to drag me here? What gives him the right? How do I know he's even my real father?"

I didn't get along with my family. My mother was busy both at work and at home. My return added even more to her workload, and she didn't mind letting me know it. I tried to help around the house, but she wasn't good at giving instructions, and complained incessantly when my work wasn't up to standard. I weighed my options, and realized she'd complain either way. I stopped helping her.

My younger brother hated me. Before I came home, he'd been an only child for nearly seven years. What little parental attention I got took away from his. He once reported to my parents that I secretly read novels, which was strictly forbidden in our family. He did so in hopes of having me expelled from the family, like a misbehaving student at school. I remained, much to his disappointment, though my mother confiscated my book. Among the four of us, my brother was the only one born and raised in Tianjin. Therefore, he was the only one with a Tianjin accent. I sometimes made fun of his accent, to which he replied, "So what, you speak with a Beijing accent? Beijing doesn't even want you."

A teacher broke my trance and sent me to the main office. Several teachers sat huddled around my test papers. One of them raised her head and asked, "Were you the top of your class in Beijing?"

"I was in the middle...a little above the middle."

After a pause, another teacher exclaimed, "Wow, Beijing really is beyond our imagination."

In truth, my answer was typical Chinese modesty. I was in the top ten percent of my class in Beijing. I had no idea my false claim would thrust the nice Tianjin teachers into such self-doubt. I kind of regretted it, but it was too late to correct myself.

As we walked home, my father held my hand. He was beaming.

That moment shaped my life. The road to my parents' acceptance would be paved with good grades.

Before long, it was time to take the middle school entrance exams.

I scored high enough to be accepted to the best school in our district. Then summer came.

On my way back to Beijing to spend summer with my grandma, I stared out the train window at fields rushing backwards. The vast North China Plain sat between the two cities and made it hard to tell where Tianjin ended and Beijing began except for the sign that marked the boundary.

But even after the white wooden sign, with two broad stroked characters spelling out "Beijing," I still had an hour on the train and ten subway stops to go. The city was sprawling and amorphous. It was even more so when I thought about permanent residency as a concept. I was an outsider.

I closed my eyes and tried to picture a map of Beijing with Tiananmen in the center. If I started at Tiananmen and walked west along Chang'an Avenue, I'd hit Nanlishi Road in six miles. Turning north, I'd keep walking till I reached Yuetan South Street. There, I'd see my grandmother's apartment building, right across from Beijing Children's Hospital.

Everything looked just as if I'd never left. The convenience store was still downstairs, the rice shop was still next door, and the bookstore was still down the street. The smoke rising from the hospital chimney felt just as chilly as before. Only I had changed. I'd known the fact that I didn't belong to Beijing.

In 1534, French explorer Jacques Cartier arrived in what is now Quebec. When he returned to France, he kidnapped two young indigenous boys. He returned to the New World a year later. As their ship entered the mouth of the Saint Lawrence River, one of the boys pointed toward the shore and exclaimed, "Chemin de Canada!" (Road to Canada). In his notebook, Cartier quickly wrote: "This land is called Kanada."

Historians realized Cartier had made a mistake based on a

cultural misunderstanding. Kanada means "settlement," or "village" in Huron-Iroquois. The indigenous people had no concept of a continent-sized nation and therefore no term to describe such a construct.

But maybe those boys were different from their clan and they'd intended to call the continent "Kanada." For the past year, home wasn't a nearby village they could return to in a matter of hours. It was a far-off land that took a month by sea to reach.

Maybe the country wasn't named "Kanada" by mistake.

Anna Wang (the first person on the right) taking parting shot with her teacher and friends in Peking University, June 1988.

Photo by Weng Tong

Chapter 3

My Best Friend Forever

My name is Yuan Wang. Like some Chinese characters, my first name can be pronounced different ways to produce different meanings. If you pronounce it "Yuan," it means a poisonous flower; when it sounds like "Yan," it means fragrant grass.

I was born just a month after the Cultural Revolution commenced. As college graduates, my parents fell overnight from the top of the social order to the very bottom. Those in power declared that "the more knowledge people have, the more reactionary they are." I believe my father chose my name as an ironic comment. Even the most fragrant, beautiful blade of grass can turn to poison in the blink of an eye.

What kid wouldn't want to be sweet-smelling over poisonous? Throughout elementary school, I called myself "Wang Yan." Unfortunately, of the two pronunciations, "Yuan" is the more obvious one.

At the beginning of each school year, when my new teacher called roll, and it came time for "Wang Yuan" to raise her hand, I sat silent and still. When the teacher asked, "Who hasn't been called?" I would thrust my hand up and say, "There is a Wang Yan here."

Part of what thrilled me was the teacher's consternation. I

imagined her whispering to herself: "Watch out, there's a child pundit here."

Although Tianjin is only a hundred kilometers (sixty miles) or so from Beijing, its accent might as well be from a different planet. My first morning at Xinhua Middle School, I seated myself according to the chart. I turned to the student beside me to say good morning, but when the words left my lips, she looked at me like I was a talking monkey.

"What did you just say?" she asked with amusement and distaste.

I was confused. "I'm sorry?" I mumbled.

She stood and called out, "Hey everybody! Come listen to this girl's crazy accent!"

Some turned their heads, staring expectantly like I was a circus animal.

I tightly pursed my lips.

The bell rang and the teacher came in. She began calling roll. When it came to my name, of course she pronounced it "Yuan." But this time, I held my old ways at bay. They would only chalk it up to my crazy accent.

From time to time, the girl who sat beside me tried to goad me into conversation, but I remained silent. She then complained to the teacher that I was arrogant.

The head teacher called me over and asked why I couldn't get along with my classmates. I replied that I'd done nothing wrong. I just wasn't one for talking.

"With this attitude, how can you expect to win an exemplary student award? How can you possibly get into the Communist Youth League?"

"Some people in the world are just born introverts, just like some are born short. Isn't that true?"

"I'm talking about behavior. It can be changed. You need to interact more with your classmates to show that you don't think too much of yourself," she smiled. "You can do that, can you?"

I couldn't. I didn't care about receiving an exemplary student award. I never once spoke to the girl beside me, which made her crazy. She later requested another seat and never stopped gossiping about me. The rest of the class stayed neutral on the issue. However, they'd all raise their eyebrows when I answered teachers' questions, which was reason enough for me to keep to myself. I maintained my refusal to learn the Tianjin accent.

I went to school alone, and left alone.

In the 1970s, getting onto a bus meant a battle. When an already-full bus lumbered up to the stop, commuters swarmed like a wave against the shore. The driver pressed a switch to open the doors, but with the inside so packed, the doors couldn't swing inward. Those crowded in the doorways would shout, "Don't open the doors! There's no room!" but the people outside would shout back, "Come on, just move in!" and fight their way in.

Those struggling to get in would push on the door with all their might while those on the other side shrieked as if they were getting pushed into an electric fence. But with enough persistence, one person managed to get in, then two, then three, then four...

It seemed the magic bus could always fit one more.

The key was to join forces, and the students were great at it. When in groups, youngsters act particularly rude and adults don't really want to deal with them. Over time, the bus stop in front of our school became notorious for combative minors. Adults avoided it entirely between 4 and 5 in the afternoon.

A sea of students had gathered around the bus stop at the front gate. I passed without pausing. I lacked the will to participate in the bus game, and I hated the vulgarity of it. I'd have to transfer three stops down, anyway. I'd much rather walk.

Three stops may not seem like much, but during one of Tianjin's brutal storms, it was no small feat. I questioned what I gained by walking alone. Was it freedom or just isolation? If it was isolation, I cherished that I was free to isolate myself.

I completed my daily hike at where the #4 bus line ended and the #93 trolley began. I could easily fit on a semi-full trolley. Sometimes I even found a seat.

One day, however, as I passed the crowd, fragments of a conversation made their way through that chaos: "Friedrich Engels says that half of the time, Johann Wolfgang von Goethe is one of the greats, but the other half, he's nobody. He can be a paragon of rebellion, sarcasm, and misanthropy, but just as easily as he can be nothing more than a cautious, happy little man."

My heart jumped. Who was speaking so profoundly? I stopped, scanned the crowd, and caught sight of a thin, bespectacled girl so caught up in her explication. She practically danced as she talked.

Her name was Zhi Hua. She was in the same grade as me, but in a different class. Just like me, she needed to ride to the last stop of the #4 bus. Ever since I overheard her little speech, I found myself casting a piece of my freedom aside, and discovered that I had no shortage of brazenness when it came to shoving my way on the bus.

I yearned to get to know Zhi Hua. We had a lot in common, but one giant difference. The things that mattered to us were beyond the pale of what any normal middle school student cared about, but we diverged when it came to interacting with others.

If anyone else disagreed with me, or didn't understand my view, I immediately shut down, not bothering to say another word. Zhi Hua was the opposite. The more someone disagreed with her, the more excited she became, and her excitement brought about the endless strings of reasons that were her conversational trademark.

Poets and philosophers weren't her only topics of discussion. She could easily switch to entertainment or celebrity gossip. She was witty and enlightening even when gossiping. Listening to her became one of my greatest joys.

At times, she'd be very close to me, though there were a few people between us. At the end of the line, the doors opened, and I moved with the crowd, while looking around for Zhi Hua. She'd always been gone before I planted my feet on the ground.

A year passed. Zhi Hua and I competed in a Tang Dynasty poetry reciting contest. She placed second, and I failed to place at all. That day after school, we saw each other at the bus stop. Since we'd formally met at the competition, I felt comfortable saying hi.

"Congratulations!" I said.

"You did well, too!"

"Not really." I sighed, then lamented, "Of a hundred poems, there are only two I don't like, and of course, I pulled one of those two out of the hat."

"It's called 'Murphy's law," she replied.

"What do you mean?"

"Anything that can go wrong, will go wrong."

Was there a law like that? Why hadn't I learned about it? I looked at her, full of admiration.

From then on, Zhi Hua was my favorite person in the world, but our friendship was limited to a three-stop bus ride.

Another year passed. One day, I strode out the front gates and realized I hadn't seen her in a couple of days. The next day, I learned her family had moved to Qinhuangdao, a coastal city in Hebei province, about four hours from Tianjin by train.

I was crushed. Day in, day out, there was nothing else I could think about. Every moment of our time together came flooding in, forming a massive monolith of loneliness. I remembered her telling me that her parents were civilian officers in the People's Liberation Army, and as a result, they were always moving from one post to another. I didn't expect her to move again without so much as a goodbye.

Time passed, and in my mind I saw her as a wanderer. Her long hair blew in the wind like a black, silken sail carrying her away, like the forgotten heroine of an obscure novel we both loved.

Then I snapped myself out of it. Why should I picture her as such a tragic figure, trapped in a sad, lonely fate? How did I know she wasn't having the time of her life out there? Qinhuangdao was a beautiful city by the sea with nicer weather than Tianjin. While I was off sulking by myself, she was probably enjoying the sun and sand, entertaining a new audience.

Two years passed.

One afternoon, as I was walking out of my last class, I heard a familiar voice at the end of the hall: "So the main office moved to the new building? Do you mind telling me which floor?...okay, thanks!"

Zhi Hua! I ran down the hall and caught her on the stairs.

"I can show you the way!" I called out.

"Wang Yuan!"

In a blissful mood, I took her to the office and waited while she took care of her registration. After, she told me her parents were honorably discharged and relocated to Tianjin.

"So you're going to live in Tianjin for good?"

"Yes."

We talked for so long that day. I can't even remember how many things we talked about. The only thing I recall is the janitor appearing all of a sudden, threatening to lock us in for the night if we didn't leave.

Two scenes play out repeatedly in my dreams. In one, I walk out of my grandmother's house just as a bus passes by. I chase after it, but no matter how hard I try, I can never catch it. In the second, Zhi Hua and I are locked in a tall, empty building. I want to leave, but there's no way out. According to Freud, dreams are the manifestations of our desires. But to this day, I can't decipher what it was I wanted in either dream.

By eleventh grade, every student had to decide whether to pursue a career in the humanities or sciences. Those who chose the sciences had all their history, social studies, and geography classes canceled for their last two years of high school, while those who chose humanities forewent biology, chemistry, and physics. The programs were designed so that students could concentrate on classes relevant to their college entrance exams. Once a path was chosen, there was no turning back.

In the summer of 1982, I came home with my application in hand. My father took one look and said, "What's there to think about? Sciences, of course."

I knew he'd say that. His wounds from the Cultural Revolution were still fresh. For all he knew, it would happen again in a blink of an eye. Fragrant grass would turn to poison. The only smart thing to do was to play it safe and shy away from humanities.

"It's not the same anymore," I tried to argue. "The Cultural Revolution is over."

"But for how long? It's too soon to draw any conclusions. No matter what kind of society we live in, the sciences are the only safe bet. As a scientist, if you say oil is lighter than water, you can prove it with evidence!"

In a strange, backhanded attempt to comfort me, he added, "Smart people go into the sciences. Only people who don't know how to use their whole brain study the arts."

"That's not true!" I protested. "Zhi Hua is smarter than me, and she's going into literature."

"Then you stay as far away from her as possible."

I couldn't disobey my father, so I chose the sciences, but at that moment, my goal of life became to be just like Zhi Hua.

There were six classes in my grade. One through five were for the sciences, and the sixth was for humanities. I was in Class Five, which was separated from Six by just one thin wall. I could hear their teacher lecture whenever we took a test. The humanities class always ended right at the bell, while ours always ran late. I could always hear the humanities students already in the hall, shouting and laughing. There wasn't a time I couldn't hear, over everyone else, the sweetest song of all: Zhi Hua.

Hearing the noise of the humanities students, our teachers would grimace or shrug silently. Occasionally, if the clamor was too distracting, they would charge into the corridor, and angrily say something like, "There are serious students in here working hard for the future of our country!" That was a common notion at the time: only science could make China great again. There wasn't anything worth studying in humanities. Otherwise, how could they always end class right at the bell?

Although Zhi Hua was back in Tianjin, our rides home were sadly behind us. Her family had moved, so she took a different bus. The only time we got together was during our lunch break.

Our school was situated in one of Tianjin's nine "concession territories." These were areas the Qing dynasty ceded to the U.S., Japan and a number of European countries. The foreign powers established settlements in these areas from 1860 to 1947. European architecture lined both sides of the street that led to our school, and each building was different from the next. Though I was taught at school that the concession territories were symbols of humiliation, I enjoyed walking the area. I hated my neighborhood, which was nothing but rows upon rows of identical 5-story apartment buildings, a fascist aesthetic.

Electricity was scant everywhere. Even European houses burned fossil fuel for heat. In winter, courtyards turned to open storage for coal. We spent our lunch times walking through a light veil of smoke. As we sauntered, blurry contours gradually became sharp, giving us a sense of optimism about the future.

On one of our daily walks, during my senior year, Zhi Hua announced that the movie *Song of Norway* would be in theaters soon.

I don't have an ear for music. To this day, I don't know if *Song of Norway* is at all important in the annals of film history. All I knew was that Zhi Hua couldn't have been more excited.

Naturally, I pretended to be just as excited: "Great! Let's go see it!"

"The theater will only have afternoon showings," she said. "If we want to see it, we'll have to cut class."

"Let's cut class!"

In the days leading up to our adventure, she often hummed the melody of "Solveig's Song" while we walked, and over time, it found its way into my head as well.

The winter may pass and the spring disappear.
The summer too will vanish and then the year.
But this I know for certain: you'll come back again.
And even as I promised you'll find me waiting then...

It became my battle cry. I anxiously awaited that day I could finally become the rebellious teenager I'd always wanted to be, but forty-eight hours prior, I got cold feet.

"I don't know, maybe we should at least say we're sick. I'm not sure cutting class is such a good idea," I said.

She had no objection.

During lunch on the day in question, Zhi Hua and I went to the school nurse one by one. After a few minutes of moaning and groaning, both of us were successfully sent home.

We left school separately and met at the bus stop. We walked briskly, laughing the whole way. When I saw a classmate returning school from lunch, I couldn't help but let them in on our secret, "Hey, guess what? We're cutting class to see a movie!"

The next day, my teacher lectured me. "Your job is to learn," he said. "Learning is the only thing that should be on your mind right now. Getting into a good college is the only way to fast-track yourself to a successful life. You need to concentrate. Otherwise, you're wasting your time."

I agreed for the most part. The issue I had was that I didn't like what I was taught. I tried to comfort myself by thinking everything would be fine once I got into a college with comprehensive programs.

My goal was getting into Peking University, which had a reputation as a safe harbor for free thinkers. I'd heard their professors encouraged students to skip class and allowed unregistered students to sit in on lectures. Peking University sounded like the solution to all my problems.

In 1984, I was accepted to Peking University in Beijing as a microelectronics major. Zhi Hua also called Peking University home, but as a student of Chinese literature.

It didn't take long for me to notice a world of difference between me and my microelectronics classmates. If you had real interest in a subject, you would ferociously absorb all the information you could. My classmates discussed the questions all the time:

How did Chinese microelectronics stack up against the rest of the world?

Was the Chinese Academy of Sciences better than Peking University when it came to semiconductor research?

If one was to set up a microchip plant, should one do so in Beijing or Shanghai?

Me? I just fulfilled my basic duties as a student, studying the text book, doing my homework and taking tests. Beyond that, I never dedicated even a minute to microelectronics.

But every time I visited Zhi Hua in her dorm room, I instantly felt I belonged. I eagerly jumped into any discussion.

Was *The Odyssey* the western equivalent of China's *Journey to the West*, or *The Water Margin*?

Did George Sand favor Alfred de Musset, or Chopin?

These were debates I never hesitated to spare my two cents. I never minded if Zhi Hua and her friends cared for my input. I had so much more knowledge in her field than in mine that I thought I could easily pass for a literature major.

Gradually, my desire to become a legitimate, full-time literature student became irrepressible. I was over 18 and I didn't need my parents to sign anything anymore.

But how could I officially transfer to the Department of Chinese Literature? Sneaking into Zhi Hua's classes was one thing, but to have my name formally put on the roster would be almost impossible in 1985.

Under the planned economic system of the time, there were quotas on everything. Quotas on how much steel to produce, how much cotton to mill, to how many teachers, engineers, and even writers to produce. If Peking University was tasked with producing one hundred electronic engineers and fifty writers, but delivered only ninety-nine of the former and fifty-one of the latter, its production line would be considered a failure.

In the 1980s, China transitioned from a planned economy to a planned economy with market regulation. The country was struggling. Change was possible, but those who wanted it should have just started the fight instead of waiting, like what I did. I didn't apply for a transfer, assuming that any effort I made would be futile. Even so, I stopped doing any work in my microelectronics classes and snuck into Zhi Hua's instead. I was killing any chance I had of graduating.

Unsurprisingly, I failed four classes in my first year. By Peking University rules, if a student failed in more than five classes, they would not be eligible to receive a degree even if they passed make-up tests. Even that daunting reality couldn't get me to re-engage in a field I had zero interest in.

I stuck to Zhi Hua like glue, and she grew tired of me. One day after class, she got up and left without a word. I followed her from a distance, being careful not to give myself away. She reached a sharp turn where there was a half-dome mirror to let drivers see around the corner. Right before that mirror, she raised her head, and our eyes met in its shiny, curved expanse.

I would have disappeared into a crack in the sidewalk if I could. Anything to avoid that horrible rush of shame. In the old days, I just liked being with her. Now, I had grown tired of myself. I wanted to be her.

If only she had cast me off completely, I could have found myself again. But she, as everyone else, had moments of weakness. Every time a deadline for a paper loomed, she would get fidgety. If I didn't go looking for her, she'd show up at my dorm. Without text messaging, Facebook, or WeChat, all you could do to track down a person was to go to their house right before bed time.

Zhi Hua usually turned up at my door around ten o'clock. We talked in the hallway since my roommates needed to sleep. She'd hastily lay out for me what she planned to write. She really had an incredible way with spoken words and I was always intoxicated by her verbal feats. When she finally rested her weary voice, I'd exclaim, "That was brilliant! Just write down exactly what you told me!"

"Just like I said it? Exactly like that?"

"Yes. Just like that. Word for word. It's perfect."

But she would never fully believe me, or even in herself. Every time, she'd ask me, "But how should I begin?"

I wish I'd turned on a tape recorder the moment she walked into the room. Her speech would've made a perfect essay.

Whenever she had a paper due, my confidence came back. I'd believe once again that she needed me too. She just didn't need me as much as I needed her. And that I could live with.

Half way through my sophomore year, Peking University made an official announcement I thought would never come: it would allow students to change majors. Literally overnight, the most impossible of feats had become as easy as filling out a form. Who did we have to thank? The school's new president: Ding Shisun.

Ding Shisun was born in Shanghai, in 1927, and started college right around the end of the World War II, when even basic resources were in short supply. Seeing that the power company in Shanghai was foreign-run, and offered a markedly higher salary than the average

Chinese company, Ding declared himself an electrical engineering major, and set about a path that guaranteed material security. But he found he was terrible at drawing, and engineering classes involved tons of it. In his first year, he never scored higher than a 60 in any of his classes. He realized his chances of succeeding as an engineer were slim, so he transferred to mathematics. He loved math, though it couldn't ensure the same kind of future as electrical engineering. He understood firsthand that universities should be a place for students' self-realization and self-discovery.

In May 1986, I took the Chinese Literature Department's entrance exam. I was desperate. The first semester of my sophomore year, I failed nearly all my classes, despite my classmates valiantly letting their papers slip toward the end of their desks so I could see their answers. As hard as they tried to help me, I eventually fell far behind I didn't even know what to copy. There was no turning back. Either I got into the Chinese Literature Department, or I dropped out entirely. I couldn't imagine what my life would be like as a college dropout. Would I show up on my parents' doorstep in Tianjin, and live under their roof for the rest of my life?

To this day, I think my passing the exam was largely due to luck. My interests, expertise, and hard work somehow all came together. My confidence returned.

For the next two years, when anyone asked me what I was studying, I would proudly state, "I'm a student of Chinese Literature." But in actuality, I learned almost nothing.

The Chinese Department wasn't concerned with fostering the next generation of great authors. Graduates were to work in one of three fields: literary theory, literary critique, or literary history. These disciplines required a strong academic foundation built on reading and research. In that sense, a literature major's life wasn't so different from a computer science major's.

I never chose any fields. I just fulfilled the graduation requirements. It wasn't that I'd stumbled into another wrong major. I was just more interested in voicing my feelings and opinions than actually studying.

My father always hoped to see me engaged in facts and reasoning, rather than expressing myself. But for all his talk of scientific exactitude, he was the one who had given me a name open to interpretation.

Chapter 4

First Asia, Next, the World!

Campus security at Peking University must all have graduated from the Philosophy Department. Every person who desired passage through the gates had to answer three existential questions:

Who are you?

Where are you coming from?

Where are you going?

All schools in China, elementary to college, are surrounded by walls. Peking University occupied a sprawling 837 acres but only had four gates, named by location: west gate, east gate, south gate, and small south gate. Those were the only ways for nearly ten thousand students, staff and faculty to get in and out every day. As one of the most liberal institutions of higher learning in China, Peking University opened its doors discreetly. Renowned radical scholars were invited to give lectures. Cutting edge bands performed at student dance parties. Artists, poets, and free-thinkers from every corner of China floated around campus grounds.

Now and then, there were tense days when only students, staff and faculty were allowed in. When this happened, it meant a student protest loomed on the horizon. Gate guards would step up their existential interrogations to keep out political dissidents seeking to capitalize on student dissatisfaction.

Three months in at Peking University, I experienced a protest for the first time.

"No-lights-out" was organized in response to new restrictions on light usage. Previously, dorm occupants were allowed to leave their lights on as long as they wished, but this was a thing of the past starting December 10, 1984. The announcement had been made by way of a notice on the school's official bulletin board.

As of December 10th, eleven o'clock was lights-out.

It's impossible to speak of Peking University's history of protest without mentioning the Triangle. It was a triangular garden in the middle of the campus with a row of bulletin boards installed beneath the trees. Its central location between the dorms and academic buildings made it a key communication hub for everyone within campus walls. Directly across from the Triangle was the school's official bulletin board. It was a cement wall with neatly-arranged glass cases holding meticulously pinned announcements.

A few hours after the lights-out notice was up, posters denouncing the policy appeared at the Triangle. I carefully read every single one. A good portion argued that grown men and women should decide for themselves when to brush their teeth, wash their face, and go to bed.

The word "grown" resonated in the deepest recesses of my mind, and my indignation swelled. All I'd ever wanted was to be independent. I'd left my parents' house only to find myself in the hands of a giant babysitter!

The school's administration had braced itself for the backlash. They responded on the official bulletin board with record speed. They insisted that freedom was indeed important, and they themselves championed it, but freedom came with a responsibility to not harm those around us. That perspective paused me. I left the Triangle in the throes of a dilemma.

I returned a few hours later to saw a new poster proclaiming,

"Our dorms are our collective home. As responsible adults, we can talk to each other, find solutions, and live together as one. The school isn't our mommy, daddy, or dictator. Autonomy is the foundation of democracy."

Words like "autonomy" and "democracy" were beyond me. They sounded foreign in a good way. I'd never thought that the right to decide one's own bedtime was a debatable subject in the realm of political science.

Another poster pointed out that notices delivered by the communist/socialist Parties all over the world were worded in almost exactly the same way, meaning that individualism must be eradicated to achieve the greater goal of unity. Though I had never personally been to any other communist/socialist countries, I felt the logic held water.

As I mulled it over, my eyes fell to yet another poster which made an even more confounding argument. "There are eight students in each dorm room," it read. "It can be hard, if not utterly impossible for eight roommates to reach consensus on issues like this. If there were only two to a room, like in America, this would be a different story. Too many cooks spoil any broth. If our country had a smaller population, direct democracy could work. But in a country as populated as China, only a dictatorship can preserve peace."

I stared at those words, unable to discern if the author was serious or not.

As December 10th grew nearer, a large yellow poster appeared bearing lines from a Petofi Sandor poem in bright red ink:

Life is dear, love is dearer.
Both can be given up for freedom.

I felt uneasy. I never expected myself or anyone else to get so confrontational. The "lights-out" policy was annoying, but exchanging life or love? That was too much. However, when I looked around, I found solemn look on my fellow students' faces as if they were preparing for the worst.

I left the Triangle frustrated.

With a storm coming, the gate guards mandated thorough identity checks. Their primary security method was visual inspection. If someone didn't look like a student, they were asked to provide identification. If they couldn't do so, they were taken to a room beside the gate, where they were questioned further.

The guards stood vigilantly at those gates day in, day out, year after year. Over time, they had pretty good intuition regarding who they should stop and inspect further. On any given day, even if I forgot my ID, I never had a problem.

A few days before the 10th, as Zhi Hua and I exited the south gate to go shopping, it occurred to me that I'd forgotten my ID. Both of us had. Zhi Hua quickly assured me it wouldn't be a problem. The guards had seen us a million times and had never once asked for either of our IDs.

When we returned to the south gate, the guard atop his high post held out his hand: "Identification, please." Even on his podium, he wasn't any taller than us, and his oversized uniform hung loosely around his slight frame. He looked like a child in clothes his parents had bought for him to grow into.

Zhi Hua replied with her trademark ease, "Sorry, we forgot to bring them with us. We're students. We come through this gate every day."

He simply made the same demand again, this time without so much as looking at us. He looked up at the sky, hand outstretched, awaiting our compliance.

"Come on, you know we're students."

He blinked, asking mechanically, "Which department?"

"Chinese Literature."

He continued his lifeless line of questioning, reciting everything he had been trained to ask, nothing less, nothing more. "Who's the dean of your department?"

"Wang Yuan." Zhi Hua answered without a hint of sarcasm.

I stood in complete shock, but the young man simply waved us on just the same.

We walked through the south gate, faces taut with a seriousness requisite for entering the palace of an emperor. About a hundred steps in, we burst into laughter.

On December 10th, the school made a noontime announcement. I can't remember exactly what was said, but I remember its tone clearly. In all its wisdom, the institution delivered a condescending and hostile message. For the life of me, I couldn't figure out why authorities tried to put the fire out with oil. It was a strategy employed not only by Peking University, but by every level of the Chinese government.

As it happened, my mind was completely focused on the fact that that night's class would be held in the computer lab. Believe it or not, I had only seen pictures of computers in magazines like *China Today*. They were massive, industrial monoliths, always grouped with pictures of hydroelectric plants and towering ships; testaments to the growing might of the nation. We were finally going to see a computer in flesh!

Chance to use the computer lab was precious. Our teacher was more than aware of that and scheduled us from 6pm to 10pm to maximize our class time. We got back to our dorm room at 10:30pm. Being the good girls we were, we reminded each other to hurry up and get ready for bed before lights-out, but we seemed to take our sweet time. I think deep down, we were still in denial and hoped the school was bluffing.

At 11pm on the dot, the shower room went pitch black. Sighs of exasperation echoed from every corner of the corridor, as flickers of flame began to grow in the featureless landscape outside. Realizing there was still soap on my face, I gave it a quick, half-hearted swipe clean before groping around in the dark for my glasses. As I walked out into the hall, I found myself deluged in shadow. I was sure that I knew the dark forms in the hall, but I couldn't make out a single face.

Slowly but surely, the mass of shadows cautiously made its way to the stairs. Clusters of dark forms clumsily guided one another down the staircase.

"Here comes another step!"

"Careful!"

"Not so fast!"

"Great, where's my shoe?!"

As we reached the bottom and made our way outside, we were greeted by a group of male students carrying makeshift torches. All were falling over each other to heroically rescue their damsel in distress. We suddenly felt like Rapunzel, while the boys looked into our eyes and saw themselves reflected back as princes. United, we were to rise against all the villains of the world. All our newly-formed front needed was a direction. Someone suggested touring from dorm to dorm to grow our ranks. Someone else shouted that we should head to the lawn in front of the library, where we'd have room to form battle lines and state our demands. Finally, someone screamed, "March straight to the Tiananmen Square!"

Despite the ongoing debate, most of us instinctively marched toward the Triangle. As we passed by the post-graduate housing, more people rolled out of the dorms. The nebulous rage that had hung in the air was now visible, audible and palpable. Shouts mixed with exploding firecrackers as students set fire to broom handles, chair legs, or anything else they could find. Normally, it would only take me a few minutes to walk from my dorm to the Triangle, but with the crowd, it took me twenty minutes to cover half that distance. Up in front, the flames that led our way grew distant. I suddenly felt grimly alone in the mob.

I wasn't a brave soul. I turned and found my way back to the dorm, only to find that my roommates had never left. Seeing me return safely, they breathed a sigh of relief and pestered me for details.

"I didn't do anything. Really," I replied.

"But you were gone forever..."

"I dunno. I never even made it to the Triangle."

"Well, whatever. You're still the craziest one of all of us," they teased. "We didn't even leave the room!"

Eventually, the rest of the dorm's residents began to return, filling the pitch-dark halls with excited chatter and vitriolic chants. The building was bursting with noise. We opened our door to hear as much as we could. Apparently, some students had marched down to the south gate and found it blocked by school authorities. The entire body of counsellors had been deployed to try to reason with the students.

A small number of students managed to slip by and headed just off campus to the Zhong Guan Yuan apartments, where Ding Shisun lived. They descended on the front door of a building, with torches in hand and screaming his name, but his wife yelled from the balcony of a neighboring building that he was at his office and to please find him there if they had anything to say.

The next day, we learned that someone had smashed the glass cases that housed the official bulletin boards, and ripped up everything inside. They tore up all of the school announcements, along with last year's honor roll.

And that was that.

The protest began with a bang but lost momentum and accomplished nothing. Dissatisfaction ran through our student body. The adrenaline wore off, and exhaustion took its place. The next day, the new lights-out policy wasn't an issue. Most of us were sound asleep long before lights out.

Four days later, at the Asian Cup semifinals, China's soccer team beat Kuwait 1-0, and entered the finals for the first time in history. The school was thrown into a frenzy. I was never one for sports, but when the whole building erupted, I was far from immune. The enthusiasm that had dampened was reignited in no time.

"To the south gate!"

Once again we rallied. We passed the post-graduate housing as our numbers surged. The frigid December air was warming up. Every twist and turn played out the exact same way as four days earlier, but this time I never lost sight of the torches in front.

"To the south gate!"

We poured past the Triangle, and onto the main road to the south gate. Somewhere along the way, the boundaries between people melted away and there was no "me" anymore. Just "us." I was still Wang Yuan, but I was bigger than I'd ever been.

"To the south gate!"

"First Asia! Next, the world!"

Wait a minute. What was that?

I looked around. There wasn't a single face I could associate with a name. I hesitated for a moment, until another shout rang out, clearer than before: "First Asia! Next, the world!"

Back in August of 1979, at the World University Games, 17-year-old Chinese diver Chen Xiaoxia defeated a formidable adversary from the former Soviet Union and won the gold. Two days later, *Sports Daily* published an editorial entitled, "First Asia...next, the World!"

Those simple words soon evolved into rallying cry for all Chinese sports, from gymnastics, to shooting, to volleyball, and football surely not far behind. Tonight, we had risen up taken the Asian Cup finals. There could be no doubt that tomorrow, the world was for us to conquer.

We were edging closer and closer to the south gate, and could see that its doors were eerily flung askew. The guards on each side kept a watchful eye over the surging wave set to crash through the gates. No sign of any authority figures to stop us. Was this some kind of trap?

My mind was racing. I inexplicably slowed, and the crowd's momentum sent the person behind me crashing down on the back of my heel, making me scream out in pain, but I was drowned out by the roar of the people.

"First Asia! next, the world!"

Not a soul stopped us pouring out of the south gate. We'd made it. It was unbelievable.

Once we stepped off campus, we were confronted by a cold, open street. I felt a wordless tension. I assumed our leader at the front of the pack felt the same way, because there was a sizable pause before the next round of shouts. What next?

It was a winter night, and the lack of people on the street made it seem even more vast and foreboding. We passed a worker just off the night-shift riding home. He didn't quite know what to make of a crazy mob of college students banging on wash basins and waving flaming broom handles.

The change of scenery brought about a new rally cry from the leader at the front:

"Unite! Unite! China will rise!"

Everyone joined in, "Unite! Unite! China will rise!"

Two more cyclists stopped to see what all the fuss was about, and leaned on one leg as they waited for what was to come. A group of shady teenagers huddled in front of a shop glanced in our direction, but simply turned away and continued with their business.

Did they not realize? Peking University was making the history! I shouted even harder, "Unite! Unite! China will rise!"

We continued our victory march past Haidian Theater, before finally heading back to campus where it all began. What a night! I was spent in every possible way, and was dead asleep before my head even hit the pillow.

According to the girl in the bunk above me, I still called out, "First Asia... next, the world!" even from the depths of slumber.

Over the next few days, I couldn't stop thinking about what had happened. The more I did, the more I realized there were greater forces at work. Why was the south gate blocked when we protested against lights-out, but open when we marched to celebrate the soccer team's victory? Authorities had manipulated us in extremely covert ways. Our thirst for freedom, our taste for rebellion, and our adrenaline had all been channeled toward a nationalistic cause. We'd been used by the Party.

Still, the Party was on edge, and increasingly so. They needed to ensure that every element was in place for the right fire to burn down the right thing. And so, whenever a storm began to brew, the school guards would once again become the nation's greatest philosophers.

I studied at Peking University from 1984 to 1988. Every year I was there, I took part in, or at least witnessed one large-scale protest.

The 1980s were a stormy time. China's Communist Party officially announced an end to the Cultural Revolution, calling it a mistake. China opened its doors to the world and sadly found itself far behind. The Party was humble and cautious, but the people were reckless and impatient. Clashes between the two were frequent, and we sincerely believed that change could come about in response to our demands in the blink of an eye.

In December 1986, students at the University of Science and Technology of China took to the streets to protest the government's illegal tampering with elections. Over four thousand students flooded the streets. Peking University, never willing to be outdone, coordinated a multi-university protest on New Year's Day, 1987, in Beijing. Protesters screamed "better dead than oppressed!" and "no democracy means no future!"

Eighty-three students were arrested, thirty-five from our school alone. This sparked yet another protest. Students trampled school grounds demanding their detained classmates be freed, and fair, unbiased reporting on the student movement. Before long, five-thousand students burst through the front gates of the school and headed straight for the police headquarters and Tiananmen, vowing not to return until they were reunited with their imprisoned brothers and sisters. By the early hours of the next morning, they returned victorious.

A friend told me stories of his interrogation.

A policeman asked him, "Are you all working together?"

The police must have thought someone was behind the scenes, pulling strings.

My friend played the part of the myopic bookworm, pretending to understand the sentence only in a scientific context, replying, "No. We're parallel circuits. That's what you were asking, right?"

Years later, thinking of that frigid night in December, 1984, I couldn't help but wonder which world I was actually screaming about when I'd shouted, "First Asia! next, the world!"

From my first day of elementary school, I was taught that "two-thirds of the world live in misery, and we Chinese people are the lucky other third." This dichotomy sheltered me in a blissful little bubble. I believed I was lucky, for whatever reason.

In 1974, as Mao Zedong played host to guests from Africa, he proposed his "Three Worlds Theory," which would later be presented to the United Nations by Deng Xiaoping. According to Mao's theory, the world was divided into three socioeconomic categories. The "first-world" was comprised of the superpowers: the United States and the Soviet Union. The second contained the world's lesser, yet still wealthy countries, such as France, Great Britain, West Germany, Canada and Japan. The third was the under-developed and exploited rest of the world, made up of countries throughout Africa, Latin America, and non-Japanese Asia.

What? China was a third-world country?

I was shocked. My teacher comforted me by telling me that China wasn't actually a third-world country, but had grouped itself in with those below us to show solidarity with their struggle. There were two bullies in the world, the Soviet Union and the United States. We needed to join together and take on them one by one.

China was a communist/socialist country, and a mortal enemy of the United States. Even so, we needed to befriend America out of mutual disdain for the Soviet Union, who had betrayed communism and become revisionists, which was far worse than outright capitalism. After defeating our common enemy, we'd move on to annihilating America, which would be a piece of cake. Our socialist system was intrinsically better than their pernicious capitalist ways. Marx had proven that. Victory was practically guaranteed.

This was supposedly why we'd opened our doors not only to America, but to every other capitalist former enemy. As the country opened up, more inconvenient truths set in. Not only was America ahead of us, but also Japan, Korea, Singapore, even Hong Kong and Taiwan.

Starting in 1977, my parents bought a new appliance every year. First was a TV, then a refrigerator, then a washing machine. Whenever we went to the store, only Chinese brands were on display. Anything made in Japan would already have been sold at the back door the minute it came off the truck.

Every night for dinner, my mother made one dish of stir-fry, which we would split four ways. If anyone wasted time talking instead of eating, she would threaten to take away their stir-fry and leave them with only rice.

A woman in my father's work unit was infamous for her lack of moral compass, and my mother forbade my father to have anything to do with her. Sometimes at the dinner table, my father would let something slip, "Today, Ms. Zhang told us a joke..." My mother's glare would instantly turn him to stone: "Are you going to eat, or are you going to talk?" Of course, she never actually did anything to my father, but every time, at my mother's warning, my father lowered his head and finished his dinner like a good boy.

Starting in 1978, China's planned economy system began to loosen up, and it became acceptable for work units to divvy up extra profits among employees, for all sorts of reasons. One such reason was to pay overtime. When the holidays came along, my mother and father were both up and off to work bright and early. There was little actual extra work to be done, so they'd just sit around drinking tea and chatting. But since we had no school during the holidays, I went to work with my father, and my brother went with my mom. On one such occasion, I was sitting in my father's office when the infamous Ms. Zhang sauntered in and asked, "Do you want a Panasonic fridge? I've got a connection."

I looked up at her. She looked quite different from other women. Her eyes darted back and forth, checking every corner of the room, her freshly-permed hair bobbing briskly. Back in those days, hardly any woman would dare perm their hair. She was spirited, social, just...Maybe a bit frivolous, precisely the kind of person who could take advantage of the opening-up policy. I had no dislike toward her at all.

That night at dinner, my father mentioned that a "colleague" had a connection for a Panasonic refrigerator. My mother immediately replied, "Really? Let's do it!"

Hmmm, I thought. *He left out one important detail.*

I blurted, "Just so you know, he's talking about Ms. Zhang."

My father's face went white, and he moved his arm around his plate to protect it from being taken.

Instead of praise, my mother scolded me. "What business is it of yours? Are you going to eat, or are you going to talk?"

I was sure she hadn't heard me correctly. "You know, Ms. Zhang, the one you hate!"

This enraged her further, and resulted in my dish being confiscated. She angrily turned it over to my brother, who fought his hardest to hold back a smirk as he ate his extra portion. I stormed off in tears. What kind of world was this? Had everyone lost their minds?

A few days later, a brand-new Panasonic refrigerator stood proudly in our living room, a testimony to my parents' immorality. I vowed to never touch any of what lay inside, no matter how refreshing, cool, or delicious.

But it was summer. Every evening, my father filled containers with syrup, milk, sweet red bean and other delicious things. The next day, my brother's tortuous walk home in the blistering heat was rewarded with a huge popsicle. Not being able to partake for moral reasons, I imagined it a pleasure of inconceivable proportion. It only took a week for me to cave.

In 1978, my first year of middle school, we had no English teacher to speak of. Before we knew it, the school's Russian teacher took the podium to least make an attempt. Three years later, as Tianjin Foreign Studies University's first graduating class since the Cultural Revolution entered the job market, one finally found her way to our school. She became the school's first English teacher with a BA in the subject. Young, beautiful, and fashionable, with a sweet voice, she quickly won us over.

Our new teacher had a soft spot for me. Whenever she had office hours and I was free, I spent every spare minute with her, playing with her tape recorder. I'd hit "record" and recite the entirety of our daily reading, only to be dismayed when I played it back and found I had a far-heavier accent than I had expected. It was a mess. My pronunciation was off, my emphasis was all wrong, and I spoke with a relentless stutter. It had sounded so perfect in my head!

Still, next time her office hours came around, I returned for more torture. At that time, tape recorders were still rare, mythical beasts that had only just recently found their way to China. My teacher's tape recorder wasn't the school's property. It was a gift from her boyfriend, an American exchange student. A year later, they were married. A year after that, he graduated and returned to America with his new wife in tow.

It wasn't the first time someone in my life had left me for America. In 1981, my favorite actress Joan Chen had done the same! I was crushed, but loved learning of my idol's new life through the local paper. I learned of California State University, Northridge, where she studied filmmaking. It was the first university in California I'd heard of, even before Berkeley or UCLA. For years, as far as I was concerned, it was the best university in the state.

The exodus continued.

There was a girl named Jin Yishi at my middle school. Four years my senior, she was famed for her academic prowess. In 1980, she was accepted to Peking University. In September, 1984, as soon as I began my studies at Peking University, one of my first orders of business was seeking her out. Yishi held a special place in my heart, as we both had names with sophisticated meanings. It was said that her father named her Jin Yishi to lament her being born during such a dark period of Chinese history when "gold (Jin) could be mistaken (Yi) for stone (Shi)." I visited her at her dorm room one night, and learned she had just passed the CUSBEA (China-United States Biochemistry Examination and Application) and was taking intensive English classes to prepare for studying in America.

One example after the next, I gradually came to the conclusion that no matter what capitalist evils lay in wait, America had to be better than China. My teacher, my idol, the star student of my middle school were all leaving for America.

It was becoming painfully apparent that China had a long way to go before it caught up with much of the world. This disparity led China to set its sights on smaller, closer targets, trying first to best its Asian neighbors before taking on the rest:

"First Asia! next, the world!"

Time flew. And it flew even faster after I transferred to the Chinese department. Before I knew it, I was facing my last semester.

I thought back to what the "philosopher" guards had asked me.

Where are you going?

It had been more than twenty years since my parents graduated college, and while there had been some changes favorable to individuals, the fundamentals of state control stayed the same. The state would hand the school a list of work units who needed new recruits, and the school, like a matchmaker, would place its graduates in those units. By 1988, graduates had the option of choosing on their own. If you could find an employer, the school would happily place you at the job of your choice. But if the job was in Beijing, it was your own responsibility to get yourself Beijing residency, and that was nearly impossible.

My career counselor told me that while entering Beijing's dog-eat-dog job market might seem daunting, there was no shortage of work units in Tianjin looking out for capable hires from the nation's top university.

"Would you consider the Tianjin Prosecutor's Office?" she suggested. "They're looking for a secretary with strong writing skills."

I didn't have any desire to return to Tianjin.

Following my triumphant change of majors, I was always met with looks of wonder and flurries of questions: "You changed majors? How did you do it? How come I didn't know we were even allowed?"

The attention played no small part in feeding my growing sense of vanity. The Tianjin Prosecutor's Office would doubtlessly be a highly sought-after work unit, but for me the devil lay in the word "doubtlessly." This decision would raise no questions, while I wanted every big decision in my life to provoke a degree of uncertainty, make a statement and stir the pot a bit. I was like a bear who had once jumped through a ring of fire at the circus, and had been rewarded with applause and honey, therefore I yearned to perform again and again.

What could I say to truly see people's jaws drop? What career would fill that need? I wouldn't be satisfied with simply surprising others. I had to surprise myself as well.

Before considering finding a job, I briefly entertained the idea of going to America. But other than taking the TOEFL, I hadn't taken any steps toward making the idea a reality. I tried to get into a graduate program in Scientific and Technological English Journalism at the

China School of Journalism, but was unsuccessful. I had assumed they wanted humanities students with some knowledge in science. It turned out they wanted science students who could write a little bit. I scored a mere twenty points out of a hundred on the scientific knowledge exam. Not exactly impressive, despite my high score for English.

May's warming breezes began to permeate the city, and with them came painful farewells to my treasured home, and my beloved friends.

I had no idea what my future would look like, or even how it would begin. From the depths of that amorphous desperation, I wrote an essay to express my confusion. It was published in the school newspaper and received favorable comments. It might not have made a job magically fall from the sky, but I felt better once I'd written out what was stuck in my mind.

It was the first time when I felt good about being a writer.

In May of 1988, a job listing appeared in the Triangle. The employer's name was the Founder Group: a company founded by Peking University two years earlier. The company was focused on technology-related ventures and would go on to become one of the nation's largest conglomerates, dealing in everything from commodities, investment, real estate, even healthcare.

Founder Group was started by Wang Xuan, a computer science professor at Peking University, and the inventor of a Chinese-character laser phototypesetting system, which allowed computers to print Chinese characters for the first time in history.

By the '80s, computers had become instrumental for word processing in many languages, but the complexity and staggering variety of Chinese characters posed a significant obstacle for digitalizing this language. Processing Chinese characters required huge data storage capacity. Wang Xuan's innovative method allowed for compression and restoration of each character, which cut down the storage requirement millions of times over.

After inventing his revolutionary system, Wang Xuan faced any innovator's ultimate task: how to bring the product to market. Instantly seeing the product's potential, Ding Shisun proposed that Peking University start its own company, which later became Founder Group.

In its initial stages, the company was entirely run by Peking University. All managers were teachers or professors, with the rest of staff being comprised of graduates. Not having its own headquarters, the company operated out of several locations. Its center of research and development rented two laboratories from the Physics Department. Sales and finance offices were established off campus on Zhongguancun Street, to save clients the trouble of being interrogated by the philosophers at the gate. Human resources was in the university's famed "Red Buildings," along with the graduate admissions offices and the school newspaper.

The moment I saw the Founder's notice at the Triangle, I knew that's where I wanted to work. I was fascinated by its start-up feel with offices throughout campus. It felt like Bohemian art colony. I could be "out in the world" without ever actually leaving my beloved campus!

They were seeking graduates of computer science, radio engineering, mathematics, physics...the list went on. Nothing remotely close to Chinese literature, but that didn't discourage me.

I strode into the HR office and filled out an application, noting that while I had graduated with a degree in Chinese, I entered as a computer science major. I was granted an exam and an initial interview.

And then, nothing.

Two weeks later, I was called back for a second interview.

Here's how they contacted me: First, a teacher from HR rode his bike to the Chinese Department, where the notice of my second interview was presented to Mr. Feng, an office clerk in his late 50s.

Mr. Feng then rode his bike to Building 32, where the female Chinese literature students lived, before being told I lived in Building 31: the Computer Science Department girls' dorm. Though I had changed majors, they never had me change dorms. Poor Mr. Feng, an elderly man getting set to retire, had to trek to the next building over, then huff and puff his way up four flights of stairs to deliver the notice.

During my second interview, I chatted with the HR director for about half an hour. He asked how my English was, and I replied, "Not bad, I got a 580 on my TOEFL."

Expecting him to be impressed, I was surprised to find him alarmed, asking brusquely, "Why would you take the TOEFL? Are you going to America soon?"

To which I replied, "That was the plan, but I don't have the money. As you know, I'm a Chinese literature major, and there are very limited grants and scholarships in my field. I want to find a job first and save the money."

His demeanor eased considerably. "You put in ten years here, I guarantee you'll have your tuition."

I knew I was probably hired.

He continued to tell me how the Founder Group had just signed a cooperation agreement with Canon in Japan to form a joint-venture called Pecan Inc., which was about to develop a new Chinese-language word processor. It just so happened they were seeking candidates who had knowledge in both computers and Chinese language. I exclaimed, "That's me! That's exactly me!"

He chuckled, and walked out of the room. After a few minutes, he returned, and announced that his boss, Mr. Lou, wanted me to help him draw up a document.

I assumed this was another test, but the boss was, in fact, about to head over Canon's Beijing office to negotiate the terms of an agreement, and needed my help.

Moments later, I was alone in a room with a stack of materials. In two hours, I produced what he needed. I took it to Mr. Lou's office.

He leafed through it and said, "I have to leave for the meeting right now. Come with me. If there's anything that needs editing, you can do it there."

I followed him outside, where a Nissan Bluebird waited on the driveway to take us to Canon's Beijing Office at the famous Beijing Hotel.

This was the first time I'd ever ridden in a car, and only the second time I'd been to the Beijing Hotel.

The man in charge of Canon's Beijing arm of operations was Mr. Murata. Mr. Lou introduced me as "Ms. Wang, my secretary," as we walked inside. Mr. Murata greeted me in astonishingly authentic Chinese with a slight Shanghai accent, and asked me if I was a member of the Communist Party. Shocked by his fluency and the question itself, I stammered out, "No...no, I'm not."

A look of disappointment came over his face as he asked me why. I wondered how on earth it was any of his business. Did he want me to be a communist? Wasn't the ultimate goal of communism to crush capitalist countries like his?

I didn't utter a word to express such a thought, but he seemed to sense me running laps in my head. He patted Mr. Lou on the shoulder and said, "After the deal, we really need to hire more Party members. Party members don't care about private property, so they don't ask for raises."

Mr. Lou let loose a hearty laugh, and it was then I knew it was only a joke.

It turned out that Mr. Murata was half-Japanese and half-Chinese. After Japan's defeat in 1945, most Japanese living in China fled back to their homeland, but Mr. Murata's mother decided to stay behind with her Chinese husband. Mr. Murata was born in 1949, the same year the People's Republic of China was founded. China had been his only home until 1978, when he decided to restore his Japanese citizenship to attend a Japanese university. After graduation, he joined Canon. Five years later, he was dispatched to China, in charge of the company's Beijing office.

I didn't think I'd impressed Mr. Murata, but two days later, HR informed me that Canon's Beijing office needed an intern and Mr. Murata wanted me to start immediately. I was close to graduation, and only had a few exams at the end of June. I could easily handle an internship.

Mr. Lou explained that I would learn first hand the Japanese style of management, which was light years beyond our own. "You're there to learn. Take in everything you can, do everything you're told, and only speak when spoken to. I don't care what it is, even pouring tea for customers. Do it with a smile. Too many Peking University graduates think they're above everything, but even the smallest matter can lead to the biggest deal."

I didn't like it, but I couldn't work for Founder Group if I failed the internship.

Three days a week, I traveled from Peking University to the Beijing Hotel.

My grandmother's apartment was roughly in the middle between Peking University and the Beijing Hotel, so when I was in the mood for grandma's cooking, I would head to her house for dinner. Unlike my parents, my grandma didn't have a refrigerator, so she only made enough for whoever was at the table. In my youthful impulsivity, I always showed up unannounced. But no matter when I arrived, there was always a plate for me at her table.

On June 2, 1988, I got off work at five, headed to my grandma's for dinner, then went to a movie before returning to school around ten o'clock. The second I got off the bus, I noticed something wasn't right at the south gate. I'd already been working for a month or so, and had a bit of money in my pocket, which I eagerly spent on clothes and makeup. I was distinctly aware that I looked less and less like a student, so before leaving my dorm, I always double-checked that I had my student ID.

The guard checked me before waving me through. I headed

straight for the Triangle.

Hundreds of students surrounded a patch of newly-posted notices. I couldn't come close to reading them. Someone stood up on a chair in front of the bulletin board and was giving a fervent speech.

It took me quite some time to figure out what had happened. Chai Qingfeng, a graduate student of Peking University, had been beaten to death by a group of hooligans.

Chai was a grad student in the Geophysics Department, and had gotten into an argument with people at a neighboring table at a restaurant off campus that evening. Somehow the fight escalated. Chai's opponents brandished knives and stabbed him to death on the spot. News of his passing sent shockwaves across campus.

It sounded like any other street fight gone out of control, but students were enraged to an extent I hadn't seen before. There'd been a growing sense of unrest at elite universities for quite some time. With China's budding market economy taking up more and more public sphere, graduates had no idea what kind of future to prepare for. Before the market economy, every student was guaranteed a job by the government. Now, they were on their own. Some sought an upper hand through back-door dealings, but most didn't have the connections.

On the other hand, Peking University students had learned how to use chaos to their advantage. Whenever they took to the streets or swarmed campus in outrage, the government would do anything to quell the riots. This had resulted in better food in the cafeteria, free movies and dance parties on campus. Sometimes a high-ranked government official would descend upon the school to meet students as a gesture of appreciation for us serving as role models for the youth of the country. Constantly cycling through being discarded and coddled left students feeling disoriented and aggravated.

The night of Chai Qingfeng's death, I sensed collective grief, anger, impatience and disillusion, but somehow, I didn't even feel a bit agitated. One of us had been killed, and that those who committed the crime should be arrested, tried, and convicted. That was that. What was the point of all this animosity?

Getting a job at a Japanese company had changed me. I thought more pragmatically now. Mr. Lou had promised that Founder Group would award Beijing residency to this year's new hires. Even my parents had never been able to make that happen! Before it could be finalized, I had to make sure I did everything right. Shouting in the streets wouldn't look good.

I turned my back on the Triangle. I started taking an out-of-the-way route to my dorm, and kept my head low in case anyone asked me to join in a show of force. The Triangle faded from view behind me until it became invisible.

I'd put off moving my things out of my dorm room for the simple reason that I had no idea where to go. My internship was complete, and I had been officially assigned to Canon's Beijing office. I could have easily applied for a room at Founder Group's employee housing next to campus, but it was almost an hour and a half by bus to the Beijing Hotel, where I would be working for the foreseeable future. Living with my grandmother would save me a great deal of time. I wanted to ask her if I could live with her again, but couldn't bring myself to say it. Maybe I was too old to stay under my grandma's roof now?

I procrastinated until the very last day I could to collect my belongings, but workers were already cleaning the halls and making their way into the rooms. I approached one and asked if anyone had seen my suitcases. He stared blankly back at me, only his eyes visible over his dust mask. He silently shook his head. I stood in the middle of the hall, lost in space as the workers deftly set about sanding down the walls. They worked like a swarm of bees, immersing the entire building in a cloud of lead-laden dust.

I took a mental inventory of what I'd lost. Besides some books and clothes, the only thing I really cared about were my application forms to American universities. The forms were free, but I had to send query letters to each school. I had spent 100 RMB in postage in total. My brochures and applications made up a major portion of my assets, but I'd waited until the very last day and they were gone forever.

It looked like I wouldn't be going to America anytime soon. Instead, I would be working for a Japanese company. I thought about that slogan: "First Asia! Next, the world!" and I felt relieved.

Was this coincidence or destiny? Hopefully there would still be time for the rest of the world.

Before starting work in August, I took a break to visit my parents in Tianjin. For the last two years, I'd kept my change of majors a secret from my parents, for fear of rebuke, or an end to my monthly allowance.

There it was, written in bold letters across my diploma: "Graduated from the Department of Chinese Literature with a B.A. degree."

As I handed it to my parents, I braced myself for their fury, but my mother looked at it with a measured curiosity. My father shrugged and pushed the diploma away: "Well, Congratulations, I suppose. You graduated. Better than we expected."

You mean to tell me that this whole time, you were just wondering if I could even graduate?

They always had to find a way to one-up me.

I couldn't take sitting in their house any longer, so I went to see Zhi Hua. I spent the next two hours traveling across town.

I wanted to surprise her. Shock her even. Anything to make up for the pleasure my parents had so deftly robbed me of.

"I want to tell you a secret," I told her, "You remember Mr. Zhang, my Chinese teacher from Xinhua High School? I was madly in love with him."

"Puh! Who didn't know that?" she replied.

I couldn't catch a break. "How did you know?"

"That time we planned to cut class to watch a movie. Why did you get cold feet? It was your idea to fake sickness to the nurse, and then you told everyone on the street that we were going to watch a movie! You wanted his attention. You wanted to get called to his office for a lecture."

I was dumbfounded. After a while, I was able to gather myself up and reply: "That's nonsense."

She continued, "And that's just one example. You always sat in the back because you were taller than most of your class, and every time Mr. Zhang walked back there to talk to you, you would squirm like your seat was on fire. You never noticed the students in front of you giggling because they had their backs to you."

My face flushed with shame and a little anger. "Everyone was laughing at me?"

"Oh yeah, everyone," she nodded. "I could see when I passed by in the hallway."

I was down to my last weapon. "You know what? I should be called Wang Yan, not Wang Yuan."

"Wang Yan?" She rolled her eyes. "Like the herb? We use it in some dishes in Qinhuangdao. Why do you want to be called that?"

That was a decisive blow.

Before coming to Zhi Hua's house, I'd been planning to visit Mr. Zhang after. He was a talented, inspiring teacher, and I was still secretly in love with him. He was almost twenty years older than me and married. I didn't dare express my love for him in high school. Now, I'd graduated from the best college in the country and was about to start work at a real grownup job. I felt as if I'd conquered an entire continent. I finally had the courage to come up close to him and say "hi."

But Zhi Hua's remarks had dampened my enthusiasm. The secret love I'd cherished was a book everyone had already read! I suspected Mr. Zhang knew it too. He must have met a legion of young girls who'd fallen in love with him over the years. Plus, the air of mystique around my name had vanished. "Fragrant grass" was only a common household spice somewhere in this world.

Chapter 5

FESCO

There is a theory in geometry that three points define a plane. I now had three points of interest in Beijing: Peking University, my grandma's home, and the Beijing Hotel. Shuttling between them made me feel that I belonged to Beijing completely.

My grandmother's apartment building was on the corner of Yuetan South Street and Nanlishi Road. If I wanted to get to Tiananmen, I had to take either the #19 or #15 bus south to Chang'an Avenue, then transfer to #1, #4 or #10 headed east. The total distance was about 4.5 miles (7.3 kilometers).

When I was in elementary school, I visited Tiananmen Square at least once a year. Every June 1st was Children's Day, which is a holiday observed in many communist countries. Our teachers would march us to the foot of the Monument to the People's Heroes to pay our respects. There would always be a veteran making an impassioned speech calling for constant vigilance. A student representative would respond, shouting out, on our behalf, the gratitude for the veterans' service and dedication. The ritual always ended with us singing the national anthem, or "The Internationale," in unison.

About a half mile east of Tiananmen, there's a commercial district called Wangfujing: Beijing's hub of wealth and pleasure.

Wangfujing means "the well of the princes." It was where princes went to pass the time in the days of the emperor. After 1949, it became a place for average citizens to pass an afternoon eating, drinking, and shopping.

When I was living with my grandma, my parents and brother came to visit every Chinese New Year. On the morning of the third day of Chinese New Year, our family would embark on our yearly trip to Wangfujing.

My mother headed straight for her favorite hair salon, while my father went right for his favorite restaurant with my brother and me in tow. We waited in a line which on its best days was an hour long. In the freezing cold, we stared holes through the doors until they finally opened. We rushed into the warmth within, frantically grabbed a table and got our orders in before the kitchen became buried under an avalanche of orders. My father never stopped watching the front door, through which an endless wave of people would enter, before coming over and asking if they could take our empty chair. My father always replied apologetically, "We are still waiting for someone who will be here any minute." The inquirers left in a huff, muttering, or "accidentally" kicking the leg of the chair. My father fretted that someone would end up taking the chair despite him, but I worried even more about how selfish we looked guarding an empty chair in a ridiculously overcrowded restaurant. Finally, my mother would come flitting into the restaurant glowing with a gorgeous new hairstyle. We breathed a sigh of relief.

The restaurant's food wasn't that great, and to me, there was no real reward for what seemed a crazy yearly exercise in testing the limits of our patience. But even so, I never refused to go with them. It was better than sitting at my grandmother's house, wondering if something interesting would actually happen this time. Besides, the experience of eating out itself gave me something to brag about. Not anyone got to dine out at Wangfujing once a year. They didn't have to know whether or not I enjoyed the food.

During our 1973 trip, as I approached the corner of Wangfujing Street and Chang'an Avenue, I noticed a fence had been set up, and a large crowd of people were gathered around it. So many, in fact, that they were blocking the road entirely. My father stopped and craned his neck to see what was behind the barrier.

"What is it? What's happening?" I asked.

"It's a construction site. They're starting work on a new building. From the depth of the foundation, it's going to be pretty tall."

Apparently, a building of that tall was a much bigger deal than I understood at the time. Economic activity had been frozen since the beginning of the Cultural Revolution. New development potentially heralded a thaw in conflict. Years and years of factional strife would end, and the government could get down to business.

The next year, we returned and found a resplendent, shining tower where the foundation had been. The magnificent eastern tower of the Beijing Hotel had been erected and was open for business. The chain link panels had been replaced by thick trimmed hedges. Just like the year before, a throng of people were crowded around, blocking the road for a peek inside.

"What is it? What's happening?" I asked again.

"It's a car," my father replied. "The best car made in China."

At that time, every feature-length film at the theater was preceded by a ten-to-fifteen-minute documentary on domestic and international news. Shortly after its opening, the Beijing Hotel appeared in these pre-film documentaries. It was known as the most luxurious hotel in the city and was often tasked with receiving foreign visitors. Therefore, it made itself newsworthy.

For car enthusiasts, watching fancy cars on screen wasn't enough. They clustered around the hedges of the Beijing Hotel, waiting to see the newest models cruise into view.

The first time I went inside the Beijing Hotel was in 1987. I was taking the TOEFL, and had to pay the registration fee in US dollars.

I didn't know how to exchange RMB for USD, so I turned to Mike, a former exchange student from America. When he'd studied at Peking University, I tutored him in Chinese for 5 RMB per hour. After graduating, he went to work for the US-China Business Council at the Beijing Hotel. He left me his number and told me to stop by if I was ever in the area, which I'd never actually done. I gave him a call and explained my situation. He replied that he was happy to help, and told me to come by his office.

My journey from campus took much longer than anticipated. By the time I set foot on the lobby's marble tile, Mike had already left for the day. I had no idea he'd gone, and proceeded just as he had instructed. I'd never ridden in an elevator before, but I could read. I followed the signs to a small lounge with doors on each of its two longer sides. I pressed the nearest up button and a soft ding sounded as one of the doors slid open.

The inside of the doors was so smooth I could see myself in them as they closed in front of me. I felt a slight jolt, then felt much heavier than normal. The heavy feeling stopped and the door opened again. I raised my right foot and planted it on the soft carpet outside. It sank a bit, which almost sent me tumbling, but my left leg intuitively followed. My two legs were once again level and I recovered from my near fall. The walls here were a rich cream color. I thought of the harsh white walls of my dorm, which had discolored here and there. At the end of the hall was a huge window letting in an enormous amount of sunlight. What a pleasant place to be!

It turned out Mike had already left for the day, but he'd left a note at the front desk telling me that he would be back at Peking University in a few days. He asked me to meet him at the front door of cafeteria #5 at 6 pm this Friday.

When the day came, I headed for the cafeteria. I could see Mike easily from a distance since he was exceptionally tall. As I got closer, I saw a stack of paper in his hand, which he was methodically handing out to every person in his midst. When he finally saw me, he stretched out his long arm and gave me one too. It was a cashier's check made out to ETS in the amount of $29.

So this was how one paid for a TOEFL! I thought I'd simply take some cash to the testing center and pay at a window, like I was buying a movie ticket. There was a quiet implosion inside my head. I spent a minute or two admiring the check, left to right, right to left, before I snapped out of my trance and reached into my pocket to grab Mike the money I'd brought him. Mike quickly replied, "Don't worry about it!"

It wasn't just me, it turned out. He hadn't taken a penny from anyone. His plan all along was to pay our TOEFL fees outright. He'd arranged for us all to meet him at the cafeteria at the same time, like he was serving Christmas dinner to the homeless. I looked up at Mike and felt slightly uneasy. He, however, looked perfectly natural; not even a bit self-conscious. It seemed like this was just what he did on a daily basis. How many people had he done this for? How many people had him to thank for their TOEFL, or even for their entire future?

As dusk settled over campus, I headed back to my dorm, check in hand, my head and heart tugging me in a thousand different directions. As grateful as I was for his generosity, I felt a bit embarrassed for accepting it. I'd really only wanted to see if he could exchange the currency for me. I wasn't looking for a handout, but evidently he'd thought otherwise.

By the late 1980s, Beijing still lacked any actual office buildings. Foreign businesses were relegated to operating out of guest rooms in the few hotels authorized to house modern-day Marco Polos. Nearly a quarter of the rooms in the Beijing Hotel were leased to foreign companies, among them, Canon Beijing, who leased a suite on the 11th floor of the east wing of the Beijing Hotel.

Now, I was officially a member of the club. I could take my time admiring the hotel's details instead of sneaking glances here and there. One day, I noticed some curious writing on the elevator control panel: "Capacity: 23." What did it mean? I asked Yang, a slim, handsome desk clerk. In those days, high-end hotels had a 24-hour service desk on each floor. I'd built a rapport with some of the clerks since I'd started.

"It means that only 23 people are allowed in the elevator at a time," he said, slightly surprised.

"What if more than 23 people squeeze in?"

"An alarm goes off, and some people would have to get out. Otherwise the elevator won't work."

I thought of the magic buses I took everyday. They seemed able to accommodate an infinite number of people. No matter how many got on, it staggered ever forward, even if we were squished to a pulp.

"Why there isn't an alarm like that on buses?" I asked.

It wasn't as much a question for him as for myself, but he answered anyway. He furrowed his brow for a time before coming up with his response: "Foreigners are more delicate. They aren't as tough as us Chinese, so they need extra protection."

Indeed, foreigners did seem to need more than us. They needed more lighting and space than we did. They had higher hygienic standards. The bathrooms at the Beijing Hotel were so clean, they looked as if they'd never been used. Having seen how foreigners lived at the Beijing Hotel, I began to wonder how people could bear to live in places like my grandmother's apartment building.

The building where my grandmother lived in was even darker and quieter than it had been in my childhood. Back in the '70s, the halls were always bright and full of life. Every door was open, even if some had half a bed sheet across the doorway to create some semblance of privacy, allowing sunlight from the windows beyond or the nighttime glow of lamps within pour out into the hall through the translucent fabric. "Privacy" was merely symbolic, as you could hear every word of every argument between husband and wife, and every sharp crack across a disobedient kid's bottom.

In 1988, every door was sealed up like a tomb. Throughout the hall, only four points let in any natural light: the stairwell, the public washroom, and the two bathrooms. Walking down the hall was like trying to navigate a pitch-black box with four pinholes in it, and that was during the day. Why did everyone suddenly decide to spend all day closed up in these little shoeboxes?

My grandmother explained that in the '70s, everyone pretty much led the same kind of life, and no one saw any point in shutting the door. Whatever was happening in your home was nearly identical to next door, so you might as well at least let some air in.

Besides, for some, keeping the door open meant there were witnesses should anything need to be proven. Rumor had it that the Xue family, who cared for their bedridden father, left the door wide open, so everyone could see they never mistreated the old fellow. Remember? In the '70s, public opinion was everything. If even one person began doubting their piety, it would spread like wildfire, destroying reputations along the way.

I remembered the Xue family. They lived next to the stairwell, with their father's bed facing the front door of their room. Every time anyone passed by, the old man would let out a series of unintelligible grunts, trying in vain to convey a message no one understood. Scared, I always sped up, ducking to avoid eye contact.

"What happened to him?" I asked.

"Two months after they started shutting their door, he passed away."

I gasped, "They abused him to death?"

"Who's to say?" My grandmother shook her head.

Even with every door sealed shut, it shouldn't have been so dark. There were ceiling lamps every few meters, and when I was a kid, at least half the lights worked. Now, all the bulbs were broken and none of the switches worked. It was as if the building never even had electricity in the first place. I asked my grandmother why things had gone so far downhill, to which she responded flatly, "No one wants to pay the electricity bill, so someone went through and broke everything."

In the '70s, the entire building shared one power meter. Each month, the collective bill was divvied up according to how many people lived in each household. This system relied on the assumption that every person used roughly the same amount of electricity, which, for a long time, had held true. But by the '80s, as the economy expanded, the gap between the rich and poor began to widen. Some had refrigerators, TV's, and other modern electronics, while others had nothing more than lamps. Those with money installed their own meters to make sure they paid exactly what they owed, leaving the cost to keep the lights in the hall going fell to those who didn't have their own meters. Why should they pay to keep the halls lit for the rich? The only solution was to make sure the halls stayed dark.

Before I moved in, I offered my grandmother 50 RMB a month in rent. She wouldn't accept until I explained that if I lived in the company dorms, I'd pay the same amount. Much better if it went to her. In the end, she relented.

For me, it was natural, but she took it a very different way. She bragged to neighbors about the money her granddaughter so generously gave her. They certainly complimented her, which she relayed to me, beaming as she described to me how they marveled at her good fortune. That was her way of saying "thank you." She also had a habit of telling me her own opinions and feelings by way of quoting the neighbors. "People all say that I've lived a hard life, but now my granddaughter is here to give me a good one," she said.

One day, she told me that she was going to have her own power meter installed, even though she and my grandfather had nothing that ran on electricity except a couple of lamps. She explained it wasn't about necessity, but about appearances. She had a granddaughter who worked for foreigners, which meant she finally had the means to keep up with the Joneses. I guess merely bragging wasn't enough for her. She had to have something concrete to show the neighbors.

One day, I came home and found a brand new meter on the wall. A wire wrapped in black electrical tape stuck out of one side and stretched toward the light above her doorway. Now, each time I went to the washroom, I could turn on the light and let its dim, fifteen-watt glow get me just down to the end of the hall.

Every morning, I traveled from our dimly lit commune-style home to a luminous temple of capitalism. Our office at the Beijing Hotel was continuously bathed in light. With six huge windows and a set of French doors leading out onto the balcony, natural light came pouring into our office all day long. When natural light wasn't enough, electrical lighting came to the rescue. Whenever I think of wealth and luxury, I think of bright lights. Not gold, not diamonds, just abundant lighting.

I had two bosses: Mr. Murata, chief representative of Canon Beijing, and his assistant, a young woman named Ms. Kawashima. Ms. Kawashima always looked radiant, and her work dresses, impeccable. I wasn't as good at blending in. I took notes on her outfits and went shopping after work to assemble a wardrobe similar to hers. But she rode in a car to work, while I commuted in buses packed like a tin of sardines. I arrived at work wrinkled and ruffled until I figured out I could wear casual clothes on the way and change once I got to the office.

Every morning at 8:30, I headed to the service desk for the key to room 1103. I unlocked the doors, changed my outfit and got to work. My job included wiping down the furniture, washing the bosses' tea cups, brewing fresh tea, and neatly placing said tea on their desks. Before I knew it, it was almost 9 am and time for the bosses to show up.

Mr. Murata was a Japanese national, but Japanese was effectively his second language, from which Ms. Kawashima derived no shortage of delight. Whenever Murata was out of the office, she would go over to the fax machine, pull out the originals he'd sent to Japan, and peruse them for mistakes. At times, she'd laugh so hard, and she'd be rocking back and forth at her desk. I didn't know what it was about, but knew it wasn't my place to ask, much less to interfere. One day, she noticed me sitting nervously in the corner, and felt an explanation might be in order.

"You look confused, Miss Wang. Do you know what I'm laughing about?"

"Not in the least..."

"It's Mr. Murata's baby Japanese! Oh my god! Hahaha..."

She was four years older than me, and had graduated with a B.A. in Chinese from a prestigious women's college in Japan. She was beautiful, and spoke in a cute, coquettish way like Japanese girls in movies. There is a Japanese word for this style: *kawaii*.

According to Japanese custom, cleaning, pouring tea, and other such duties were exclusively the purview of women. But Ms. Kawashima felt that since Mr. Murata wasn't really Japanese, she didn't have to follow convention to serve him. No matter how bad his Japanese might have been, Mr. Murata was the head of our office, and, more importantly, a man. There was no way he would brew his own tea, much less hers. It took me a month, but I finally figured out my importance in the office. If not for me, they would probably have died of thirst on the job.

In addition to my tea and cleaning duties, I wasn't really responsible for anything else, except occasionally answering the phone. Before I came along, if Mr. Murata was out of the office, Ms. Kawashima had no choice but to stay, as someone had to be present to answer the calls at all times. After the arrival of the tea-girl, they were both able to attend any meeting they wished. My job wasn't nearly as glamorous as I'd thought. I was simply here to solve a personal spat.

I felt somewhat dejected after discovering my real role in the office. I started sneaking out to chat with Yang at the service desk when I was really bored. Yang had his own problems too, and would demand a solution for his issues before I'd have a chance to tell him mine.

"Do you think I should change jobs?" he would ask.

"If you want to change, you should do it!" I told him how I'd changed majors from computer science to Chinese literature.

"At least you are passionate about something," he'd sigh. "I don't love anything."

He'd worked at the hotel for over ten years. At the time, most men of thirty looked a little weathered from commuting by bus or bike. He, however, living in a dorm building at the back of the hotel, barely exposing to the wind and sun, looked young and pale. A rich elder woman from Hong Kong had been wooing him, claiming he looked exactly like her late son.

"Why did you choose to go into a hotel management school in the first place?" I asked.

"I don't know. Working in a hotel isn't too bad. I guess I could've ended up working in a foundry or something."

"You're happier here than there, right?"

"I guess so," he nodded. "I don't regret it. Working here suits me, actually. It's just really boring sometimes. Are you bored by your work?"

"A little," I said. It was my turn to tell him my problem, but Canon's driver, a guy named Zhao, walked over right at that moment.

"I just started," I said to Yang in a hurry. "I don't really have time to feel bored yet."

I left the service desk and went back to work.

There were four people in our office. Mr. Murata, Ms. Kawashima, me and Zhao. Zhao's job was to drive the two bosses to meetings, and depending on the length of the matter at hand, he would either wait there, or head back to the office until he was called to pick them up. Every time he left, I prayed it wouldn't be the latter. When it was just the two of us, he wouldn't stop talking no matter how many hints I dropped.

He only had one topic of discussion: how he was superior to me. Every time, he'd put his feet up on the massive desk in front of him and start the same lecture again: "Just come to FESCO! I hear they're hiring!"

There was a state-run company called the Beijing Foreign Enterprise Service Co.—FESCO for short. In the '80s, foreign companies couldn't do any direct hiring in China, which is where FESCO came in. FESCO had a reserve of various workers, secretaries, translators, accountants, drivers, you name it. If foreign companies needed a worker, they went to FESCO to answer the need.

For foreign companies, there were two main problems with going through FESCO. FESCO paid its employees around one-fifth of what it charged foreign companies, which substantially raised the cost of manpower. The other issue was that every employee effectively had two bosses to answer to. Plus, rumor had it that some FESCO employees were corporate or government spies. That's never been officially proven, but one of my FESCO-employed friends did tell me she was told to take a peek in the wastebaskets when necessary. Thankfully, she never went that far. It's not surprising at all that some foreign employers wanted to circumvent FESCO altogether, directly signing employment contracts in flagrant disregard of the law. If they were caught, they were fined heavily. But for some, the risk was worth the reward.

Zhao knew I hadn't been hired through FESCO. Early on, he tried different ways of finding out if I was a distant relative of Mr. Murata. I told him I wasn't an illegal employee, but was hired through a joint-venture.

"What's a joint-venture?"

I tried to explain it as plainly as I could, knowing it was still a novel concept for most Chinese. "Canon is a company from a capitalist country, and Peking University is an entity from a socialist country. They want to do business, so they form a new company together.

That new company is called a joint-venture. As a result, Canon can sell its products in China, and Peking University receives investment from Canon."

I further pointed out that FESCO was owned wholly by the state, and was the obsolete child of a planned economy, while Pecan Inc. was the fashionable fruit of the new hybrid economy.

He kept silent for a few days as he thought of a new way to one-up me. After my first payday, he asked if I got my lunch allowance in RMB or FEC.

"RMB, of course. Why?"

"Ha! Even I get FEC, and I'm just a driver! I think Mr. Murata is bullying you because you don't work for FESCO."

Foreign Exchange Certificates, FEC for short, hold a unique place in Chinese history. Officially called "Bank of China Foreign Currency Exchange Certificates," they first appeared during the initial stages of the "reform and opening-up" period. They were created as a means of guaranteeing the value of RMB against incoming foreign currency. Foreigners coming to China could only exchange their foreign money for FEC and only spend their FEC at designated shops, hotels, restaurants, so forth. Thus, circulation of FEC was restricted to a small circle. But Chinese citizens also wanted to get their hands on the items sold only in the designated shops, and a black market for FEC emerged. On paper, the value of 1 FEC was supposed to be equal with 1 RMB, but in reality FEC was always worth much more. At its peak, 1 FEC was worth as much as 1.9 RMB.

If a foreigner stayed in China long enough to figure it out, they would first go to the Bank of China to buy FEC, and then sell it on the black market. After that, they could avoid the designated shopping destinations and went to neighborhood shops, spending RMB like ordinary Chinese people. While the practice was illegal, I'd never heard of a foreigner being arrested for spending RMB.

FESCO employees received two sources of income. One came from their mother company, and the other came in the form of "lunch allowances" paid by their foreign employers. I got paid the same way, with 120 RMB per month coming from Pecan, and another 200 as a lunch allowance. My lunch allowance came in plain RMB, while Zhao got his in coveted FEC. The difference was rooted in our employment affiliations. Foreign bosses dared not pay FECSO employees in RMB because foreigners weren't legally allowed to have RMB. But Mr. Murata was a representative of Canon Inc., as well as vice president of Pecan. It was perfectly legal for the joint-venture to have RMB.

Zhao's unceasing attempts to brainwash me were starting to work. I began to feel that FESCO employees actually were a grade above me. And I was a graduate of Peking University!

No matter the currency, I received my first paycheck at the end of August. I was officially a person of means, and had finally overcome feeling disoriented in a luxury environment. Still, I felt uneasy, like I'd missed a homework assignment and couldn't remember what it was. I felt there was something I should have done. As I was riding in the elevator, I overheard two men talking about the US-China Business Council. There it was! I had to find Mike and return the money he lent me. I followed the men all the way to an office with "US-China Business Council" engraved on a metal plaque on the door. I told the receptionist I was looking for an American whose first name was Mike. I'd forgotten his last name. Maybe I never even knew it. The receptionist thought for a moment and remembered that someone named Mike worked there at some point, but he'd returned to America.

I asked if he'd left a forwarding address so I could send him a cashier's check. I made sure to point out that as an employee of a foreign firm, I was familiar with such business. I wasn't some stupid girl who would simply mail him cash in an envelope. With legitimate curiosity, she asked me, "How much did he lend you?"

"Twenty-nine dollars."

She shrugged. "It's not even thirty bucks. I wouldn't worry about it."

I was embarrassed. Thirty dollars was almost an entire week's pay for me. I didn't want to be remembered as someone who took advantage of other people's generosity, but according to that girl, thirty bucks wasn't a big deal, so the effort it would take to return it would be for nothing.

This different attitudes toward money signified a hierarchy among Chinese who worked for foreign companies. Those worked for American companies got paid more than their counterparts at Japanese companies.

"First Asia, next, the world," I thought enviously.

My friends at the service desk had naturally assumed I was a FESCO employee, as Canon was a massive international name, and thus was too high-profile to try anything illegal. In their eyes, you either worked for FESCO, or you were working illegally. They didn't know there was a third option.

Back then, China still employed a six-day workweek, while most foreign countries had a five-day week. Japan was part of the latter group, so Mr. Murata and Ms. Kawashima took turns working Saturdays. Some other companies would be completely devoid of foreign employees on Saturdays. FESCO saw an opportunity, and asked its subordinates to come to the main office for "political studies" every Saturday afternoon.

One such afternoon, it just so happened that I spent my lunch chatting with Yang, when two young women, apparently FESCO employees, appeared in the hallway. They walked toward the elevator complaining about how boring "political studies" would be. When the elevator opened, they let out an audible sigh. As soon as the elevator door closed, Yang turned and asked, "How come you never have to go to political studies?"

"I don't work for FESCO," I replied matter-of-factly.

The look on Yang's face made me realize I needed to expand on my statement: "But I'm not a private hire. I was sent to Canon by a Sino-foreign joint venture."

"A joint venture?" Yang repeated in disbelief.

I explained it to him in the same way as I explained it to Zhao. Yang couldn't help but marvel, "That Mr. Murata is one crafty fox. If he got a secretary from FESCO, he'd have to pay at least 2000 FEC per month. Who knows how much he saved going through a joint-venture?"

"How should I know?" I murmured, not even trying to conceal my annoyance. He saw what his seemingly innocuous comments had done, and immediately went into damage control:

"I mean what's so great about FESCO, anyway? I wouldn't work for them if they begged me to. Did you know they don't even allow employees to date foreigners? I know people who've gotten punished for it."

I couldn't help but scoff. I wasn't even looking for a foreign boyfriend, but who were they to tell me I couldn't have one? What a joke! It later proved to be an actual rule. One of my friends from FESCO showed me their employee handbook. There it was in black and white: *No FESCO employee shall enter into a romantic relationship with any foreign businessman.* But the employees were behind closed doors with foreign businessmen every day, and FESCO definitely didn't have the resources to watch everyone's every move. I had to guess that it was just like so many other rules in China: purely for show. What a laughable bureaucracy!

They did, however, have a trump card up their sleeves. If the two wanted to marry, they wouldn't be able to hide it anymore, and it would be time to pay the piper. They would have no choice but to come clean, because in China, if you wanted a marriage certificate, your employer had to sign off on it. The only way to get that certificate would be a long process of apologizing for whorish and shameful behavior.

In those days, sexual harassment was a totally foreign concept to Chinese people. I'd heard a case of which a Chinese secretary at a Brazilian company complained that she was subjected to a daily barrage of sexual advances. Her Brazilian boss would often samba in the office, and stretch his arm out, asking, "Come, sleep with me! Am I not handsome enough for you? " She didn't know how to deal with it and asked FESCO for re-assignment, but they wouldn't grant her a transfer. They asked her, "What if a girl much weaker than you was in that same position? She would be corrupted by the decadent lifestyle of the capitalists." They asked her to stay "for the good of the country."

HR should have at least protected the poor woman's privacy, but somehow, the conversation leaked and the girl became the talk of the town. People went out of their way to walk past the Brazilian company's office to see the legendary samba man. "He *is* handsome!" They'd say. "And the girl? Very plain." Everyone wondered what he saw in her. She'd been made a laughingstock.

I assumed the real reason she couldn't be transferred was probably very simple: another candidate fluent in Portuguese wasn't easy to come by.

I rode with her in an elevator once. She was tiny, like she hadn't hit puberty yet, but her heavily made-up face told a different story. Her eyes were drowning in eyeshadow. Perhaps she'd wanted them to look bigger, but to me, they looked like they carried the weight of the world.

Chapter 6

Searching for an Ally

Zhi Hua was studying for her master's in Comparative Literature at Peking University. One day, she met me at Wangfujing for a visit. It was already after 6 pm by the time she arrived. I treated her to dinner at the restaurant my parents had brought me to once a year in my childhood.

While we were talking, she dropped terms I wasn't familiar with, like "orientalism." I couldn't keep up and felt uneasy. Academia was so far away it seemed like a different galaxy. After dinner, I took her to my office to continue our chat, hoping the hotel would impress her.

I invited her to have a seat on the couch while I made us some Japanese tea and turned on the television. We had access to channels from all over the world. In as nonchalant a manner as I could, I flipped through every channel. The foreign tones of English, Japanese, Russian, French, and other languages filled the room. I was observing her out of the corner of my eye, hoping to catch a glimpse of admiration or awe, but she inspected the room with a critical, unsatisfied eye. Suddenly she stood up, walked over to the work area and asked if she could go inside.

"Of course! Go for it!"

She opened the door and went in. I was hot on her heels, eager to see how she'd react. I flipped on the lights. The room was bathed in ample light. Cabinets and dressers of lacquered hardwood glimmered, holding sleek and expensive fax machines and printers.

"It may not look like much, but it's temporary," I explained. "Until now, Beijing hasn't had a real office building. The International Trade Center's being built not far from here. We're moving in next year."

She didn't say a word. After a while, she went back into the reception room and took a seat on the couch, looking ready to say something.

"What exactly do you do here?" she asked.

"I'm a secretary."

"Secretary?" She furrowed her brow. "I thought you worked for the development team."

"They're still building the team! Pecan sent me here first to learn Japanese culture and management techniques. It's super important for development." I knew it was bullshit. Still, there wasn't much room for her to argue. She didn't know that Mr. Murata's Japanese wasn't "pure," and that Ms. Kawashima wasn't even willing to pour tea for him. I could see disapproval and pity in her eyes. Whatever I was doing had nothing with the ideals we'd cultivated together from middle school on. She felt I was wasting my time.

In some Asian traditions, there is a rigid distinction between mind and matter. The material and spiritual realms are in conflict with one another, and one had to choose. Both traditional thinking and communist beliefs exalted the spiritual path while the material path promised to drag you to the depths below. Zhi Hua and I were both brought up with disdain for material things. Her look of pity expressed the pain she felt for how far I'd fallen. If we hadn't been such good friends, she probably would have just come right out and said something.

It was true. I'd become enchanted by material things. I'd been completely engulfed by this brightly lit, lavishly furnished world. If Zhi Hua thought such a feeling proved my corruption, I agreed. I could admit that Zhi Hua was pursuing a more spiritual goal than I. She lived in a spartan dorm at Peking University. But how about my grandma and her neighbors? Did living in a ramshackle apartment building make them any better spiritually?

I began to doubt if there was any conflict between material and spiritual pursuits. Still, Zhi Hua wasn't completely wrong. I had only been at Canon for a couple of months and I hadn't read a single book. Next evening, I headed straight for Xinhua Bookstore at Wangfujing, bought a stack of books, and hurried home to delve in.

My grandmother was delighted and welcomed me home with a proclamation: "Finally, you're home on time. Now they'll have nothing to talk about."

I responded, "Yeah? What are they talking about?"

She wanted to say something, but stopped short. "Don't worry about it. Eat your dinner."

While I ate, she opened her mouth again, "You should find a good boyfriend. It's the only thing missing in your life. That'd finally shut 'em up."

"What's that even supposed to mean? What did you hear?"

"I didn't hear anything. Who'd say something like that to my face? But people are saying that foreigners are corrupt. Since you come back late every night, you know they're all gossiping."

"So let them!" I retorted. "Who cares what they say?"

"Shhh! they might hear us!" she hissed.

In the '70s, saying one word against Chairman Mao could unleash nightmares at the hands of the government. Back then, everyone kept their doors open partly to prove they had nothing to hide. We'd already marched into the '80s, a time of the individuals. Everyone kept to themselves now. Who cared what I was doing?

"You're wrong," my grandmother said. "Nowadays people hate each other more than ever because of the economy. Everyone is either rich or poor. Many feel they've been handed a raw deal. More than ever, they love to watch others fail, and they hate it when they don't get to see you do so. Like you getting into FESCO. I'm sure everyone's jealous."

"I'm don't work for FESCO."

Her face went pale. She went to the front door and pressed her ear against its cold surface. After a few minutes, she let out a sigh of relief. "We're lucky. There's no one in the hall."

I laughed, "Every house has their door shut, and the hall is pitch black. Who's gonna walk around listening to us?"

"See, that's what you don't get." She shook her head, tired of explaining. "You may not care. But they do. Never let them know your weaknesses."

I found myself drifting further and further from Zhi Hua. I was simply captivated by the transient beauty of commercial products. Once, I wrote her a letter just to show off our letterhead with its delicately ornate watermark. I used a newly imported three-color retractable ballpoint pen designed to promote Canon's color printer. The pen wrote in red, green, and yellow. Its inks were made of the brightest and purest pigments, nothing like the brownish red and grayish green popular in Beijing at the time. I was a bit ashamed of my messy chicken-scratch, but surely I would dazzle her with my stunning tricolored chicken-scratch on exquisite snow-white paper.

One day, Zhi Hua invited me to participate in a discussion at Peking University. She was taking a sociology course taught by a professor from the States. The professor wanted to hear what someone with a white-collar job thought of China's rapid modernization. Enamored with the sound of my own voice, I rambled on and on. Afterward, I prided myself on having contributed a constructive, entertaining perspective. I was positive I'd been well-received.

A week later, I called Zhi Hua to touch base, and she complained about "dealing with the notes from your so-called speech. Who on earth can figure out what the hell you were even talking about? It's all so subjective, incidental, and fragmentary. There's absolutely no theoretical frame to it at all. How can I do anything with what you said?"

I was too dejected to ask what kind of theoretical framework she'd expected me to use. Existentialism, expressionism, impressionism, naturalism? I'd read a little of everything at college just as she did. But she was a graduate student now and had all the time in the world to read the −isms. I'd fallen behind.

As for calling my remarks "subjective, incidental and fragmentary," she wasn't entirely wrong. I was in and out of this new material world. Sometimes I longed to lose myself in it completely. I'd spend my days talking about salaries and lunch allowances, then escape to Shen Zhen on weekends to splurge on the latest Chow Sang Sang diamond earrings, but whenever I found myself consumed by the material world, I grew impatient and restless.

I had a particular weakness for high-quality printing products. In my childhood, the majority of my grandmother's neighbors worked in a printing factory, so I knew a thing or two about materials and production. Not long after I started, Ms. Kawashima ordered boxes of catalogs, along with a trove of small gifts from company headquarters. A month passed before the order finally arrived.

I took a catalog out of the box and turned it over in my hand. It was a beautifully printed piece of work. Everything about it, from the smart design to the smiling models placed next to each product— every printer, copier, camera, and medical instrument, all bathed in a rosy aura, promising that every workday with a Canon product would be better than the last.

Ms. Kawashima chuckled. "When you have time, mail those out."

"To whom?" I asked, dreamily.

"Anyone," she shrugged.

"Just anyone? They look expensive."

"Canon doesn't have authorization to do direct sales in China yet," she explained. "Our Beijing office can only do a little bit of marketing for now. As long as those catalogs find their way into the hands of potential customers, I couldn't care less who they are."

"So just potential buyers, then," I repeated.

She tilted her head and thought for a second. "Yeah, you're right. But do try and broaden your horizons a bit here. Even though some people are unlikely to become customers now, they may be able to in the future. Let's see...Who lives with you?"

"My grandmother. She can't even afford a roll of Fuji film, let alone a camera."

"Alright, who else lives with you?"

"My grandfather. He's as poor as she is."

She paused before asking, "Okay, who else do you know?"

"How about my aunt? She doesn't live with me, but she's not far."

She asked my aunt's age, and nodded. "Good. People below 45 will eventually be able to afford nice things as long as China's economy keeps booming."

We kept at it, and I finally thought of a superb candidate: Lu Hua, my second cousin. She was the granddaughter of my grandmother's half-brother. From the time my grandmother was dropped at my grandfather's doorstep, she never made contact with her father's family. Who would have thought that over forty years later, someone from that far-off village would come seek her out? Lu Hua and her husband had opened a small factory in the village and manufactured picture frames. They had customers in Beijing and came often to make deliveries. The first time they came to visit, my grandmother was ice cold. The second, she warmed slightly. The third, she insisted they stay for dinner. In her old age, she'd learned to let bygones be bygones. That, or she simply couldn't resist the temptation of finally being respected. Besides, every time they came, they brought baskets of fruit and snacks.

I asked my grandmother for Lu Hua's address, and sent her two catalogs. Some weeks later, I received an enthusiastic letter saying how much she loved them, and how many great design ideas she'd gleaned from them.

I showed Lu Hua's letter to Ms. Kawashima, who praised my good work:

"This is what I was talking about. You've planted a seed."

With her approval, I sent more and more catalogs out to friends and relatives. Soon after, I got ahold of a phone book, and page by page, found every business big enough to afford a Canon product.

The Beijing Hotel had three towers, the east, the center and the west, each built at different times and connected by one long corridor. There was a post office in the center tower—a historic building that dated back to 1900. Every morning, if I didn't have other assignments, I would seal envelopes and pack packages before setting out with a trolley piled high with mail. I took the elevator to the ground level, where I would trek to the post office, feeling proud and professional.

Lu Hua was born in 1960 in Hebei province. Her grandfather, my grandmother's half-brother, grew up without a single worry under his mother's protection. My grandmother had been driven away from the family by her stepmother to protect her son's inheritance, but in 1949, every land-owner in China lost their rights to their land leaving nothing to inherit.

By the time Lu Hua came along, they had become a simple family of farmers. Not a trace remained of the family's wealth and breeding. Lu Hua joined a production team at the age of 16. Production teams were a socialist attempt to organize farmers to work collectively on state-owned land. The goal was to maximize productivity.

According to Lu Hua, this attempt was a farce. The farmlands were far too large for one team leader to watch over everyone. Team members spent most of the day finding ways to avoid work. In the end, after turning in their quotas, farmers were left with only the bare minimum to live on.

By the end of the Cultural Revolution in 1976, China's agricultural systems teetered on the brink of collapse. Eight hundred million farmers were barely producing enough food to sustain the nation's population of nearly a billion.

Toward the end of the '70s, a few provinces began experimenting with contract responsibility systems. The point of the new system was to disband production teams and redistribute land back to team members. Every family signed an individual lease with the government. After each family met their annual grain quota, they could keep what was left for themselves. It was a step back for communism, but sparked enormous drive and motivation.

Lu Hua married a man from a neighboring village at twenty-two. Her husband wasn't interested in farm work, so he sublet his land to another family with three sons who needed more land to sweat on. In 1986, the couple used that rent as capital to start a picture frame factory.

Their workshop opened the same year I changed majors. At the time, I was convinced my transfer was due to two things: Ding Shisun's progressive leadership, and my own sheer will. Lu Hua's appearance in my life brought with it new perspective. I'd never thought about the key role China's economy had played in my personal life. Before, I'd thought there was no direct relationship between what happened out in the country and what happened in the cities, but now I saw the links. Only in a market economy could people make choices according to their own interests. Those small farming villages had propelled the exalted intellectual vanguard of Peking University.

Three months in, I started receiving my lunch allowance in Foreign Exchange Certificates. I was finally an official employee of Canon Beijing. It was ultimately a good thing, but I now needed to exchange my FEC for RMB, which seemed like a pain.

I asked Zhao where I could do it, and he advised, "Go to Xiushui Street."

Xiushui was a well-known bazaar, popular with foreigners as it was within walking distance of some foreign consulates. I had been there and seen high-end smuggled Hong Kong merchandise and a huge selection of knock-offs from Southern China. The knock-offs were made with such skill it took an expert to tell they weren't real, and Xiushui became known as "Cheat Street." I asked Zhao if he thought I'd end up with counterfeit bills. He replied scornfully, "Who'd go through all that? They could just knock you over the head and rob you."

Zhao loved showing off his street smarts. He liked to exaggerate danger. Still, I took what he said literally.

The day before New Year's Eve, I returned home to find Lu Hua waiting for me. She told me that their company had made it onto the official registry of the Bureau of Beijing Light Industry. I congratulated her. She wanted to give the bureau's section chief a gift to ensure that her next year went as smoothly as the last.

She wanted to buy something from the Friendship Store: a department store for foreigners. Chinese customers could also shop there as long as they paid in FEC.

"You have some of those FEC's, right? Can I trade you?"

"The market price is about 1.8 RMB per 1 FEC right now, but I can give you a better price. How much did you want?"

My grandmother butted in, "What's wrong with you? How can you make money off family?"

"I'm not making money. Its value is decided by the market," I protested. "I'm even giving her a better price. I'm losing money this way."

"There's no better price than 1:1," she said grimly. "1:1. It's an even trade to me!"

I'd already had the feeling my grandmother liked Lu Hua more than me. She always listened to my grandmother's stories with rapt attention no matter how many times my grandmother repeated them.

Lu Hua turned to my grandmother, "It's okay. I actually need a good amount of FEC. It'll take a lot more than just her lunch allowance. If she gets it from friends, they won't give her 1:1. There's a market price for it."

"Not in my family." My grandmother had given her final verdict.

How did she know how much my lunch allowance was? Was this some kind of good cop/bad cop routine to trick me into giving up my money?

I announced I was going out for a walk. I put on my coat and left without another word.

My fury cooled after walking in the biting cold for a while. I pictured my grandma bragging to Lu Hua about her ability to convince me to do things. *It's no problem. I raised Wang Yan. She'll listen to whatever I say.*

"It's not about whether she favors Lu Hua over me," I told myself. "It's about my grandma saving face."

I straightened out my thinking and went back home. I agreed to give my FEC to Lu Hua in exchange for the same amount of RMB. I just pretended that my lunch allowance was still paid in RMB. Problem solved.

The problem emerged again when I got paid the next month. FEC was worth more than RMB, but I had to exchange it in order to spend it. Otherwise about two-thirds of my salary was dead money.

It was then that Min came into the picture.

A foreman lived on our floor, whom I called Uncle Li. He was a tall man, refined and gentle. He looked very different from the other workers. It was common knowledge that he was highly skilled and very intelligent. He should have been promoted to management long ago, but remained a foreman because his father had fled to Taiwan before he was born. Even though he'd never seen his father's face, the government would never trust him, and no city girl would marry him. In the end, he married a woman from a village about two-hours away by bus.

There are two kinds of household registrations in China: urban residents and rural residents. Urban residents can receive benefits that range from retirement pension to free education and health care, while rural residents are often left to fend for themselves. Uncle Li's wife, whom we called Auntie Zhao, was a rural resident. She had to work in the fields with her production team full-time, so the couple spent long stretches of time apart. At the height of farm season, Uncle Li helped her work the fields on weekends. When farm work slowed, she came to him, and helped with the housework. They had a daughter and a son. Both lived with their mother, and as was prescribed by Chinese law, both children took their mother's residency status.

In 1987, the Taiwanese government loosened restrictions and allowed veterans from the mainland to return home to visit. The move was welcomed by the Chinese government. Hearing that Uncle Li's father would be visiting, leaders at the factory rushed to his doorstep to inquire in what ways they could make his life happier. Having a relative in Taiwan was suddenly an advantage. The Party wanted those who had fled to see how good they could have had it.

Uncle Li proposed granting his wife and two children Beijing residency. The previously impossible task was achieved in a matter of days. Auntie Zhao moved in with Uncle Li permanently with two children in tow. She liked standing in the hallway, government-issued rice voucher proudly in hand, asking passers-by, "Please, take a look at this rice voucher. Is it the same as yours? I know you're from Beijing and all."

"Haven't you gotten your residency yet? You know it's the same."

"Hmm, I guess you're right. Must be my stupid hick brain. I keep forgetting!"

But time wasn't on Auntie Zhao's side. Had she gotten her Beijing residency in the 70s, she could have been assigned a job at the factory. In the time of the planned economy, Beijing residency could solve all your problems. Food, clothing, housing, and employment were all taken care of. By the mid-'80s, due to competition from rural factories like Lu Hua's, the factory Uncle Li worked in would shut down at least two days a week. They simply didn't have enough work. City workers just didn't have the same drive that farmers did. They were employees of the state, and at the end of the month, they got the same pay no matter what. The end result was that state-run factories stopped hiring.

Auntie Zhao didn't really mind being a housewife, but was worried about the future of her children. Youth unemployment had ballooned to overwhelming proportions. The government had encouraged urban youth to employ themselves, and countless bazaars sprung up across Beijing. Each had hundreds of small stalls selling imported (or smuggled) goods. If you ran even the smallest stall, you earned a great deal more than one would working at a factory. Even so, most saw running a stall as a less desirable life.

There were roughly ten young people around my age in my grandmother's building. Only one ended up running a stall. After two years in prison for his role in a fight, he had no hope of getting a factory job. His story reinforced the notion that running a stall was often the last possible option, profitable as it was.

Retiring workers pleaded with their factory leaders to let their children take over their positions. These requests were often fulfilled. Thus began the "replacement" era, in which hordes of older workers, many barely fifty, opted for early retirement to make way for their children. Management liked it too, since younger workers were paid far less than their fathers and mothers. There was not much work to do, anyway.

Auntie Zhao was steeped in elation for only a couple of weeks. Soon, she found something else soured her sweet charade: Every other household had both the husband and wife who worked in factories, which meant they had two positions to be taken over. When her husband retired, only one of their children would be eligible for a job. This would never do. How could she continue her life as a city parent when one of her children would end up jobless?

She began pressuring her husband to request that he be replaced by both of his children. He refused. They fought. It was said that during one of their particularly nasty fights, he called her an "old woman," which sent her into a frenzy.

He didn't really mean she was old, but meant her greedy. He was referring to the "old woman" in the *Grimm's Fairy Tale*, "The Fisherman and His Wife." The reference simply went straight over Auntie Zhao's head. It was their daughter, Min, who explained it to me with amusement.

They fought like cats and dogs for days, but Uncle Li stuck to his guns, and wouldn't go back to his bosses with another request. His son was only seventeen, after all. He still had a year at high school to go before college. Min was already twenty-one, and needed work. They agreed to let Min replace her father at the factory.

Min was a year younger than me. She sometimes visited in the evening. I'd open up my cot, and we would lounge on it, talking about whatever came to mind. From when she was a small child, her mother, who believed that only a woman with a skilled hand could get a good husband, had taught her to make clothes. No one could have imagined that at twenty-one, she would trade her country life for that of factory worker, and her love of dressmaking for the repetitive clacking of a printing press. In her mother's eyes, it was a huge step up, but Min hated the factory. There was no beauty or poetry in sitting at a machine all day.

She especially hated getting the ink on her skin. As we chatted, she would stick out her hands, "Look at them! They were made for stitching, and look at what they've become!"

She, like me and Lu Hua, loved Canon's catalogs. One day, while gazing at one of the beautiful office ladies on its pages, she declared, "You'd look good in a dress like that. How about I make you one?"

I agreed, and we went straight out to buy the fabric. A few days later, she showed up with the finished dress. As I tried it on, she flitted and fussed, exclaiming, "You look so beautiful! So beautiful!"

The next day at the office, I finally had a mirror to admire her handiwork, and I was taken aback. Min had made an absolutely beautiful dress. Even Ms. Kawashima couldn't help but comment, "Miss Wang, you look so cute!"

Min asked if I could loan her 100 RMB so she could buy more material. With that much, she could make a dozen dresses to sell. I replied awkwardly that I only had FEC. She laughed, "If you can loan me a hundred in FEC. I'll give you back one eighty RMB in a month."

And just before Chinese New Year, Min made good on her word. She'd taken the dresses to Cheat Street to sell. Japanese style dresses were very popular with businesswomen, especially those who worked for foreign companies.

I immediately asked if she wanted to expand her operation, "Do you need more money? I could loan it to you."

"I do! thanks! But for now, there's something else I need your help with. I have a boyfriend. He's awesome, but he doesn't have a good job. I don't really care; I love him anyway. But my mom and dad wouldn't ever let us be together. You know how it is."

"What does he do?" I asked.

"He runs a stall on Xiushui Street."

I didn't know what to say. Her mother was a tough woman, and I didn't want to offend her. The second Min fell out with her mother, she'd be at our door, cursing me.

Feeling me pause, Min chided, "I never thought you'd be soft. A Peking University grad who changed majors? I thought you were fearless."

Her words hit me right where it hurt. I had bragged to her about my supposed bravery, my anti-establishment views, and my resistance to norms.

I proposed that I meet her boyfriend. I needed to see him with my own eyes. She said he'd take us to dinner at Szechuan Restaurant.

It was the best place for Szechuanese food in the city. I found Min already waiting for me at the gate. She put her arm in mine, and we stepped over the red lacquered threshold with lion statues on each side to keep out evil spirits. Min guided me to a corner table where two nearly identical young men were seated. Min pointed to one, "This is my boyfriend, Xu Weidong." She pointed to the other, "And this is his brother, Weiguo."

She sat down next to her boyfriend, leaving me to sit beside Weiguo.

Weidong was a lot chattier than his brother. He pointed out that the restaurant was his favorite because this was where Deng Xiaoping uttered his famous cat theory for the first time. "Deng Xiaoping came from Szechuan, whose grain farmers fought a constant war against rats," Weidong said. I nodded. I'd imagined him as less intelligent, and he was clearly aware of the stereotype. To counteract, he constantly talked of politics.

"Oh, come on," Weiguo interjected, "no more politics, my brother."

"Fine," Weidong smiled. "No more politics."

"Let's talk about food," Weiguo said. "There's a famous Szechuan dish, Roasted Goose Feet. You know how it's made?"

We shook our heads.

"They put charcoal in a pot, get it nice and hot, then they stick a live goose inside. Its feet get blistered from stepping on the hot coals, then they take it out, cut the feet off, and immediately marinate the feet in soy sauce and other special seasonings. That's why they taste so flavorful."

Min was about to burst into tears, "Why can't they kill the goose first? Does that really make it taste different?"

Weiguo shrugged. "That's what they say. Maybe we can try it someday."

"You two go ahead," Min frowned. "I'm good."

I first assumed that "you two" referred to the brothers, but then I noticed her leaning into Weidong's arm around her shoulder.

It dawned on me that she'd split the table into two sides: her and Weidong, and me and Weiguo.

After dinner, Weidong proposed to drive us home, but I told Min I got carsick easily. She didn't want me taking the bus alone, so the brothers climbed into their car and drove off. Very few people owned cars.

"So," Min asked, "what do you think of Weiguo?"

"Don't you want to know what I think of Weidong first?"

"Don't be mad," she chuckled. "Do you like him, or not?"

"No, and his story about the goose feet didn't help."

"Maybe he just wanted to impress you," Min said. "He's not like that normally. "

The point was that I didn't like being set up.

Chapter 7

Love in the Time of Protests

About a thousand yards north of Wangfujing was the Capital Theater, home of the Beijing People's Art Theater Group: China's most renowned theater company.

Zhi Hua had been there once. It was in 1985 when she was taking Western Drama Studies. The professor required the class to watch a play as a course assignment. It was before I transferred, so I didn't get to take the course. Zhi Hua spoke highly of the venue's grandeur, which made me yearn to see it myself.

My dream of going there wasn't fulfilled until after I'd started at Canon. In 1988, the theater mounted a production of *The Caine Mutiny* translated into Chinese by Ying Ruocheng. Ying was a famous actor, playwright, director, and had once served as China's Vice Minister of Culture. At Ying's invitation, Charlton Heston directed the play. This was unprecedented in the world of Chinese theater in the 1980s. There were long lines at the box office every day starting at 5 pm. However, I was able to saunter over and buy a ticket for that evening's show during lunchtime with no wait.

The Capital Theater was built in 1952, when relations between China and the Soviet Union were still in their honeymoon phase. It's said that the theater was designed under the guidance of an expert architect from Russian Turkestan, meaning the building was representative of Central Asian architecture. It was exotic and imposing. I always arrived at the theater at least half an hour early. That way I had ample time to find my seat, leaf through the playbill, and watch the audience file inside, dressed up and glowing. When the second bell rang, the huge chandelier on the celling and the bud-shaped wall sconces would dim. The audience brought their attention to the stage, still empty expect for the curtains swaying almost imperceptibly. I watched the wall sconces go dark little by little, until the tiny bright cores of each one was completely extinguished.

The Capital Theater was a great getaway from everyday life. Even the lowest ranked clerk had an air of drama about them. I remember a middle-aged ticket clerk who carried himself gracefully, with a beautiful, yet melancholic voice. I also recall a female ticket inspector with a delicate figure and spirited eyes, like an elf. Their every gesture, expression and word seemed to signal that I'd entered a different world.

One winter night toward the end of '88, the main auditorium of the Capital Theater was only about seventy percent full. I sat in the seventh row with empty seats on both sides. As the show was about to start, a man sitting a few seats away came over and took the seat next to mine. He asked if I was a reporter for *Beijing Youth Daily*. I said I wasn't, to which he asked, "Well, which paper do you work for then? I'm Guo Yan. *China Culture Daily*."

"I'm not with any paper. I work for a Japanese company that makes optical instruments, like cameras."

My introduction was met with a look of shock. I guess he'd thought girls like me only went to fashion shows.

"Do you know what the play is about?" he asked.

"Of course," I proceeded to give him a summary of the plot.

Uncle Doggie's Nirvana is about a farmer named Chen Hexiang, nicknamed Uncle Doggie. He fights his entire life to claim a strip of land of his own. In the old society, he was not only denied the right to own property, but is subjected to corporal punishment by landowner Qi. The founding of the People's Republic brings about land reform, and Qi's land is split evenly between all the farmers in the village. Uncle Doggie finally has a piece of earth to call his own.

Before long, the collectivization movement requires farmers to turn their fields over to production teams. Uncle Doggie can't accept the change and has a mental breakdown. He moves to a cemetery in the distant hills, where he claims a small plot of land and plans to live out his days in isolation.

The play then jumps forward to the 1980s when new contract responsibility systems were in place. Upon hearing that peasants can own land again, Uncle Doggie awakes from his trance and returns to his village. His son has grown up and as fate would have it, has married Qi's daughter. Instead of farming their land, the young couple plan to start a stone-processing plant. Uncle Doggie is adamantly against it. Bulldozers are scheduled to come clear the field the next morning. In the deepest dark, Uncle Doggie torches the kindling under the arch of the home's gatehouse and sits on top of it, letting the flames consume him.

"Impressive," he said, taking a quick glance at the program. There was a synopsis in there, but I knew my version was better.

"I've seen this play four times," I said.

"What?" His eyes opened wide.

"Yup. Today is my fifth."

I'd never thought about why I liked the play so much. Guo Yan's surprise made me wonder if my fixation on a tale of rural China was abnormal in some way. Mayby Uncle Doggie reminded me of my grandmother? And the young couple were a lot like Lu Hua and her husband? The play wasn't that far from my own life.

But even if the play wasn't at all like my own life, the point of art was to break down barriers between people, wasn't it? The second bell rang and the lights began to dim. Guo Yan asked in a whisper what scene would provide the best photo ops. Before the lamps were completely dark, I whispered he should wait until Uncle Doggie moves to the cemetery and comes across Qi's ghost. The scene was dramatic in an eerie way and would make a great picture.

I didn't give him my number because I didn't have one. Mobile phones and email were still light-years away. But he looked up Canon's number in the phone book. When I answered the phone in my usual professional manner, I heard Guo Yan laughing on the other end.

"It's me. Guo Yan! What time are you off? I'll take you to dinner!"

We arranged to meet at a restaurant at Wangfujing.

I arrived early and sat near a window. I pulled out my copy of Garcia Marquez's *Love in the Time of Cholera* and began to read. Soon, I looked up to find him sitting across from me, asking what I was reading. I handed it to him. "Ah, yeah," he murmured. "I read *One Hundred Years of Solitude*, but not this one. Is it good?

"It's amazing," I replied.

Guo Yan had graduated from Fudan University in 1982 with a degree in Chinese literature, so we had a lot to talk about. He'd gone straight into reporting and had more or less stopped reading. He was woefully unfamiliar with any recent literature, but his job was to roam the city, and he was up on just about every cultural event. Talking to him brought back my memories of talking to Zhi Hua in middle school, when she was less judgmental than she was now.

He didn't look down on the growing class of white-collar workers, but his knowledge stopped at the stereotypes. He assumed that a girl like me only cared about fashion and marrying my boss. According to him, that wasn't a bad thing. I laughed at him. We ate amid a fierce debate, and before we knew it, it was nine. I had to get home. He walked me to Chang'an Avenue, where at night buses came only once in a blue moon. We waited for a while and decided to continue walking west along Chang'an until the bus found us. Just as we passed the front gate to Tiananmen Tower, I saw headlights, and turned to see a #10 bus barreling down the street. The bus stop was about a hundred feet ahead. It seemed there was no way I would make it, but I had to try. I shouted a hasty goodbye and ran. The bus lumbered by, stopping just ahead of me. I felt triumphant and slightly regretful. I looked out the back window to see Guo Yan standing under the towering might of Tiananmen.

I didn't like him that much, but he filled the void left by Zhi Hua, and he was rooted enough in the real world to take Min's place too. Whenever he had tickets to a show, he'd call and invite me. One night, when we were out at the Capital Theater again, he showed me a door down a hallway next to the entrance to the main auditorium. He pushed the door open, revealing a staircase. Stepping in first, he waved for me to follow. I looked back and saw the elf-like ticket inspector. She knew what we were up to but didn't seem to care. I followed Guo Yan up three narrow sets of stairs before we reached a tiny room above the auditorium. It was the director's room. The wall that faced the auditorium was a giant one-way mirror. Guo Yan told me he was a friend of the director's, who didn't mind us sneaking in.

The view was superb and everything sounded excellent, but I had no idea what I was watching. I was distracted by my unexpected closeness with a man. We were so close I could hear his heartbeat. When the play ended, the chandelier and the wall lamps awakened. Gao Yan grabbed me and kissed me, just as I'd expected. The actors came back onstage for curtain call, and the audience exploded with applause. It felt as if they were cheering just for us.

After we'd emerged from our secret cave, we walked in silence through the winter air as if we didn't know each other. I wanted him to talk to me nonstop, but all he said was a simple goodbye as I climbed on the bus. I was frustrated. How on earth were we strangers after we'd just kissed so passionately? When I was in college, the girls' dorm was locked down at 11 pm. Every night when 11 drew near, I saw lovebirds under the trees in front of the dorm, kissing and hugging desperately, refusing to let each other go until an administrator appeared, threatening to lock girls out if they didn't come in immediately. That seemed like love. What was it between me and Guo Yan?

When I was the only one in the office, I'd give him a call at the paper. He was hardly ever there, so I'd leave messages when I couldn't reach him. He'd call me back when he came in. I was by the phone nearly every day from 9 to 5. I hated myself for being so easy to reach. I imagined I'd refuse to take his calls, but I couldn't. I had no way of knowing when it was him calling. If it rang more than three times without being answered, Ms. Kawashima would pick up, and there's no way she'd appreciate having to relay my personal calls. I felt my relationship with Guo Yan was unfair, but I couldn't name the pain I felt. Maybe it was love?

One evening, as the cold tendrils of winter gave way to the green vines of spring, we went to see another play. The theater was within walking distance of my grandma's, and we'd barely started walking when we had reached Yuetan Park. Suddenly, I had an idea. I was going to show him a secret spot of mine.

I had played in this park as a little girl and knew it like the back of my hand. Built in 1530, it hosted full moon ceremonies for the Autumn Equinox during the Ming and Qing dynasties. As we walked, I punctuated our journey with anecdotes. The park was silent, as if listening to us chat.

The southern part of Yuetan Park was originally an orchard. When I was in elementary school, our teacher often brought us here to do volunteer works like picking weeds or apples. In 1983, the park expanded to absorb the orchard. The majority of the fruit trees were still there, but a large pond and several pavilions were built. The destination I had in my mind was a shrine in the southeast corner.

The shrine was dedicated to the "old man under the moon." He is a Taoist god responsible for bringing men and women together in marriage. It is said he possesses a registry of all the men and women in the world, and when he finds someone's perfect match, he writes their names together, sealing their fate. He reads his registry only by the light of the moon, hence the name. From the moment it was erected, the shrine became the go-to destination for young singles.

We found ourselves at the foot of the shrine at the southern-most point of the park. It shared an iron fence with the backyard of my grandmother's apartment building. I pointed to the statue of the old man, glimmering in the pale moonlight. Guo Yan's eyes shuffled between the marble face and the marble registry. He smiled. He drew me to his chest as if indulging a willful child. We kissed again, and I felt relieved. Guo Yan wanted to seal our fate.

The next day, Min came looking for me. I hadn't spoken to her since her matchmaking attempt, other than occasional empty pleasantries if we met in public.

She said she had something to talk about. "I saw you last night." She started like a policeman interrogating a suspect.

"Where?" I asked.

"Yuetan Park."

I flushed beet-red, and stammered, "What were you doing in the park?"

"What do you mean what *I* was doing in the park?" she said.

"OK," I growled in irritation. "What exactly are we talking about?"

"If you don't like Weiguo, that's fine. That's your choice. But why would you run into the arms of a married man? You're destroying yourself!"

"Married? You know Guo Yan?"

"I don't need to. I can tell from one look at his face. He's married and feels guilty."

How could she even see his face? It was pitch dark!

I didn't want to admit it, but I believed her. I'd long suspected Guo

Yan was married. Something about him wasn't right. He wanted to spend time with me, but he wasn't as direct and passionate as a single man. I'd never asked him about his marital status. On one level, there didn't seem to be a need for me to ask. On another, I was afraid to know the truth.

I promised Min I'd get to the bottom of it. If he was married, that would be the end of it. But as soon as we parted, my courage disappeared. All I could muster was the determination not to call him anymore. Two weeks went by. I didn't call him, and he didn't call me either. What did it mean? Was it always me who courted him?

It wasn't so bad when I was at work, but when I had my thoughts to myself, I couldn't stop them from spiraling in his direction. I couldn't go near my old haunts. What if I saw him with another woman? I went straight home after work, but my grandmother's claustrophobic apartment did nothing to quell my anxiety. There was a bookstore not far away: Sanwei, the first privately-owned, independent bookstore in Beijing. It stayed open until 10 pm.

I stood in the spacious serenity of Sanwei. The towering shelves were completely filled. I felt I was small in the presence of giants, which brought me a strange kind of peace.

I went to the office seven days a week. My favorite days were Sundays, because no one else was there. Peking University, the Chinese side of the joint-venture, had gifted Canon Beijing a laser typesetting system. It was essentially a computer with proprietary software. I methodically worked my way through its manual and eventually I learned its basic functions. Rather than laying out newspapers, as it was designed to do, I used it for word processing.

Until then, writing was strictly done pen-to-paper, which meant draft after draft. But with a computer, I could edit with ease. Before long, I lost the ability of writing a complete sentence with pen and paper. I simply couldn't do it if you paid me.

When it came to documents in Chinese, Mr. Murata liked a rough draft done by hand, so he could make edits before I typed it up. Now, I gave him printed rough drafts.

He looked at it as if it were an alien artifact. "Didn't I ask you to write a rough draft first?"

"It's a rough draft, don't worry! It's just easier for me to write on the computer. I can still make changes. It's fine."

Mr. Murata didn't think so. A printed draft had an air of authority that made him feel too intimidated to do any edits. He thought it was incredibly cocky of me to make a draft final before he could edit it.

I found his befuddlement hilarious, and it fueled my desire to mess with the device. My love of playing with the computer converged with my love of writing. Every Sunday, I went to our office to write, and by the beginning of April of 1989, I'd had a four-thousand-word essay published in *China Youth Daily*. It was the first time my work had been published on a national scale. I bought as many copies as I could find, and mailed one to Zhi Hua.

As April marched forward, when I trekked to the office on Sundays, it wasn't just a secret lair where I worked at creating the next great masterpiece, but also the only place Guo Yan could reach me. I knew it was unlikely he would call on a Sunday, but if I stayed home, the chance of us meeting each other would be zero.

On the evening of April 15, 1989, I heard on the radio that Hu Yaobang passed away.

Hu Yaobang was a deposed leader of the Party. He became General Secretary of the Chinese Communist Party in 1982. He supported reform and opening-up policies, and was well liked by intellectuals. However, his radical tendencies were met with severe criticism from Party conservatives.

In December 1986, over four thousand students took to the streets in Anhui Province demanding democratic elections. Not to be outdone, Peking University coordinated with several other schools to stage an even larger protest on New Year's Day. Students took to the streets screaming, "Death Before Oppression!" and "No Democracy, No Modernity!" The protest was soon crushed by authorities, but Party conservatives felt Hu Yaobang should be held responsible for the turmoil. They thought the student revolt was a direct result of Hu's tolerance for bourgeois liberalism. Several founding members of the People's Republic unanimously agreed to remove Hu from his position.

Hu's firing wasn't done through normal procedure. A few elite members within the Politburo decided he was unfit for the job and simply forced him out. It was a political play plotted in secret chambers, and a slap in the face to the youth who had protested for transparency and democracy. I was studying at Peking University at the time. When word spread, we felt angry, powerless, and humiliated.

After Hu's dismissal, economic progress didn't slow one bit, though talk of political reform was suppressed. When their material lives became easy, average people didn't care whether or not they had freedom of speech. Founder Group continued to sell laser-typesetting machines, Canon continued to advertise in China, and Pecan Inc. was born. I graduated, entered the white-collar world, and found myself among the emerging middle class with their newly gained economic advantages. I gradually forgot about Hu Yaobang and the students' cause until I heard the news of his death. It reminded me of his larger significance, and of the special place he once held in my heart and mind.

The next day was a Sunday, and I went to the office again. I worked undisturbed until about 3 pm when the phone rang. The person on the other end unloaded a barrage of English on me, asking for god-knows-what.

"Sorry, wrong number," I interrupted.

As soon as I set the receiver down, it rang again. I didn't answer, but it kept ringing. I picked up. It was Guo Yan.

"How come you're calling me up on a Sunday?" I was thrilled.

"I'm heading over to Tiananmen, so I thought I'd take a chance and see if you were in. You wanna meet up?"

"Tiananmen? What show?"

"Are you kidding? You don't have any idea that Hu Yaobang died? Are you sure you went to Peking University?"

There was Guo Yan's usual condescending tone. I was speechless.

But he made some sense. You see, Hu Yaobang's death stirred up a sadness in me, but the emotion wasn't strong enough to elicit any action. I wasn't a student any more. Protesting in the street had long disappeared from my list of interests.

Still, from Guo Yan's reaction, I realized there were protests already going on. At Tiananmen Square, there would be marching, shouting, and probably fighting. I found myself nostalgic for a more exciting time in my life.

I met Guo Yan at 4 pm outside the Beijing Hotel, and we set out for Tiananmen Square. I never asked why he hadn't called for weeks. I stole a peek at his face, and found it cast with stern resolve. He was a reporter: a man of information. I didn't care if he was married. A storm was approaching. How could I care about a trivial promise I'd made to Min?

The scene at Tiananmen was far different from what I'd imagined. The majority of people there were tourists. Protests were scattered and sporadic. A student who had brought a funeral wreath made a short speech. When he didn't get the response he expected, he asked, "Do you know who Hu Yaobang was? He used to be General Secretary of the Central Party."

He pointed to the couplet attached to the wreath. This helped. Some tourists pointed their cameras at the text written on it.

I felt somewhat disappointed until Guo Yan poked me and with as small a motion as humanly possible, pointed out a man not far away: "He's a plainclothes policeman."

I saw a short, stocky man with a flat-top haircut. His cold gaze passed over us before he moved on.

We laughed, almost hysterically. It took me a couple minutes to calm down. Guo Yan put my arm in his as if it were the most natural thing and said, "How about you come to my house tonight?"

Chapter 8

April Is the Cruelest Month

We ate dinner in Qianmen, then headed for his house. He lived in the southeast part of the city, in a sprawling neighborhood called Fang Zhuang. I wasn't familiar with it, and I didn't pay attention to the bus routes on our way there, which would cause problems on my way back to work the next morning, but I didn't care. Guo Yan was all that existed for me in that moment.

He told me that he was married, but was separated from his wife. "We're getting a divorce," he said while put his hands on my shoulders, looking me in the eyes. "I didn't tell you because I was afraid of losing you. What else do you want to know?"

"I know enough," I said. Tears almost flooded my eyes. The weight had been lifted.

It was deep into the night when we got to his house. He lived in a three-bedroom apartment provided by his newspaper, which he shared with two other people. As he opened the front door, a completely bare living room materialized. The only light came from a bare bulb hanging from a wire in the ceiling. Just like the hall in my grandmother's building, this was a place everyone used and no one cared about. I glanced at the two doors. A range of hues emanated from underneath either. One of the two could've flung open at any moment.

We quietly snuck into Guo Yan's room. When he flicked on the light, I saw a room of utilitarian furniture not too different from my grandmother's. In those days, furniture in every household was purely functional. Guo Yan had a collection of souvenirs from business trips all over the country, which set his home apart from my grandmother's. Her lack of souvenirs made it all too clear that she hadn't been anywhere since being dumped on her husband's doorstep. I was perusing Guo Yan's collection when he interrupted my train of thought.

"Want some water?" he asked.

A glass of water sounded good.

He poured me a glass of water and set it on the dining table with a heavy thud. He seemed angry but I couldn't tell why. I sat at the table and drank my water quietly. He asked sternly if I wanted more. I said I did, but I didn't. Somthing in his tone suggested that it would be offensive to say no. He had to get it from the public kitchen and left without another word. When he came back, he had a kettle in one hand and a knife in the other. His demeanor had changed completely.

"What's the knife for?" I asked.

He pointed the knife at me. "Take off your clothes," he said.

"What?" I was stunned.

"Do as I say, otherwise..."

"This is ridiculous."

I stood up. His room was small and his dining area was only two steps from the door. Just as I reached for the door handle, he dropped the knife and hugged me from behind. "Don't leave," he said. "I'm sorry."

Warmth crept up the back of my neck.

"I didn't mean it." He said, hugging me tighter. "It was just stupid and awkward of me."

My heart softened.

The next morning, I got up and started getting dressed as the single window began to bring the room to life.

"Don't you work at nine?" Guo Yan asked.

I couldn't look him in the eye. I felt like we were bank robbers who'd decided our only guarantee of freedom was to never lay eyes on each other again. I'm pretty sure he said he would call, but I was already halfway out the door. I had to get out before anyone woke.

I was out on the street and kept running until I was at a bus station on the other side of the street. Where the hell was I? I studied the bus routes and found a #25 bus to Yongdingmen. Beijing is arranged like a set of Russian nesting dolls, with a set of walls placed one outside of the another. The area in the center is for the emperor, and is known as the Forbidden City. Tiananmen, or "The Gate of Heavenly Peace," is the south gate to the Forbidden city. Yongdingmen, "The Gate of Forever Peace," is the south gate into the outer city. Both Tiananmen and Yongdingmen are on the same axial line. Once I got to Yongdingmen, I was sure I could find a northbound bus to Tiananmen.

I rode bus #25 north with a new sense of confidence. I'd been to a part of Beijing I'd never been to before. My sphere of mobility had increased. I was exhilarated, but when I looked back on what happened last night, something wasn't right. Things definitely hadn't played out the way I'd expected. I'd dreamt for years about what my first sexual experience would feel like. Most of my expectations were based on romance novels. In that world, a man makes love to a woman because of his deep affection and appreciation for her. Was there any affection and appreciation between me and Guo Yan? I didn't think so.

He apologized a couple of times. His explanation was that he didn't know how to break the ice, so he chose to imitate a rapist. When he said it, I was nestled contentedly in his embrace and found his words funny. But now, in the cruel light of an April morning, it felt humiliating. All I wanted was to get rid of these unhappy thoughts. I had my Walkman on me with a copy of Cui Jian's *Rock 'n' Roll on the New Long March* inside. I put on my headphones and pressed play. Cui Jian's rough voice blasted through the space between my ears.

Cui Jian instantly made me think of Hu Yaobang. Today, Cui Jian is regarded as the godfather of Chinese Rock 'n' Roll, but before 1986, Cui and his band had long been working underground. The first half of the 1980s had seen heavy censorship of popular music. There was even a regulation stating that no musical event was allowed more than three rock bands on a given night.

Cui Jian rose to fame after performing at a 1986 concert called "Fill the World with Love." It was the largest pop concert China had ever seen. It was broadcast live on television, but I didn't watch it. The day after, Zhi Hua burst into my dorm room screaming, "Did you see Cui Jian on TV last night? He just wore whatever he wanted! His pant legs were different lengths! Man, that guy was cool!"

The concert was inextricably linked with Hu Yaobang's tolerance for bourgeois freedoms. After Hu stepped down, Cui Jian was fired by his employer, Beijing Song and Dance Troupe. It seemed that veteran revolutionaries within the Party couldn't tolerate a ragged, unkempt rock star.

Cui Jian didn't enunciate when he sang, so I never paid much attention to his lyrics. But on that particular April morning, as I fled the scene of the crime, I heard what he was singing for the very first time:

The earth is turning under your feet,
The waters of life are flowing free...

His voice cut straight through my emotional fog. His deafening proclamations agitated me even more. How I wished the world would suddenly flip upside-down so I could forget my trivial frustrations! My curiosity rose. I wanted to see how the situation at Tiananmen Square was developing.

However, when the #25 dropped me off at Yongdingmen, I couldn't find a bus directly to Tiananmen. My only option was a trolley that circled around Tiananmen Square and would drop me off a block from the Beijing Hotel.

I arrived at the office and, and half asleep, carried out the same rituals as I did every morning. After Mr. Murata and Ms. Kawashima arrived, a call came in from headquarters in Japan. It seemed that Murata and Kawashima had been expecting it.

The call lasted about ten minutes. Mr. Murata barely spoke, save for the occasional "yes, yes". As soon as he hung up, he and Ms. Kawashima plunged straight into a heated discussion. They spoke at lightning speed, far beyond the scope of my textbook Japanese. As I handed them their tea, they didn't mutter a cursory "thank you" as they normally did.

Today, I was invisible, which suited me just fine. I started my computer, which took a couple of minutes. Before I could get to work, Mr. Murata called my name.

"Ms. Wang. You were in Beijing in 1976, right? Do you remember the protests when Zhou Enlai died??"

I was surprised by the question. "I...I...I was still in elementary school then. Our teacher wouldn't let us go."

Ms. Kawashima let out a strange, guttural chuckle, like a child who just got away with a prank. Mr. Murata couldn't help but laugh either, and with that I was excused. They went back to speaking Japanese, with Ms. Kawashima mixing in some English.

After a while, I pieced together what they were talking about. The phone call from Tokyo was asking about the protests at Tiananmen Square. Foreign companies who wanted to expand into China had to pay attention to the possible chaos on the horizon.

Ms. Kawashima quoted reports from the Associated Press, explaining that Hu Yaobang's death didn't have any real significance since he had long since fallen from power. Mr. Murata, however, claimed that the populace at large was growing more and more disgruntled. Inflation, corruption, no freedom of press...take your pick. There were hundreds of reasons for people to get angry. "Don't forget," he said, "the Chinese have a tendency to use the deaths of leaders to air grievances that have bottled up for years." He was well versed in the ways of the country of his birth, and he had looked to me to back him up.

The main office had impressed upon Mr. Murata the importance of understanding the nuances of the situation. Both he and Ms. Kawashima agreed that they should send me to the Square to take pictures on my lunch break.

I felt like a prisoner granted parole. "Can I use the office camera?"

"Whichever one you want."

I'd coveted the cameras since day one. Every time a new customer came to the office, it was my job to introduce them to every piece of Canon technology. There'd been no shortage of chances to hold Canon cameras, but I'd never had film to shoot.

I asked Ms. Kawashima for 200 RMB and headed straight for Wangfujing. At that time, there were three main brands of film on the market: Kodak, the most expensive one, Fuji, a close second, and Lucky, a Chinese brand which was by far the most affordable. Lucky was a typical Chinese brand in that when it was good, it was just as good as the other two, but its performance was not guaranteed. I put reliability first. Both Kodak and Fuji were reliable, but there was now an affinity between me and Japan, so Fuji won.

Lunchtime rolled around, and it was finally time to hold a brand new Canon EOS in my own two hands. A 28mm lens would capture the entirety of the square, even if the crowd ended up bigger than the one in '76. The 135mm lens could show every wrinkle of a student's sleeve, and every hand thrust up in anguish.

The students were more than the day before and appeared more organized. Each battalion flew its school flag. Two stronge students held it, while hundreds more surrounded them in tidy rows. Some students joined hand-in-hand to form protective barriers around their fellow classmates.

The Monument to the People's Heroes was the nucleus from which all else radiated. Wreaths were piled high at its base, forcing newcomers to climb even higher to place theirs. They took absolutely no safety measures, but the young men looked agile and confident. Whenever they were able to find balance on a narrow protrusion, they'd bend down and reach for wreaths held up to them by classmates. The crowd cheered as the couplets attached to each wreath unfurled like a waterfall. When a student climbed down, two more were ready to take their place.

A funeral song blasted through the square from the Peking University student group.

I headed into the fray but was stopped by the increasing density of the crowd. I pled for people to give way. Seeing the camera bag on my shoulder, everyone assumed I was a reporter. I plodded forward, inch by inch, until I reached a circle of two dozen young men, hand in hand, wearing armbands emblazoned with the word "security."

I asked one to let me through, but he didn't budge, and instead barked, "What school are you from?"

"Peking University," I answered just as I had a million times before.

"Which department?"

I wanted to say "Chinese," but remembered I wasn't a student anymore. My hesitation clearly made him uneasy. He muttered something to the person on his right, who looked at me before relaying a warning all the way down the chain.

I couldn't help but feel excluded. The students of Peking University thought it was their mission to stand up to totalitarian authority. The rest of the populace would do nothing but wait for enlightenment. I'd only graduated a year ago. Though I still had a Peking University work badge, I began to wonder if I'd been downgraded to average citizen.

The music stopped and a student with a megaphone led the crowd in singing "L'Internationale" before giving a speech. He described how Hu Yaobang had been struck down. Whether his story was true or not, I had no idea, but it was the first time I heard the students' understanding of events.

According to the speaker, the Central Committee of the Communist Party held a meeting ten days prior at Zhongnanhai to discuss educational development. The Director of Education, Li Tieying, made a speech about the seriousness of the shortage in education funding. As the meeting dragged on, Hu Yaobang's expression grew graver. Finally, his heart couldn't take it anymore and he crumpled to the floor. Paramedics rushed him to Beijing Hospital. A few days later, he left this world.

The student pointed out that Hu Yaobang had died of anger and anxiety. He was anxious about a shortage of funding destroying our nation's educational system. And where was the money going? Straight into the pockets of bureaucratic profiteers. Thus, he managed to establish a relationship between the public outcry for Hu Yaobang and numerous other causes. A solemn expression fell over all within earshot. After a moment of silence, megaphone still in hand, the student cried out:

"Overthrow the bureaucratic profiteers! Eradicate the corrupt! Education will save the nation! Long live freedom! Long live democracy! Long live law and order!"

The crowd joined in, roaring.

When the chants waned, the megaphone was passed to another student, who led the crowd in singing "March of the Volunteers." If past ceremonies were any indication, things were coming to a close. I needed to get a good shot of the students joined together in song and I looked around for a better spot. Suddenly, a crowd of people flooded toward the Monument. Bystanders, including me, were blindly swept up in the current.

I couldn't see the ground. I heard feet shuffling. People struggled for traction on pavers strewn with leaflets and paper flowers. The security detail gave up and disbanded.

I felt the strap of my camera bag leave my shoulder. I turned to find a man trying to snatch it from me. I screamed "Help!" and held on firmly. The man let go and disappeared. I blinked wildly. The crowd flowed on toward the monument.

I opened the camera bag and took stock. I'd taken thirty-six pictures. It was standard capacity for a 35mm roll. On an automatic rewinding camera, you could sometimes squeeze one more in, so as I came out of the elevator, I asked Yang if I could take his picture. He lit a cigarette, trying to pose as cool as he could.

I had the film developed at a nearby one-hour photo shop. I gave Yang his picture. "Hmm, those Canon cameras are pretty good!" He said and asked to see the rest.

I laid them out on his desk and explained them one by one:

"For this one, I used automatic brightness. For this one, I used auto-focus; See how it makes the couplet on that wreath super clear?"

He nodded in approval. When we were done, I said casually, "Time to get these to Mr. Murata."

Yang's face sunk. "You took these for him?"

"Yeah, so?"

"You'd better be careful. Don't let the state police think you're some kind of spy."

"It's not like there's national secrets in here."

"You...you're too naïve."

"The square was full of people taking pictures," I explained.

"Yeah, but you took these for a Japanese corporation. That's different."

"OK. I'll be careful." I said, though I had no idea what I was supposed to be careful about.

That afternoon, Mr. Murata's phone rang off the hook, each call longer than the last. With each, he seemed to bow even deeper in response. I felt sorry for him. As we were finishing up for the day, he asked if I could take the camera home with me, and take a few more pictures of Tiananmen on my way.

"No problem," I answered.

When I was finally alone in the office, I recalled Yang's warning. I also started to wonder whether the man who'd tried to steal my camera was a thief or police.

I started to miss Guo Yan. He would have known what to do. Or maybe if he'd been there, the guy wouldn't even have tried. I'd read enough spy novels to know that one of the best ways to blend in was to pretend to be a couple. With Guo Yan by my side, I would have been safer. But he didn't call and I wouldn't be calling him. My grandmother taught me that women shouldn't approach men or they'd be regarded as cheap.

Time crept by and the phone never rang.

There was no way I was taking an EOS back to Tiananmen alone at night, so I grabbed a model AF35M. It was a compact camera, nicknamed the "auto-boy," though in China, it had won itself the nickname "idiot-boy" for its fool-proof point-and-shoot technology.

As I turned it over in my hands, I noticed the phone's red message light blinking. When I called the message center, there was no message for me. Was I hallucinating?

I got home after eight. My grandmother's house was pitch dark. By a sliver of moonlight, I made out her silhouette sitting cross-legged on the bed.

"Is electricity so expensive?" I asked, turning on a lamp.

Grandma was wearing sunglasses in the dark. She lowered the glasses to reveal a pair of red, swollen eyes.

"What happened? Are you sick?"

"I thought something terrible had happened to you. I've been crying all day." She put her sunglasses back on.

"I'm not a kid anymore. What did you think happened?"

"Bad things only happen to kids? Just last month a woman was killed in Yuetan Park."

Fresh tears fell behind her dark glasses. I hurried to bring her a handkerchief. "Don't cry...don't cry. I'm sorry. I shouldn't be staying out overnight without telling you. I won't do it again. I promise."

She calmed slightly. "Where were you last night?"

"I went to Tiananmen with a friend."

"You went to Tiananmen? Your grandpa said that's probably where you were. I said no way. I thought you'd probably found a boyfriend."

My mind raced for the right answer. If I wanted to put her mind at ease, I should tell her she'd guessed correctly, but saying that would unleash an avalanche of questions. Who is he? What does he do? When is he coming over?

She took me by the hand, imploring, "Stay out of Tiananmen! Nothing good ever comes of going against the government! You're not even a student anymore. When students get crazy, the Party can forgive them. But you..."

"I didn't go there to join the protests," I said. "I just took pictures for my boss."

"Is that allowed?" She clutched my hands even tighter.

I felt uncomfortable sharing physical contact with my grandmother. I took back my hand and immediately regretted it. She'd become increasingly sensitive lately. I'd better not to say or do anything that would make her feel like I didn't love her anymore.

"I guess so," I patted the back of her hand.

She relaxed a bit. "Are you hungry?"

I was, but wanted to avoid her. I said I wasn't and that I needed to sleep. I opened my cot and climbed right in wearing the clothes I'd had on for two days. I turned out the light. My grandmother's cross-legged silhouette remained upright in bed, rocking gently from side to side.

Whenever I closed my eyes, I could see her sitting there rocking back and forth as if sitting on a turbulent sea. I knew her behavior well. When I was little, she'd sit like that at night for weeks after my grandfather visited.

It was most likely that she didn't believe my lie. She had no reason to worry about me spending a night at Tiananmen, but if I was involved with a man, I'd be absent again from time to time. And if that man became my husband, I'd move out entirely to start a family. That was her real worry.

I'd moved in with her in August 1988, just as the Party tried and failed to break the price ceiling. Officials claimed the nation's planned economy would be phased out over the next five years, making way for a free-market alternative. People panicked and mobbed the stores, snatching up anything they could. Banks were overrun with people clearing out their accounts. In order to placate the public, the Party aborted the plan. It only lasted 10 days.

My grandmother spent the entirety of those 10 days stocking up. When I came home in the evenings, she urged me to go out to buy up whatever I could. I told her no. I wasn't worried about inflation because I had a job. Inflation was only occurring because wages had increased. What was the worry?

"You'll be fine, but there's no way your grandfather's pension can keep up."

My grandfather had been retired for eight years. His pension, my grandparents' only source of income, hadn't increased a penny. His pension was paid according to the living standards of the early 1980s, which were basically the same as the 1950s. Chinese people hadn't seen inflation since the founding of the People's Republic. But marching into the 80's, inflation began to soar. During the transition from a planned to a hybrid economy, China's Gross Domestic Product increased by more than 10% every year. 1987 alone saw the retail price index rise by 7.3%. Between 1980 and 1988, my grandparents' purchasing power dropped about half.

The situation reminded my grandmother of how bad things were during the great economic crash of 1948. "People had to trade wheelbarrows of cash for a single pound of corn," she said.

"Don't worry," I told her. "You have me now."

I promised that as long as I had the ability to work, I'd provide for her.

"That sounds good," she said, crumpling her nose. "But I know what young people are like. Once you have a family, you'll forget all about me."

"No, I won't."

"That's what your mom did. I supported her all through college and how did she repay me? By running off to Tianjin with a man."

"Tianjin isn't that far, and I'm different. I love Beijing." I was half joking.

"We'll see."

In the quiet of the night, her words echoed in my mind. In hindsight, I'd gained an upper hand in our power struggle. Had I realized she was so vulnerable, I would've tried to put her more at ease.

But I was preoccupied with my own impending loss. The more she worried about me leaving her for good, the more I worried Guo would leave me stranded. And I hated her for torturing me by torturing herself.

The next morning, I opened my eyes to find her still rocking back and forth on her bed, sunglasses over her tender eyes. I had to get out of the house.

Students marching in honor of Hu yaobang, April 1989.

Photo by Yanguang He

Chapter 9

The Song of the Stormy Petrel

I gave Mr. Murata the photos I'd taken, and he spread them out across his desk. He lifted each one slowly and examined every last inch before separating them into three piles. As he left for the day, he reminded me to not touch anything on his desk. He'd barely passed the threshold, then turned and asked me to pass on the same instructions to the service desk. I waited until he was long gone before I went over to his desk, my curiosity running rampant. By what logic had he organized the pictures? What was I not seeing?

I picked up the first stack but couldn't for the life of me see what they had in common. I picked up the second stack and saw no difference from the first.

The next day, I handed him more pictures. He organized them into three piles except one, which he scrutinized closely.

"What are you doing, Mr. Murata?" I asked.

He paused, and then replied, "I'm trying to see who's behind these students."

He sounded just like the Party, assuming that anytime students got riled up, someone was pulling the strings.

"So did you find who you were looking for?"

He shook his head.

No kidding, I chuckled silently. *You can't find what's not there.*

As if reading my mind, he took a pile of photos and laid them out on the table with the precision of a blackjack dealer. He did the same to the second pile, then the third. "Take a look," he said.

I went over and took a look at the photos. Standing at his side, I saw that they were grouped according to the slogans on the flags and banners. In the first pile were slogans that most likely voiced the students' concerns, things like, "Education will save the country." In the second pile were slogans that pushed for things like freedom, democracy, law and order. In the last pile were slogans calling for economic reform.

"Where should this one go?" he asked me, holding up a picture. The slogan read, "Punishing the bureaucratic profiteers."

"This one's calling for economic reform," I said.

Bureaucratic profiteers were a product of China's dual-track price system. At the end of the 1970s, the Party wanted to give its planned economy a shot in the arm, and began allowing state-owned enterprises to manufacture extra products after meeting State quotas. Those extra products were then sold for whatever the market would pay. Therefore, nearly every product on the market had two prices. Goods produced in fulfillment of state quotas would be sold at the state-mandated price, while excess stock would be sold at much higher prices.

Bureaucratic profiteers bought goods at the state-mandated price, only to turn around and sell them on the open market for an outrageous profit. Rumor had it that some bureaucratic profiteers never even set eyes on the goods they traded. All it took was a phone call and truckloads of commodities were rerouted before any money exchanged hands.

The failed attempt to break the price ceiling in 1988 was designed to solve this problem by doing away with the planned economy entirely, but citizens were terrified by the idea of a market economy. I had no reservations whatsoever and thought that the students shared my opinion. Mr. Murata disagreed.

"The students hate inflation, don't they?" he asked.

"You bet," I said. "When I was a freshman, a meal cost 0.5 RMB. When I was a senior, the same meal cost almost double."

"Inflation, bureaucratic profiteers and the dual-track price system are the price we must pay to transition from a planned to a market economy," he contemplated. "How do students think we'll get rid of them? By returning to a planned economy or by implementing a market economy?"

"A market economy, of course!" I shouted confidently.

"You've benefitted from the market economy. You found a job at Pecan. But what about all the others?"

I saw what he was driving at. The students hated inflation. There'd been protests over rising prices at the school's cafeterias, but that was a relatively small thing. The real issue was job prospects. Rumor had it that starting in 1990, the government would no longer assign jobs to college graduates. Very few looked forward to being dumped into an unfathomable job market.

Mr. Murata suspected that Party conservatives were secretly behind the student movement, but this was far too cynical for me. Sure, they might be afraid of the implications of a free market, but they still wanted democracy, free speech and a free press.

I grabbed the pictures from the second pile and flung them across the desk in a clumsy fit of rage, "See this? 'Long Live Democracy!' 'Long Live Freedom!' What do you think that means? Do you really think that can happen under a stupid planned economy?"

He leaned his full weight on the front of the desk, hands outstretched, "I've seen these a hundred times."

Ms. Kawashima came over, tea in hand. "Mr. Murata just thinks young people don't know what they're doing," she commented.

I smiled. She was registering her displeasure with Mr. Murata by pretending to relate to me. She and I were of the same generation, after all. Mr. Murata's generation had grown too cynical. They couldn't see the passion and power behind the students' idealism.

"Ms. Kawashima! Is your tea bitter? Would you like me to get you some sugar?" I found myself saying.

"No, I'm good. Thank you."

The next day, I gave her an extra cube anyway.

I'd grown up when a family couldn't get more than a pound of sugar a month and I couldn't wrap my head around why anyone would willingly limit their sugar intake. So what if it made you fat? A few extra pounds only meant you had the resources to eat, drink, and be merry, and that got you respect.

Mr. Murata suspected that while the students might think they're promoting democracy, their anger was rooted in fear of a market economy, which made them easily manipulated by conservative wing of the Party, who intended to use the chaos as leverage to pressure the party's moderate reformists into their camp. He made some sense, but the students were actually fighting for democracy, which couldn't coexist with the doctrine of communism. We argued for a while. In the end, he asked me to look closely for any adults standing around behind the protestors. I agreed to do so.

On the evening of April 17, two-hundred students gathered in the Square, and decided to draft a manifesto. The end product was a document called the "Seven Demands." It called for a re-evaluation of the merits and contributions of Hu Yaobang, allowing people to publish their own newspapers, freedom of speech, transparency regarding the income and assets of government officials and their families, among other concerns.

The next day was centered on submitting the "Seven Demands" in the right hands. On the morning of April 18, the students marched together to the Great Hall of the People. The instant the front door opened at 8 am, Wang Dan walked straight in and handed the document to the Complaints Bureau at the General Office of the State Council. As Wang Dan exited and showed his record of receipt to those waiting outside, he considered his mission accomplished, and took his leave.

But after Wang Dan left, someone in the midst of the students reminded them that the full session of the National People's Congress only occurred once a year in March, and the next session was 11 months away. Maybe handing their demands to a clerk felt momentous to Wang Dan, but if they were to get real results, they'd have to get them straight to an actual member of congress.

Li Jinjin stepped up to pick up where Wang Dan left off. The sit-in at the Square continued. In an effort to draw the attention they needed, several students moved a thirty-foot long massive "Chinese soul" couplet from the Monument to the People's Heroes and planted it straight on the steps of the Great Hall. By that evening, three members of congress, Liu Yandong, Song Shixiong, and Tao Xiping, finally emerged from its massive front doors, and personally accepted a copy of the "Seven Demands." Li Jinjin once again proclaimed their mission accomplished, and ordered all in attendance to disperse, which he did first.

But once again, while the shepherd may have left, the flock stayed behind. By this time, every government employee in the Great Hall had gone home for the day. Someone suggested they set out for Xinhua Gate. A half-mile away, it was the entrance to Zhongnanhai, the official headquarters of Communist Party's Central Committee, and China's State Council. With shouts of approval from the crowd, they hoisted their massive "Chinese soul" battle flag and headed for their next theater of war.

I'd gone to the Square several times on April 18. I hadn't seen any adults in with the students but I felt an orchestrating presence. I knew as a rule the students would start off strong, then the protests would die down. This time the students' list of demands was growing. As soon as one was met, several more emerged. Someone had to be fanning the flames.

After work, I went to Tiananmen again. It was around 6 pm, just in time to see the tailend of the mob heading toward Xinhua Gate. I followed.

Leaving the Square, the students crowded themselves onto the narrow sidewalk right as all of Beijing was getting off work. Before long, the two seas of people had somehow sequestered themselves to opposite sides of the street. The students commandeered the north side, while everyone else took the south. Yards away from Xinhua Gate, the students grounded to a halt. Seeing that the southern side of the street was less packed, I headed across the street to join the civilians. Once got to across, I could finally see what was going on. A mass of students streamed in from the west, joining the students headed to Xinhua Gate headlong.

Armed police had formed an airtight wall in front of Xinhua Gate but were enveloped in a sea of students, demanding to speak to the Premier of the country, Li Peng.

"Li Peng now! Li Peng now!" they screamed.

Next to me stood a man in his fifties, wearing a neatly pressed, white shirt. He looked at the students across the street disapprovingly, "Are they serious? Whatever this is about, Li Peng's not coming out! He's the Premier, for God's sake. He's dealing with the entire country every day. These brats think the Premier's going to come out and listen to them because they throw a fit?"

Someone, most likely his wife, immediately shushed him, "Mind your own business!"

"How is this not my business?" he shot back. "They say they want democracy. I'm Chinese just like them. Why shouldn't my voice be heard?"

"Long live the students!" a worker in overalls shouted, pumping his fist in the air.

"Long live the people!" the students shouted back.

The worker shot the couple a steely glare. The husband was more than happy to engage, but his wife dragged him away as quickly as possible.

I was surprised by the students' demands. As far as I understood, democracy was a system intended to resolve conflicts through set procedures that took time. The students wanted Li Peng to give in to their "Seven Demands" right here and now. Can they even call that democracy?

I shook my head and went on my way. After I'd boarded my bus, it occurred to me that Li Peng leaned conservative, which meant that even if there were adults orchestrating the students, it wasn't the conservatives. That was a relief. Tomorrow, I'll tell Mr. Murata what I discovered in great detail.

When I rode in a westbound bus, I saw more students marching to the city center. The majority of the city's universities were in the western part of Beijing. Peking University, Tsinghua University, People's University, Beijing Normal University, the University of Political Science and Law, Beijing Foreign Studies University, Beijing Medical School... the list went on and on.

After I finished dinner in the peace and quiet of my grandmother's house, I couldn't stop wondering what was happening at Xinhua Gate. Was I missing a pivotal moment? Was it possible that the students were making history at this very minute? I looked out the window just in time to spot a #15 bus heading right toward the center of the action. I wanted to be back at Xinhua Gate, and I wanted it now!

I turned around to get ready. What I saw left me not knowing whether to laugh or cry.

I had changed into my lounge clothes after I got back, and my grandmother, figuring I was in for the night, had thrown my street clothes into the wash. I only had two sets of street clothes. Now one was soaking, and the other was pinned between her butt and the bed.

My grandmother had a strange talent. After washing clothes and letting them get 90 percent dry, she would fold them neatly and sit cross-legged on top of them for hours, resulting in neatly pressed clothes that looked like they had been pressed by an iron.

She was sitting atop my clean set of street clothes doing some needlework. Her eyes clearly hadn't fully recovered from crying the night before. She could manage only a few small stitches at a time before having to pause and rub her eyes.

My heart sunk, and my enthusiasm died. A sharp realization struck me: My restlessness was motivated by a desire to meet Guo Yan somewhere. I couldn't predict where he was, but I was damn sure he wouldn't show up at my grandma's home. Every corner in the city had potential for him to appear. Every single one except my grandmother's house.

You are so cheap, I scolded myself. My courage diminished. I couldn't bring myself to ask for the clothes she was sitting on.

I wouldn't be going anywhere tonight. I looked out the window and saw smoke gushing from the chimney at Beijing Children's Hospital. They still burned coal? Hard to believe.

On the morning of April 22, 1989, I rode the bus to work as I did every day. When we reached Tiananmen West Station, the driver kept going, ignoring the passengers pounding on the doors. The shouts of irate passengers and the sharp thuds of their fists rose to a level the driver couldn't bear. He came out from his inertia and cried out, "Until further notice, all service to Tiananmen is suspended!"

"Why didn't you say anything before?" his accusers snapped back.

"I've been saying it this entire time! Is it my fault you weren't listening?"

Seeking support, a female passenger called out, "Who actually heard him? If you didn't hear him, back us up here!" She was met with silence. Everyone on the bus had their own problems.

Our busload of frustration and indifference rolled onward. The Square came into view. It was teeming with students. Uniformed soldiers stood in formation, blocking the students from entering the Great Hall. The scene reminded us that Hu Yaobang's funeral was about to start. The tension silenced even the most outraged passengers. The bus passed Tiananmen East Station without stopping.

April 22 was a Saturday. It was Mr. Murata's turn to be in the office, but Ms. Kawashima turned up along with him. Zhao arrived half an hour later, looking solemn.

"These students are nothing but trouble," he muttered angrily.

"What happened?" I asked.

He explained that the rerouting of traffic around Tiananmen meant he couldn't drive to the hotel's main parking lot. He had to drop his bosses at the service entrance, then park the car half a mile away.

I shrugged, knowing better than to get personal.

Mr. Murata and Ms. Kawashima sat talking in the reception area, and soon called me and Zhao over to join them. It turned out Ms. Kawashima had come to watch the broadcast of Hu Yaobang's memorial with us. She could have watched it at home, but she wanted to hear what Mr. Murata had to say about it. Although she didn't think highly of his knowledge of Japanese, she admitted that when it came to China, there was little he didn't know.

His knowledge of China was indeed impressive. In no uncertain terms, he explained the significance of memorial services for Chinese politicians. China's political workings weren't as transparent as in Western countries. A memorial service was a perfect example. As for Hu Yaobang's memorial, there were two mysteries to be revealed: First, who would attend? Second, would he be called a Marxist during the eulogy?

The live broadcast began. We saw the interior of the central hall of the Great Hall of the People, spacious and elevated. A massive portrait of the deceased hung in the front of the hall. Hu's body lay beneath the portrait, encased in a crystal coffin. His makeup had been applied with a heavy hand, making him look a bit like a wax statue. He was covered with the flag of the Communist Party of China. Sickle and axe. The violence symbolized by those two things made me feel uneasy.

Over six thousand people attended Hu Yaobang's memorial. Mr. Murata asked us to carefully observe the people in the first row. These were the select few who decided the fate of every man, woman, and child in China. The most notable were Zhao Ziyang and Li Peng. Zhao, the Party's General Secretary, had a solid track record of implementing economic reform measures, and could be considered a moderate reformist. Li Peng, the Premier of the country, was a conservative.

According to Mr. Murata, the nation's current chaos was likely rooted in the power struggle between Zhao Ziyang and Li Peng. But neither Zhao nor Li could actually decide the other's fate. They were both puppets, more or less. The people who pulled the strings were called the "eight immortals." They were Mao's contemporaries and founders of the People's Republic. All were at least half-retired due to age or health, but still retained enough power to run the country behind the scenes. The two most prominent were Deng Xiaoping and Chen Yun. Deng was a moderate reformist and Chen a conservative. Chen was a fierce supporter of the planned economy, and had authored the "birdcage theory," which conceives of the free market as a bird, and the planned economy as the cage which keeps it safe.

I stared at the old men in the first row, trying to read the expressions of the "eight immortals," but I got nothing. They were all basically the same height, and had the same staunch, stoic face. They all wore the same dark tunic suit made famous by Sun Yat-sen, except for a few military officers in uniform. They looked like statues carved from the same block of stone. Was China's fate really determined by these deadpans?

Suddenly, Mr. Murata blurted out that Chen Yun was absent. The three of us stared blankly at him. He shrugged helplessly, meaning he didn't know much more. I turned and stared at the TV again, but no matter how hard I tried, I couldn't fathom the depth of the old men. This was way beyond me. I gave up.

It was time for the eulogy. Zhao Ziyang stepped into the spotlight and began reading from a script. Mr. Murata asked us to listen for the word, "Marxist." Communists believed that after this life, it was Karl Marx that they would meet on the other side. Therefore, it was very important for them to be called a "Marxist" upon death. The day Hu Yaobang died, as the broadcasts spread across the land, not once did the exalted "M-word" come up, which meant the Party didn't forgive Hu's leniency toward bourgeois freedoms. But after the battering they'd taken from the students, who, in their "Seven Demands," asked for re-evaluating the merits and contributions of Hu Yaobang, the Party might change their tune.

We all perked our ears, and then it came. "Marxist."

Zhao Ziyang called Hu Yaobang a Marxist in the eulogy, meaning the students had earned points in their battle against Party conservatives.

Still, I wondered if "Marxist" was an appropriate accolade for Mr. Hu. The sole reason students loved him was that he championed western capitalist freedoms. Why would the students want him labeled a Marxist?

Then, Mr. Murata asked us to take note of how long the funerary music played before and after the service. The length of time indicated the importance of the deceased. The shortest the music had ever played was a mere thirty seconds. The longest was three minutes, thirty-five seconds, at Mao Zedong's memorial service. When the ceremony came to an end, we all held our breath and counted. Hu Yaobang received a minute, seventeen. Not bad.

The broadcast dedicated to what was happening inside the hall, and completely ignored the Square. But I can't forget what I saw on my way to work. I knew the students wanted to play a role in the memorial but I didn't see a single student in the broadcast. I wondered how that would shake out.

The broadcast lasted about an hour, after which Murata and

Kawashima took their leave. I grabbed our newest EOS, along with every lens I could think of, and headed for the Square. It'd been five days since that man tried to snatch my bag, and the terror I'd felt had long faded.

I entered the Square from the east and met a sea of backs. The entirety of the students was facing west toward the Great Hall. Some students were ready to withdraw, but the majority refused to leave. They wanted to block the hearse to say goodbye to Hu Yaobang in person, but were told that the hearse had left through a secret tunnel. They were furious. The Square was growing more chaotic by the minute.

I felt a looming unease. The scene reminded me of the delirious, broad brushstrokes of Van Gogh's "Wheatfield with Crows." It was the first time I'd felt scared amongst my fellow students. I was enveloped by the enormity of the crowd and it pushed forward, taking me with it. I saw a person stumble, and realized a stampede could easily happen. I kept scanning my surroundings, trying to pinpoint danger as it emerged. Suddenly, the students in front of me halted, bringing me to a stop. A hush descended over the mob. The air became heavy and suspenseful, like the eye of a storm.

Everyone looked straight ahead. There were three figures on the front steps of the hall. They were squatting down on the steps. Were they stooping like a line of runners waiting for a starting shot? There was no way they were going to force their way into the hall, was there?

"Li Peng! Out! Now!"

Cries rang out.

"Li Peng! Out! Now!"

The students had turned into an angry mob. Their rage had finally boiled over.

I still had no idea what was going on, then I remembered I'd brought a 18-250mm zoom lens. I snapped it onto the camera and applied the auto-focus. A split second, and I was able to see the three figures on the steps as clear as day. What I saw sent chills through me. All three knelt on the steps to the hall. The one in the middle had his hands outstretched high, as if presenting a sacrifice.

I couldn't believe my eyes. Were they begging Li Peng to speak with them?

I was no biology major, but I knew of atavism: ancestral traits coming back full circle. How could these students, citizens of the 1980s, plunge back a hundred years in an instant? Forty years earlier, Mao Zedong had stood in this very square and declared that the Chinese people would never kneel again. Four decades later, almost to the day, the treasured future of the nation knelt on the steps of power, begging for democracy and freedom like children begging for candy.

Waves of shame coursed through me.

However, I found those around me were furious at the arrogance of the authorities. The three students were baked in the afternoon sun, knees aching on the hard stone steps, while the people in power stayed sheltered in the shade of the inner hall, oblivious to the suffering of the nation's elite youth. How different were my feelings from theirs? It seemed I wasn't one of them anymore.

I put my camera back in my bag without taking a single picture. I didn't want my Japanese bosses to see this. This occurrence was an embarrassment; one best kept within our race.

The next day, I went to the office as usual to work on my book. Upon opening the file, I noticed it was last saved on the 16th. I hadn't heard from Guo Yan since last Sunday.

Then and there I realized that the protests were instrumental for my survival. Suppose the world outside had stayed quiet. Every second would have been a prison. I needed courage to break free and carry on with each passing minute. It was fortunate to have something to focus on.

During lunch, I went to Tiananmen just as I had every day that week. I noticed the wreaths were gone. There were no students either. Just as suddenly as it had begun, it was over. I didn't want to believe it.

I went back Wangfujing to find something to eat. Around the corner, the aroma of Taiwanese fried chicken wafted through the air, and with it, my memories of the days before the protests. Would it still taste the same as it had a week ago? Or had it too, been forever changed? I stopped at the window and bought an order of chicken. It tasted exactly the same. I wanted to cry.

Nothing happened in the afternoon except for a couple of wrong numbers, which drove up my level of adrenaline, and eventually put me into a darker despair. I heard people come and go in the hall. The quietness of my own office made me incredibly unsettling.

Our office had a small balcony facing Chang'an Avenue, but due to Beijing's frequent sandstorms, no one ever opened the door. When it got dark, I tried the door. It was rusty from years of inactivity. I pulled with all my might until I thought it might break, and finally managed to wrench it open. The night air cut through all it touched, ruffling through the office recklessly.

I stood on the balcony, looking down over Chang'an Avenue. People strode along as they always. It was no different from any other April evening. Under the silent spring sky, the air quickly turned from warm to cold. The street lamps began to glow, and the cars scurried by. Dark clouds stretched from one end of the earth to the other, allowing only threads of yellow sunset through.

It was at that moment, I thought of lines from Maxim Gorky's "The Song of the Stormy Petrel."

"Let the storm come! Let the rains try to wash me away!" I shouted down to the street.

Not a single pedestrian looked up.

Hundreds of thousands of students from Beijing universities marching through the streets of the capital toward Tiananmen Square, April 27, 1989.

Photo by Yanguang He

Chapter 10

A Trip to Shanghai

I returned to my grandmother's house.

As I opened my cot, I heard a knock at the door. I opened the door and found Min. Remembering her campaign against Guo Yan, I made no move to let her inside. All smiles, she asked, "You're not gonna invite me in?"

We sat shoulder to shoulder on my small cot. Min produced two ice cream cones, one for me, and one for my grandmother, who sat on her bed "pressing" one of my outfits and knitting a hat. She thanked Min but insisted she didn't eat such things. Min of course insisted, and the two entered a stalemate until finally Min conceded, just as it was supposed to go. I knew my grandmother would never take it, but I also knew she was overjoyed that it was even offered. All she wanted was for someone to respect her.

As we opened our melting frozen treats, I asked what she'd been up to.

"I'm getting married!" she announced.

"Really?" It was the last thing I expected. "Your parents are OK with it?"

"Yeah, they're fine with it."

"How'd you talk 'em into it?"

"It's a long story. For now, I just came to ask what you're doing on Sunday the 30th."

She wanted me to be her bridesmaid.

I told her it would be my honor. As to why the wedding was so rushed, she explained that every weekend in May and June was booked solid. The only day they could find a decent place was April 30th. It made sense.

As soon as she left, my grandmother said there was at least an eighty-percent chance she was pregnant. Why else would anyone want to get married so desperately?

I felt insulted, as if she were badmouthing me. "Why are you so mean, grandma?" I said. "She thinks of you every time she visits me." I was implying the ice cream.

"She's a good kid," my grandmother shrugged. "But even good kids make mistakes, and some mistakes are expensive." I realized what she was implying. "Be careful," she chided, rocking back and forth.

On the afternoon of April 25, a call came through from Mr. Nikaidou, a senior manager at Canon's head office. He had a niece studying at Peking University. Her father had heard of the student strike, and feared what could ensue. He'd been calling the foreign exchange dorm since the strike began, but had failed to get in touch with her.

Ms. Kawashima took the call. She gave me a brief synopsis and instructed me to go to the school to "rescue" Ms. Nikaidou. I had met her once before. She was pretty much Ms. Kawashima's diametric opposite. She looked more like a boy. She had short hair, a penchant for smoking, and a dreamy, languid air about her. She was also much easier to talk to, but that could have been because she wasn't my boss.

The last time she visited our office, she asked me if I could take her to Wangfujing after work. She wanted to eat the best food in Beijing. I took her to Cuihua Lou, a famed restaurant specializing in Shandong cuisine. At the time, Cantonese food was all the rage in Beijing high society. Young, modern, new money diners looked down on Shandong cuisine as outdated peasant fare, but being half Shandongese myself, I knew exactly how to pair dishes to reflect the true essence. Being an epicurean herself, Ms. Nikaidou loved the real deal served at Cuihua Lou.

Ms. Nikaidou wasn't exactly a conventional Japanese girl. I had a hunch that studying in China was most likely her excuse to escape Japan. It was no accident that her father couldn't reach her at her dorm. She probably lived off-campus.

"You better find her," Ms. Kawashima ordered. "If you find her before six, bring her back here. If not, bring her to my apartment."

She had Zhao take me to the school. I'd never ridden with Zhao before. He was exclusively on standby for Murata and Kawashima. This arrangement meant that bringing back Ms. Niakidou was Ms. Kawashima's No. 1 priority for the afternoon.

We entered campus through the west gate and were met by near complete silence. "This place doesn't look like a school. It looks more like a park," Zhao commented. Ahead was a pond with fallen lotus leaves. I felt a pang of regret. I'd lived here for four years and not once had I stopped to appreciate the lotus flowers.

The foreign exchange dormitory was the grandest on campus. Inside, I saw a woman at the front desk.

"I'm looking for Ms. Nikaidou."

The woman dialed the extension, listened for a couple of seconds, and said with a hint of triumph, "She's not here."

"Her father's looking for her. He's been calling since yesterday. Is there any way to find her? This could get big."

"And what do you have to do with her father?" she asked.

"I work for Pecan Inc., a Sino-Japanese company. Her father is one of our managers." In reality, her uncle was the manager, but I didn't have time to get into all that. I took out my work badge.

She squinted, reading the badge. "It says Peking University, Department of Scientific and Technological Development."

"Yeah, Pecan is a joint venture between Founder Group and Canon, and Founder Group is part of the Department of Scientific and Technological Development."

She gave up trying to understand, and repeated, "She's not here."

"My boss said I have to find her. This could turn into an international incident. How I can get ahold of her?"

She thought about it and said, "If you can get a letter from the Department of Foreign Affairs, I can page her."

"She has a pager?" Finally, some useful information. "Do you have the number?"

"Of course," she rolled her eyes, "but I can't give it to you unless you have a letter from the Department of Foreign Affairs."

I knew she was bullshitting. It was typical China. People don't want to help others. They only want to show off their own importance. I returned to the car and told Zhao what happened. Zhao quickly responded, "Do you have a gift? That woman could be bought with anything worth around 20 RMB. If it was a guy, I could go give him some smokes and before you know it we'd be best buddies. But it's a woman. You're gonna have to do whatever it is women do."

I remembered my camera bag. I went inside again and offered the woman "a sample of our product:" a roll of Fuji film. She didn't have to know that it wasn't produced by Canon. It worked. Within moments, she looked up the pager number and called. After a few minutes, the phone rang. "You have a friend here looking for you," she said into the phone and handed the receiver to me.

I snatched it out of her hand, shouting, "Hey, it's me! Ms. Wang from the Beijing office! Remember?"

"Of course I remember." I could hear her disappointment. "What's up, buddy?"

I explained her father was worried about her and wanted her to evacuate the university. Obviously, she was resistant to the idea. Whatever she was up to, it had to be more fun than living with prudish Ms. Kawashima.

I pleaded, "Ms. Kawashima sent me. I'll get fired if I don't bring you back."

It turned out she had sympathy for a poor Chinese girl. She muttered something unintelligible, before saying in the most reluctant manner possible, "Fine. I'll be back in two hours."

I emerged from the dormitory victorious. I told Zhao that we had two hours to kill. He suggested we split up and meet back at the dorm. I agreed. I headed for Building 43, where Zhi Hua lived. As I was getting closer to her dorm, I couldn't help but wonder what I was going to talk about with her. We couldn't avoid talking about the protests. It was on everybody's mind. But what would Zhi Hua's opinion be? I knew I had lots of doubt about the students' motives, and lots of criticism about how student leaders hand organized things. Would that offend her? Very likely.

I'd better not to visit her at time like this. I turned to left, feeling like a weight had lifted.

I started walking toward the Triangle. I was eager to find out what was going on. Since Hu Yaobang's memorial, Tiananmen Square had been quiet and orderly. It seemed the movement had lost momentum. But over in Japan, Mr. Nikaidou had heard that the protests at Peking University were continuing and that the students were on strike. Was that even true?

It turned out it was. The students' anger had been greatly spurred by the three students' who had knelt down in front of the Great Hall. Many posters pointed out that authorities' refusal to talk with students face-to-face was pure ignorance.

The writings in the Triangle were more volatile than I'd expected. Every inch of the bulletin was covered in posters. Across the way, on the walls of the shops, posters had been pasted all over too. Placards hung from every tree, and a rusty pole had been planted in the ground, bearing a large bed sheet which read, in large characters:

Give me liberty, or give me death.

It looked like Hu Yaobang had already been left in the past. He had merely served as the catalyst for a much larger movement. In his place had risen calls to fight for freedom, eradicate corruption, and go on strike to make the voice of the people heard. These students wanted a say in how their country should be run.

One important theme was anti-corruption. I noticed that among the numerous bureaucratic profiteers, a company named Kang Hua was mentioned. I thought it was notable and took a picture of the poster.

Kang Hua was founded and chaired by Deng Xiaoping's eldest son: Deng Pufang. It just so happened that Canon's repair business in Beijing was contracted out to a company affiliated with Kang Hua. Mr. Murata's favorite game was guessing who was backing the students, and this information might give him some kind of hint. Plus, he'd have to be prepared if Kang Hua collapsed for any reason.

Something big is about to happen, I thought.

I didn't know if I should be excited or worried. On one hand, the turbulence would easily distract me from my trivial emotional matters, but on the other, I didn't want the fundamental social order to be completely overthrown.

I took out my camera and captured every poster I thought might be important. A sea of students popped into frame. I lost count of how many times I had to ask people to move to the side.

I felt a tap on my shoulder. It was a male student who carried a stool. He walked past me and right up to the bulletin boards. Standing atop his stool, he bellowed out, "Government officials have gone to Tsinghua University to speak with students!"

The crowd ignited. The students of Peking University had thought themselves the biggest dissidents. What did Tsinghua have to do with all this?

A cry rose behind me, "March to Tsinghua now!"

It was met with a thundering response from the crowd, "March to Tsinghua now!"

A small group of teachers attempted to reason with the crowd,

"This is a ruse by the government to turn students against each other! Don't fall for it."

Still, some students marched northwest, toward Tsinghua. More followed suit.

I noticed several men with dead but knowing eyes mixed into the crowd.

Tsinghua was about a mile down the road, but my two hours were almost up. Leaving the Triangle, I walked toward the foreign exchange dorms. As I walked down a small, deserted path, I heard two people behind me talking loudly, "You think she's Japanese?"

"Nah, her legs are too straight."

"Korean?"

"Nah, her face isn't big enough."

They were testing me to see if I understood Chinese. The first time I'd been insulted this way was on Wangfujing Street. I shot the hooligans an angry stare and they burst into laughter, shouting, "Fake foreign devil! Fake foreign devil!" It was a derogatory term for Chinese people who pretended to be foreigners by dressing or speaking like them. The term highlighted that while you might think of yourself as foreign, you were still a fake. The best way to shut them up was to ignore them. A real foreign devil knew no Chinese.

That was exactly what I was doing, but I didn't get rid of them. They followed me all the way to the foreign exchange dorm. I went inside, but a different woman was behind the desk. I told her the entire tale again, adding the fact that Ms. Nikaidou would be coming to meet me in minutes.

"If you're going to wait, wait outside," she instructed. "This building is for foreign students."

My pursuers stood across the street, and seeing I had been cast out of my shelter, laughed scornfully. "Told you, she's just some fake foreign devil."

I looked away. One of them called out, "Hey! Hot stuff! Let me see your camera!"

I'd been trying to cover it with my hands, which only called more attention to it. One of them tried to pry my hands open, while the other ripped the strap from my shoulder.

Zhao suddenly returned, calling out amicably, "Hey, brothers. What're you up to?"

"Mind your own fucking business!" one snapped back.

"We work for the same company!" Zhao said, pointing to me.

One of the assailants hastily opened the camera and took out the film to expose it. I almost burst into tears. He put the camera back in the bag and thrust it into my hands. I shot into the car and locked the door.

"Hoooo, Peking University students robbing people?" Zhao exclaimed. "That's a new one."

"They weren't students!"

"How's that possible?" Zhao continued. "The security at the gate was so strict. I barely got past the interrogations."

We sat in silence. I was too tired and scared to explain. A taxi cruised by and stopped in front of our car. Ms. Nikaidou got out.

We got Ms. Nikaidou back to the office by six o'clock. Ms. Kawashima was so elated she ran and hugged Ms. Nikaidou tightly. They chatted in Japanese, before Ms. Kawashima remembered I was still there, and turned to me, "Ms. Wang, thank you for today. Thank you so much. You can go home now."

I almost made it to the door when she added. "Oh, someone with the last name Guo called."

My heart leapt, "What did he say?"

"He said he'll call you tomorrow."

The next day, the phone rang off the hook. Not a single call was for me.

The day after, the phone rang just as I was about to leave for lunch. I was typing and balanced the receiver between my cheek and shoulder, "Canon Beijing office. How may I help you?"

It was Guo Yan.

"How may I help you?" I repeated nonchalantly, as I hit the keys slightly harder to emphasize my lack of emotion. Random characters appeared on the screen.

"I want to take you to lunch."

"Thank you, but I already have plans. Maybe next time," I hung up on him.

As soon as I hung up, I regretted it. Hadn't I wanted him to call? Why did I turn down his invitation? The amount I hated him was about equal to the amount I wanted him. I didn't know how to balance the two. Maybe I hated him more. Plus, I didn't lie. I planned on going to the Square.

The day before, the *People's Daily* published a stern editorial entitled "Combating Chaos: Take a Stand or Fall to Pieces." The article argued that the protests were a premeditated plot—part of a conspiracy by counterrevolutionary forces, and the nation's students had been used as pawns. The article read:

> *This is a war against the leaders of the Communist Party of China.*
> *This is a war against the fundamentals of socialist society.*
> *This is a war against us all...*

My experience at Peking University told me that if there was one thing students hated more than anything else, it was telling them they had been used. The paper was probably trying to stamp out rebellion, but they'd only added fuel to the fire.

I didn't doubt for a minute that there would be an even stronger confrontation. I couldn't shake the feeling something big was about to happen. The second the clock struck twelve, I dropped whatever I was working on, and was out the door.

The elevator was packed. Two blond men stood in front of me. They were likely western journalists judging by the camera bag and tripod they carried. I silently sized up their camera bag, wondering what it held.

The doors opened at the first floor, and everyone poured out in a hard line, cutting through the crowd of people waiting to enter. An arm shot out of the crowd and pulled me over. It was Guo Yan.

"What are you doing here?" I asked, unable to mask my shock.

"Waiting for you!" he replied, beaming. "I was going up to your office, but I was afraid you'd come down while I was going up, so I waited here."

He held my arm tight. His energy coursed into me. My resolve faltered a little. Still, I was annoyed.

"I told you. I have plans."

"Coffee then? Just for a few minutes? I need to talk to you about something," he pleaded.

The Beijing Hotel had a coffee shop at the center of the long hallway between the east and center wings. Low-slung tables with sofas on either side were arranged along the windows facing the bustling expanse of Chang'an Avenue. Seeing us take our seats, a beautiful young woman in a traditional Chinese dress shot us an indifferent look. It was a typical look when waitresses saw Chinese customers. If we were foreigners, they would rush to serve us.

Guo Yan took a quick look over the menu. Even a can of Coke was three times what it cost anywhere else in the city.

"I can only stay for about ten minutes," I quickly declared. "Don't worry about the menu, that waitress won't get up from her comfy seat for at least fifteen."

I rested my arms on the table with my watch in full view. Guo Yan's hand reached out to cover it. "Don't be like that. I'm already sad enough."

"Sad." The magic word meant I hadn't been dumped, but had been separated from him by an insurmountable obstacle. I had held my sadness at bay with anger. Now tears came flooding.

Guo Yan handed me a tissue. He explained that after I left him that day, his wife came back to work things out. He had no interest in doing so, but he couldn't just kick her out. They were still married, and they had been college sweethearts. Their lives and social circles were entirely intertwined. Nearly every day, a friend they had in common came to his house unannounced, or called him up at work, attempting to play peacemaker. He was sick of it.

I couldn't shake the feeling I'd been played. They hadn't separated at all, nor did they plan to. He'd invited me home because his wife was out of town that night. The more he tried to explain, the more he disgusted me. I dried my eyes, and asked coldly, "How do you want me to help you? What do I look like, a divorce lawyer?"

He told me he'd arranged a business trip in order to avoid his wife. He was leaving on the 28th.

"OK. Well, bon voyage."

"I want you to come with me."

"How exactly would I do that? I have to work."

The second those words came out of my mouth, I regretted them. It sounded like I wanted to go.

"Don't you have a week off for Golden Week?" he asked.

How did he know about that? Golden Week is a week of Japanese holidays. Every year it starts on the 29th of April and ended in early May. With a weekend on both ends, Japanese employees would have nine days off in total. Mr. Murata and Ms. Kawashima had already announced their plans to return to Japan. I had no plans of my own, and had honestly forgotten about the whole thing. I could work on my novel at the office without any interruptions.

"See, I remember every word you said. Even you forgot," he smiled.

He wasn't without charm, and had created an opportunity to be with me. He desired me as much as I desired him. I felt I was standing at the edge of an abyss, threatened by its gravitational pull. I summoned the strength to tell him where to stick his business trip, when the waitress sauntered over, "What would you like to order?"

"I'll have an orange juice," I replied.

Ten minutes later, she returned with two glasses of orange juice. I slowly sipped mine as I gazed out over Chang'an Avenue, to find a painfully quotidian scene unfolding. It was peaceful and mundane, like any other day.

Guo was clearly lying about getting a divorce, but I could tell he honestly wanted to be with me. Now the burden was back on my shoulders: Do I continue a relationship I know is adulterous, or break up with him entirely?

I couldn't bear to go forward without him, but simply continuing our indecent relationship wasn't a good solution either. The thing that enraged me most was the lie about divorcing his wife, and he wanted me to travel with him based on that lie. If I went with him, it meant I believed him.

The students hated how the Party underestimated them by assuming they'd been used by political dissidents. They thought of themselves as smart, independent and provocative on their own, just as I thought of myself. The sheer thought of being fooled or underestimated was humiliating.

I finished my orange juice and set down my empty glass.

"I could travel with you, but only on one condition."

He stared at me intently, "Tell me, then."

"You have to admit that you lied to me. You have to admit that there wasn't ever a separation in the first place, and that you're not going through a divorce."

"Is that what you want?" He was genuinely confused. "I don't know what to say."

"I can travel with you," I maintained, "but I won't be made a fool of. Admit those things to me, or we have no future."

"No future..." he muttered, "I could admit those things, but I wouldn't mean it. I just want to get away with you."

I spent that afternoon in a haze. Around three o'clock, my mind was still worlds away when Ms. Kawashima's piercing voice brought me crashing back to Earth: "Ms. Wang! Come quick! The students are protesting again!"

She was standing on the balcony. I hadn't seen her open the French doors and go outside. Awakened from a dream, I stumbled to join her. The protests had never been large enough to be visible from the Beijing Hotel, but on April 27, the students spilled out the square, and filled the entirety of the city center.

The people in the street below flowed unstoppably like the waters of the Yangtze River. Their rallying cries blended with the sharp snap of the banners and flags in the spring wind. I couldn't see what was written on them, but didn't need to. A massive swath of bright red cloth twisted itself mid-air like a dancing dragon. With every flicker and wave, it spoke to me in a universal language.

Nearly every balcony in the hotel was full of people of every color. Some waved and cheered the students on, while others feverishly snapped pictures. Even Ms. Kawashima couldn't contain her excitement. Already 5'6", the heels she wore made her even taller. She towered over the railing, which didn't even reach her waistline, waving her arms as she cheered. I was afraid she'd send herself tumbling and I grabbed her arm just to keep her safe. As she whipped her head around to look at me, I saw her eyes filled with wild excitement, her voice trembled. "This is awesome!"

I understood what she meant. She once told me she hated Asian cultures because in most of Asia, people were promoted in order of seniority. "Young people are sick of it," she told me.

She had interpreted the student protests as youth rebelling against their elders. This explanation was far too simple, but I didn't want to correct her. We were of the same generation after all. I looked back and saw Mr. Murata still sitting at his desk looking confused and morose.

"Awesome!" I responded to Ms. Kawashima with a big smile.

The next day, I went straight to the Beijing Railway Station after work. This time, I made sure grandma was emotionally prepared. I told her that I would be vacationing for the next nine days and would be back on May 7. She was less than pleased, and made no effort to hide it, but at least now she would have no excuse to torture me when I came back.

Guo Yan was going to Shanghai, which about seven hundred miles southeast of Beijing. We took our time, getting off the train at places of interest, and staying the night before continuing on the next day. We stopped at the artesian springs of Jinan, climbed the towering peaks of Taishan, marveled at Confucius' former home in Qufu, and wandered the misty, river-latticed depths of Yangzhou. We did and saw it all.

Everywhere we stopped, one of Guo Yan's friends conveniently appeared to take care of the hotel registration. In those days, if a man and woman planned to sleep in the same room, they were required to show a copy of their marriage certificate, which we obviously didn't have. That's where Guo Yan's friends came in. They'd go to the front desk, wave around an introduction letter from some local authority, and get a room. They then handed the room key off to us so we could slip inside without being interrogated by the desk clerk. His friends knew I wasn't his wife, but pretended to know nothing.

I made him confess to me every night before bed. I asked him say something like, "I'm being honest with you. I never intended to get a divorce." He begrudgingly obliged, otherwise I wouldn't let him touch me. One night, he refused to say it and I refused to make love with him. We slept separately. The next morning, I woke up first and went downstairs for breakfast and the paper.

Newspapers in China never featured student protests on the front page, but instead ran lengthy articles about what Party leaders were doing to stop them. Hundreds of miles away, I tried to gauge what the students had achieved by what counter measures the government was taking.

According to the newspaper, there was a meeting between an official spokesman for the State Council and forty-five students representing sixteen of universities. There was also a meeting on the municipal level. Chen Xitong, the mayor of Beijing, met with a group of twenty-nine representatives from seventeen schools. It read like dialogue was happening. By the time I was back in Beijing, I was sure the protests would die down.

I took my time, reading the news as I ate. We were in Nanjing, a city known for its delicate cuisine. The hotel buffet provided all sorts of steamed Dim Sum, and I tried everything. Around 9 o'clock, it occurred to me that we were due to catch a train at 9:30. I rushed back to our room and found Guo Yan packed and ready to go. I angrily asked him why he hadn't joined me for breakfast. He said if I wanted to come with him, I'd better pack quickly. He was leaving in 5 minutes with or without me.

I didn't have much to pack, so I made it in time. In the taxi to the train station, we didn't speak a word to each other. As the train engine started, I asked him if he would have left alone had I not come back to the room. He said yes.

"Do you want to break up with me?" I asked.

He hesitated.

"I don't feel the happiness I wanted to feel," he said. He admitted that he'd lied to me about getting divorce, but he maintained that that lie held a sliver of truth.

"I'm weak and selfish," he said. "But I still hope that we can be forever together." I'd ruined his fantasy by forcing him to confess.

The key element to keeping the game going for him was believing we had a future. Though I'd managed to satisfy my vanity, I'd ruined his appetite.

"Let's be friends," I said, "if we still can."

Our next stop, Shanghai, also our last. We'd planned to spend two days there before returning to Beijing. It just occurred to me that I hadn't seen Guo Yan do a single thing that could remotely be construed as business. I asked him, and he replied, "Shanghai is the business. I need to meet an old friend in the newspaper business."

"The *World Economic Herald*?"

He nodded, "You're quite smart."

I shrugged. That's the benefit of being friends. Once we went back to just being friends, he instantly knew how to appreciate me again.

But honestly, there wasn't a single literate person in China who didn't know of the conflict between that newspaper and the Shanghai government.

The *World Economic Herald* was founded by the China Society of World Economics and the Shanghai Academy of Social Sciences. It was one of very few papers in China that wasn't owned and run by the government. Four days after the passing of Hu Yaobang, The *World Economic Herald* held a joint symposium with a magazine named *New Observations*. They invited writers Ge Yang, Hu Jiwei, Yan Jiaqi, Pan Weiming, Su Shaozhi, Qin Chuan, Dai Qing, Zhang Weiguo, and more. At that symposium, some spoke of the powerful momentum toward change reflected by the citizens' desire to mourn for Hu Yaobang's death. Some spoke frankly of the tragic fates of Party leaders over the past few decades, calling for formalized procedures for more peaceful and orderly transfers of power.

After the event, the *World Economic Herald* dedicated several pages of its next issue to minutes from the meeting, but Jiang Zemin, secretary of the Shanghai Municipal Party Committee, deemed the material "alarming, harmful and encouraging acts of unrest," and ordered the seizure of over three hundred thousand copies. However, roughly a dozen copies still made their way out into the world.

Jiang Zemin then announced that Qin Benli, the paper's editor-in-chief, would be stripped of his leadership role. The owners of the paper resisted Jiang's order, saying that Qin Benli was not appointed by the government, but a professional manager hired by the paper's proprietors. The Shanghai Municipal Party Committee had no right to decide the inner workings of a private company.

The next day, over eight thousand citizens took to the streets of Shanghai in the biggest demonstration since Hu Yaobang's death, demanding freedom of the press and the return of Qin Benli to his rightful position.

The *World Economic Herald* affair was significant in many ways. The paper was the voice of the intelligentsia, which meant that students weren't the only ones with grievances in the wake of Hu Yaobang's death. It was also important that it happened in Shanghai, China's second largest city. While Beijing was the nation's political center, Shanghai was its center of commerce. Last but not least, the outcome would show just how powerful private industry was, and if it could win against the government.

Guo Yan's boss in Beijing had sent him to Shanghai to gather information on the paper through his personal connections.

Guo Yan had gone to Fudan University, Shanghai's equivalent of Peking University. Most of his classmates had stayed in Shanghai after graduation, and nearly all were in the news business. On the evening of May 3rd, six of Guo Yan's former classmates took us to one of the nicest restaurants in the city.

Shanghai is a city that draws a lot of influence from the West. This fact was apparent before we'd even taken our seats. In Beijing, going out to eat meant the traditional Chinese battle of insisting someone sit at the head of the table. Everyone tried to sit in the worst seat possible to show their humility. The worst seat was generally close to the spot where the waitress put food on the table. But in Shanghai, they followed British tradition, in which the host decides everyone's seat. I personally disliked putting on a grand show of false modesty, though that evening, British tradition robbed me of the chance to sit with the only person I knew.

At first, I didn't think it a big deal that I was separated from Guo Yan. All the people present were big shots in Shanghai's news industry, and everyone was nice, but I soon found myself overwhelmed by the Shanghai dialect. I would have had a better time if they were speaking Japanese.

On my left sat a Mr. Jiang: an elegant, refined gentleman who, noticing I couldn't understand the local dialect, switched to heavily-accented Mandarin to help me feel more at home. He told me he had been to Beijing a few times, mentioned some of the places he had visited, and asked what I did for work. It was standard small talk. He tried his best to sustain some sort of conversation with me, but seemed to be more invested in the larger conversation at the table. He would often interject in their foreign tongue before returning to the forlorn Beijing woman to his side. The language barrier made me feel somewhat excluded.

I tried to figure out who at the table was from the *World Economic Herald*. I came to the conclusion that it was the guy next to Guo Yan. His demeanor was bold, and he was very chatty. He seemed the center of the attention. I wanted to confirm my guess, so I asked Mr. Jiang.

"No. He's the editor of *Liberation Daily*," Mr. Jiang said.

Liberation Daily was the official daily newspaper of the Shanghai Municipal Party Committee. I was surprised that the editor from an official newspaper dominated the table. I quietly sized up everyone a second time.

Our hotel accommodation for that night was arranged by the editor from *Liberation Daily*. He was an old classmate of Guo Yan's, which meant he was also a friend of Guo's wife's. He'd booked us two separate rooms.

After dinner, Guo Yan and two of his closer friends went up to his room to continue the festivities. It was obvious I wasn't invited, so I went to my room. Around eleven, Guo called to inform me there'd been a change in plans. He was born and raised in Nantong, about 80 miles (130 kilometers) northwest of Shanghai. He'd just gotten off the phone with his parents and learned his father wasn't in good health. It was rare he made it this far south, so he wanted to take the chance to check in on them.

He invited me come with him, but I refused. He said that his family was nice and didn't meddle in his personal life. They would treat me as an honored guest. I said I didn't have the ability to play it that way. What if I slipped up?

"If you stay here, what're you gonna do for two days on your own?" he asked.

"There's plenty to do," I answered effortlessly.

It just so happened the next day was May 4th: Youth Day. There'd be massive protests in ever major cities across China. I could go see firsthand how Shanghai students did it.

The next day, I saw him to the bus station. Through the window, he shouted, "Come down if you want! There's a bus every hour!"

I replied, "Come up if you want! There's a bus every hour!"

He shook his head.

The bus shuddered forward, taking Guo Yan away. I had no idea I wouldn't see him again for a year.

The moment Guo Yan disappeared, I headed straight for Waitan. Known as the Bund to the foreigners, Waitan is a waterfront area in central Shanghai. The mile-long stretch was part of the British Concession from 1844, and as a result, was lined with intricately designed buildings constructed by different nations. Waitan had been nicknamed "the street of a thousand countries." Today, it serves as the hub of China's financial industries and looks a bit like Michigan Street in Chicago.

It was only ten o'clock when I arrived, but tens of thousands of people had already descended on the streets. While Tiananmen offered a massive, sprawling square that could easily be choreographed and host speeches, Waitan was a narrow street. People simply had to surge forward, unable to stop. It was impossible to put on any kind of organized demonstration. Even if they did try, I wouldn't know what they were saying.

I followed the current of people but soon lost interest. Passing an intersection, I noticed a sign pointing to Yu Garden: a tourist hotspot, and the home of Shanghai's renowned Nanxiang steamed buns. My mouth watered, so I quickly slipped into the alley.

A block away from Waitan, Yu Garden's tranquil, pond-filled courtyards are surrounded by high walls. I tasted the famous buns. They were good, but nothing to write home about.

Leaving the garden, I called a taxi and told the driver to take me to Shanghai Library, and before I knew it, I was standing in front of the biggest library in the city. A former British horse racing club, the library is a magnificent, red brick behemoth with stone ornaments and towering Tashkent pillars. I wasn't there for any particular purpose, so I spent my time admiring the details of the building, and occasionally stopping to look at books that caught my eye. My mind drifted. I enjoyed being able to wander aimlessly like this.

On the evening of May 5th, I received a phone call from Guo Yan. I asked what was so important that it couldn't wait till the next day. "We're going to meet at Shanghai Station tomorrow, aren't we?"

After a silence, he stammered, "My father wants me to stay here. He doesn't want me to go back to Beijing."

"Is he OK? Has he gotten worse?"

He explained that it wasn't his father's health. His father just forbade him from going back to work. According to his father, all signs indicated that a schism had formed between Zhao Ziyang and Li Peng, and that the power struggle would continue for a while. If Guo Yan went back to his job, he would be forced to choose a side. Not wanting his son to fall as collateral damage, his father wanted him to wait it out at home.

"I went to Waitan yesterday. There were tens of thousands of people there. It's too big. There's no way the government can take them all on." I didn't really know what I was saying.

"But Shanghai Municipal hadn't budged an inch," he said. "My father was in the newspaper business his whole life. He's seen it all."

I couldn't help but groan. He was twenty-nine years old, and he still had to listen to his daddy? What had I seen in this man in the first place?

At seven that evening, I left for Beijing alone on a twelve-hour, overnight train. Around five o'clock the next day, as dawn began to break, the train's stewards flitted about like hummingbirds, cleaning the car and making beds as if we'd already arrived. I got up reluctantly and moved to a seat by the window, staring blankly at the dim outside. Suddenly I saw the word "Tianjin" on a sign beside the tracks. Were we already in Tianjin? I thought back to that day I took the train alone for the first time. It seemed I had been always riding in a train, but never reached my destination.

Then I remembered I'd completely forgotten Min's wedding the week before. A chill ran through me.

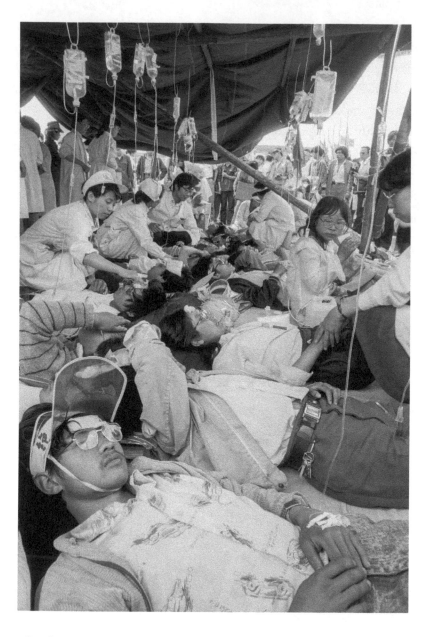

Students on hunger strike at the Tiananmen Square, May 1989.

Photo by Yanguang He

Chapter 11

The Hunger Strike Begins

In the early morning on May 7, my train slowly ground to a halt at Beijing Station. Spring in Beijing brought only a fleeting sliver of fanciful sky for about a week or so, separating summer and winter. I had been only absent nine days, but spring was already over. The trees in front of my grandmother's house were already in full bloom.

I groped my way toward the end of the dark hall while fumbling for my key. I was about to put it to the lock, when the door flew inward, revealing the silhouette of a young woman: Lu Hua.

"Wang Yan's back!" She shouted over her shoulder. My heart was touched. Only very few people knew my name could be pronounced as Wang Yan.

My heart sank when I saw my grandmother rocked gently on her bed, sunglasses on. "What's wrong?" I asked, hurrying to her side. She faced me, pressing her right hand to her chest, "My arrhythmia. It's getting worse." I could see my own helpless reflection in her dark glasses.

Lu Hua handed me the hospital's diagnosis:
Patient complained of light-headedness, chest pain, difficulty breathing.
Test results show blood pressure and heart rate normal, lungs normal.
Recommended treatment: plenty of rest.

It seemed there was no real problem with her. With me gone for so long, she'd likely spiraled into another nervous breakdown.

I put aside the doctor's diagnosis, "The doctor says get some rest...Rest up! What do you want to eat? I'll go get you whatever you want!"

She waved her hand in dismissal. "No need to worry about me. You go on about your business. Lu Hua is here to take care of me."

Lu Hua quickly interjected, "Wang Yan is back now. I need to get back home." She gathered her things, then knelt next to my grandmother's bed. "See? Wang Yan is back, just I told you. If she said today, she meant it!"

My grandmother gripped Lu Hua's hand, reluctant to let go. There was desperation in her eyes. She'd never looked at me that way. Was I not dependable? I told her exactly when I'd be back, and returned precisely when I said I would.

I walked Lu Hua to the bus station. She'd come to Beijing on business and happened to drop by. Seeing my grandmother in pain, she took her to the hospital and stuck around to look after her. "You know how it is," she said, "old people get lonely. Thank God you came back as planned."

"I'm sorry. I know she can be a lot of trouble," I replied.

I knew most of my grandmother's pain was psychological. She just didn't want to be left behind. Now that I was back, I tried to make it up to her by doing double housework. I spent the whole day washing, wiping and scrubbing. I cooked lunch and dinner. Still, she wouldn't look at me like she did Lu Hua. Maybe god had mixed us up at birth. Lu Hua had all the warmth and understanding I lacked.

Doing housework involved multiple trips to the public washroom. Every time I rounded the corner of the L-shape, I walked on tiptoe to avoid Min. At about 8pm, on my last trip of the day, a door flung open revealing Uncle Li, Min's father, smiling ear to ear.

"Hi, Uncle Li." I had nowhere to hide.

"Wang Yan! It's been ages!"

Another person who knew the alternative pronunciation of my name. I forced a smile, "How are you doing? Is Min home?"

"Haven't you heard the news? Min got married! She moved out!"

He seemed to have no idea I'd broken my promise to be Min's maid of honor. I could breathe easy for the moment.

"Congratulations!" I said enthusiastically.

"Come in, come in! Have some wedding candy!" he responded, gesturing me inside.

In China, newlyweds and their families give out candy to celebrate a marriage, sharing the "sweetness" of the event. I followed him inside. He showed me the wedding picture on his dresser, before handing me a huge tray of candy. In 1989, weddings were much simpler affairs, but no matter how simple, the bride and groom had to take a studio portrait in a rented black suit and white wedding gown. Min didn't exactly have porcelain skin, but with makeup and the right lighting, her face looked flawless. A dull ache of jealousy crept into my heart. Had I missed the wedding on purpose?

I was a devout Freudian, and every time I forgot something, I wondered if I had simply chosen not to remember. My own love life was going nowhere, and being as self-absorbed as I was, I naturally avoided any scenario that would force me to face my shortcomings.

I took two pieces of candy and asked for Min's new address. The next day, I went to the post office and sent her sixty-six RMB. In China, the sweetness one receives is to be repaid with thanks. Sending her a red envelope with a few bucks in it was the least I could do, and sixty-six is an auspicious number, meaning double luck.

Mr. Murata and Ms. Kawashima came striding in the office looking years younger. Their vacations had apparently done them some good. They spent their first day out of Beijing in Tokyo, attending meetings before going on to see their families. Mr. Murata's father had long passed away, but his mother lived in Osaka. Ms. Kawashima's parents lived in a suburb of Tokyo. Neither spent the entire vacation in Japan. Mr. Murata had flown to Shanghai for a couple days before returning, and Ms. Kawashima visited Taiwan. This was pretty much all I was able to gather via eavesdropping. There was surely more to the story, but my rudimentary Japanese would keep it a secret for now.

Before long, Ms. Kawashima dragged Mr. Murata into a full-blown interrogation. I knew from her rising end-tones that she was asking questions. He answered each with a bashful look on his face, then Ms. Kawashima would utter another question. The look on her face communicated the pleasure she derived from teasing him.

Ms. Kawashima was never once able to hide her amusement. As soon as Mr. Murata wasn't around, she turned and asked me in a stage whisper, "Do you know why Mr. Murata detoured to Shanghai? He went on a blind date!"

It occurred to me that Mr. Murata was over forty, but had never been married. I gave it some thought, and took into consideration the rather unfortunate life he'd had. Back when the country was still in the throes of the Cultural Revolution, no Chinese woman would have him. When he returned to Japan at thirty years old, he was already past his prime.

"She's young and pretty," Ms. Kawashima exclaimed. "I've seen a photo. I told him to go for it."

Two days later, she asked me out of the blue if the phrase "change of heart" had other meanings in Chinese. I replied that it was basically impossible to answer without knowing the context. She fell silent. A few minutes later, she bashfully handed me a letter, addressed "Dear Ms. Kawashima" in traditional Chinese—the kind they use in Taiwan and Hong Kong. Before I even had time to read it, she was pointing to the words in question. I obediently narrowed my attention to the words in question.

"In Chinese, 'change of heart' has two meanings," I explained. "One is that the writer's heart is with someone else. The other is that the writer is able to place their heart in everything they see, hear or touch. If he sees a beautiful flower, he imagines himself smiling at you. If he hears the song of a bird, he hears himself singing to you. It sounds complicated, but simply take it that he can't do anything without thinking of you."

Ms. Kawashima beamed.

It occurred to me that the person Ms. Kawashima had visited in Taiwan might be the writer of that letter. Both Ms. Kawashima and Mr. Murata had taken their love affairs to new heights over the Golden Week. No wonder they appeared rejuvenated. I was the only one who'd come back to work with a broken heart.

When I was on vacation, I gathered that the student protests would come to an end when I got back to Beijing. It turned out I was right. From May 8th to May 12th, small uprisings still popped up, but nothing large enough for average people to even notice.

On May 9th, Beijing reporters handed a petition to the Chinese National Reporters Association. It demanded Qin Benli's reinstatement, and major media reform. The petition had been signed by thousands of reporters and editors. This was momentous, but only within media professional circles.

On May 10th, students staged a protest on bicycles. Past efforts had all been on foot, and quite frankly, were exhausting. It was time to try something new. Riding bikes was a whole lot easier than walking, but proved to be less influential. A protest was supposed to be a show of suffering. How could people sympathize with kids riding bicycles like they were on vacation? Bells rang out as girls' hair blew carelessly in the wind. It looked like they were enjoying a day off.

Everything indicated that the chaos had ended. Our office was steeped in optimism. I'd heard for some time that Canon was considering building a large manufacturing plant in Dalian. Mr. Murata wrote a lengthy report, claiming that China was back on track and vehemently pushed for the advancement of the Dalian project. Ms. Kawashima double-checked the report while he was out, and nodded as she read it. Not a word about his grammar this time. It seemed both of them were eager to make the plan a reality.

On May 9th, Mr. Inoue, an executive from headquarters in Japan arrived at the office. He was the highest official overseeing the Dalian project, and his presence indicated that the project was a go. Mr. Inoue was on his way to Dalian, and had stopped by our office to meet Mr. Murata before they headed to the airport. Mr. Inoue was a tall, striking man, who bore a resemblance to the Japanese singer Hideki Saijo, but with whiter hair. Ms. Kawashima adored Saijo, and didn't make any attempt to hide her admiration for Mr. Inoue. Every time he spoke, she giggled like a little girl. I wondered if *she* was having a change of heart.

Two days later, Mr. Murata and Mr. Inoue returned, with the addition of Ms. Chen, Mr. Inoue's interpreter. He was pleased with her work and brought her to Beijing to serve as his tour guide. The two were planning a trip to the Great Wall.

Ms. Kawashima was not a fan of Ms. Chen. The second they were out the door, Ms. Kawashima directed her anger at me, "What's your problem, Ms. Wang? Why can't you get better at Japanese? You've been at Canon a year. It should be you taking Mr. Inoue around town. Instead, the company has to bring an interpreter all the way from Dalian? To take him around *your* city?"

"Her expenses were paid by Mr. Inoue, not the company," Mr. Murata chimed in.

Ms. Kawashima had nothing else to say, but we knew she didn't really care about the budget.

According to Zhao, Ms. Kawashima had hoped to lead the Dalian office, but Mr. Murata aspired to grow the Beijing office to manage all of northern China, including Dalian. It looked like Mr. Murata had gotten the upper hand, which was natural. A Japanese company would rarely, if never, let a woman take a position of actual power. It was the 1980s.

Still, her bullet struck me. I hadn't made any progress in learning Japanese. Time had flown. I hardly noticed that I'd been there a year already. Suddenly, I was overcome with urgency. I needed to enroll in Japanese classes.

I flipped through the classifieds in the *Beijing Evening News,* and found that # 28 Middle School, just on the west side of Tiananmen, offered night classes. I stopped by to sign up on my way home from work. Classes ran for three months at a time, with the next session beginning in June. I paid my tuition and left, textbook in hand.

May 13th was a Saturday. It was Ms. Kawashima's turn to do time, but as soon as lunch was over, she had Zhao take her straight to the International Club, after which he went to FESCO for his weekly political meeting. Once again, the office was all mine. I poured myself a cup of tea, fired up the computer, and wrote until around two o'clock, when the silence was broken by the telephone. It was Zhi Hua.

"Wha...wow," I exclaimed. "I didn't think you knew I even existed anymore. To what do I owe the pleasure?"

She ignored my sarcasm and after a few pleasantries, she asked, "I have a friend who needs to make some photocopies. Can you help her?"

"Yeah, of course. She'll need to come to my office. Is that too far?" I asked.

"No problem, she's headed that way anyway."

She gave the phone to her friend, who introduced herself as Xiao Ling, and I told her how to get to my office.

What on earth could be so important that Xiao Ling needed to come all the way here to copy it? It had to be something she couldn't do at school. Campus had enough copiers, but I'd heard that authorities had asked the copy shops not to do business with protestors. It had been declared illegal to produce fliers, posters, or any other sort of document that advocated for the students' cause.

Around four o'clock, I heard a knock at the door. I opened it to find a waif of a girl in jeans and a checkered shirt, with a backpack tight around both shoulders. She introduced herself, so I invited her in and offered her a glass of water, which she finished in a single gulp. She pulled a piece of paper from her bag and got right to the point, "Can you help me make a thousand copies of this?"

A thousand? I was expecting a big number, but not a thousand. I took a closer look at the title at the top: "The Hunger Strike Manifesto."

"You guys are going on a hunger strike?" My voice trembled.

"Yep," she nodded, as if a hundred people had already asked her the same question. "We've been considering it for a while now. In the end, we think it's the only way to make people listen. Otherwise what's this all been for? People will forget the fight."

"You're right," I replied.

"Can you do a thousand?"

"Well, I don't know if we even have that much paper."

I got up and went into the office. She followed. In the cupboard, I found five reams of paper. I could make a thousand copies, but two-fifths of our entire stock would be gone in an afternoon. Someone would notice.

"The students are already at Tiananmen. Everyone has written a last will and testament." She spoke with a soft voice. A grim shame washed over me. There were people ready to give their lives for what they believed in, and I was worried about how many packs of paper should be in a cupboard.

"Great. We have enough paper," I said.

At about eight hundred copies, the copier jammed. I checked all the usual spots, but couldn't see where the trouble was. Xiao Ling was getting impatient. "Eight hundred is fine. I've gotta go."

I found her two Canon gift bags, and put half in each. She left looking content, just like any other Canon customer.

I dug out the manual and took the copier apart. I finally discovered the source of the problem. A piece of paper had gotten crumpled into a Chinese paper fan, tucked tightly under a roller. I spent the rest of the afternoon getting it all out with a precision screwdriver, bit by bit.

That Monday, Mr. Murata came into work with a black cloud looming over him. I brought him his tea, but he pushed it aside with impatience. He robotically picked up the phone, and once again, began his pleas for forgiveness.

The higher-ups were none too pleased that his assessment of China's current state of affairs had proven erroneous. According to Mr. Murata, an escalation of the student protests should not have been happening, and this assumption had motivated Mr. Inoue to travel to China. The tyrants in Tokyo were furious, and poor Mr. Murata looked miserable.

I felt sorry for him. How could he have possibly predicted the students would go this far? No one in China could have foreseen it. It certainly caught the Communist Party off-guard, too.

And, what did a hunger strike have to do with a Canon factory in Dalian?

Even Ms. Kawashima wore a scowl. Why should she care? Even if the Dalian project did fall through, and I didn't believe it would, Ms. Kawashima would be the least impacted of all of us.

At 10 am, we heard the wail of an ambulance for the first time that day. It was the third day of the hunger strike, and students had been passing out left and right. The wails began to overlap and thicken. The scream of sirens became so deafening that the fortress-like walls of the Beijing Hotel felt as thin as rice paper. I was too distracted to work and went out on the balcony. Each time an ambulance went flying from the Square, I nervously traced its movement along Chang'an Avenue.

Ms. Kawashima finally noticed what I was doing and said coldly, "Ms. Wang, please close the doors to the balcony. It's too noisy."

I went back inside and closed the doors behind me. The sound of sirens abated, but I'd learned to tell from the sound which hospital they were headed to. Beijing Hospital saw a steady increase in volume, as it was a straight shot down the avenue. A pause followed by a few seconds of cacophony meant Peking Union Medical College Hospital.

There was a moment when the office was bathed in a strange silence. No ambulances crying out, no telephones clanging. Total quiet.

Mr. Murata broke the tension, pointing at me with his pen. "Ms. Wang, why did the students go on a hunger strike?" he asked bluntly.

"I can't speak on their behalf," I said slowly. "But as far as I gather from various documents, they want a sit-down with the government, they want the editorial denouncing the protests be retracted, and they want the government to recognize them as a patriotic movement."

"Don't you think this is all a little idiotic?" he asked. It sounded a verdict as much as a question.

"What? Why?"

"Whether they are patriotic or not. If they're so sure of it, why do they care if the government agrees?"

"Well, China is different from Western countries. In the west, strikes and protests are legal methods of negotiation with the government. Afterward, both sides move on. In China, the government might agree to some demands in order to appease the masses. After life returns to normal, authorities might attack those who led the protests. That's why the student body had asked the government to retract the editorial, which had denounced the protests as a counterrevolutionary conspiracy. If they couldn't get the government to see the protests as patriotic, there would be hell to pay when the leaders got back to school."

"So they have to occupy the whole square and make a scene? What good is an agreement if it's forced? Useless spoiled brats!" With each word, he became further enraged. He hurled his pen across his desk in disgust. It slid off the edge and hit the carpet below.

I didn't say another word. It was almost lunch. When the clock finally struck twelve, I shot straight out the door. Outside, I was caught amidst a confluence of emotions. Chinese people have long been known for a supposedly lack of facial expression, but on that May afternoon, every pair of eyes I saw were silently screaming to be heard. They radiated anger, worry, even helplessness. The only emotion they didn't communicate was indifference.

Like most of my countrymen, breaking the ice is not my strong suit, but on that day, I felt I could talk to anyone. The opening sentence of every conversation was prewritten:

They're on a hunger strike...Can you believe it?

In hindsight, I think a hunger strike struck a chord with people because memories of mass starvation during the Cultural Revolution were still fresh in our minds. Eating was deemed the most core of all human rights. Nowadays, you start a hunger strike and people would only begin feeling for you on day five or so. They would count the first four days as exercise to lose extra fat.

On my way to Tiananmen Square, an unbroken streak of ambulances rushed by. The sound cut right through my heart. What was there to think about? Right or wrong, there were a bunch of kids suffering and dying. Maybe Mr. Murata was right, but it didn't matter anymore. Logic had been replaced with the most visceral pity and sorrow. With every red cross I saw speeding out of the square, I knew another young person lay on the brink of leaving this world, just because they believed in something.

The Tiananmen Square was a roiling sea of people. I tried my hardest to push through to get closer to the students on hunger strike, only to find that they were separated from the crowd by a roped enclosure, and multiple rows of guards. The guards kept the order, and ensured the ambulances parked nearby could get in and out quickly.

In the end, I gave up on taking pictures. They were suffering, and that was all I needed to know. Thousands would bear witness to this day. The sun slowly drained them of their energy. The wind blew harshly across their weakened, failing bodies. They all bore witness to this day. I went back to the Beijing Hotel empty-handed, but feeling that I'd made the ethical choice.

On my way back, I bought two reams of copy paper at a stationary store. I returned to find the office as cold and brooding as it was when I left. When no one was watching, I opened up the cabinet and replaced the paper I'd used. It was then that I noticed that our office used a Japanese brand of copy paper, while I'd bought a Chinese one.

Buying office supplies was Zhao's job. I asked him where I could buy that brand of copy paper.

"What do you need to know that for?" he asked.

"No reason," I replied. "Just wondering."

"Who asks a question like that for 'no reason?'"

I realized my question had raised red flags. A sudden interest in his daily duties could only mean I was looking to step on his toes. I had to come clean. "The day before yesterday, a friend's friend from school...Hunger strike..."

"Psh. That's all? Why didn't you just say so?" he said with relief. "I'm headed that direction to see a friend tonight. I'll pick some up."

The next day, he appeared with my lifeline tucked under his arm. I tried to pay him, but he shrugged me off, just like most Beijing citizens would in those days. They were honored to contribute to the students' cause.

For the next five days, the office was an oppressive tomb. Mr. Murata did his best to keep a brave face, but I could see his desperation.

One morning, Ms. Kawashima arrived without makeup on. Japanese women never left the house without makeup. Ms. Kawashima once joked she'd put on makeup just to take out the garbage. "The key is to never expose your wrinkles to anyone," she told me playfully.

Today, she'd broken her own rule. I noticed that while she was only four years my senior, her skin easily looked ten years older than mine. She must have felt her career in Beijing was over and didn't mind to exposing her flaws. I reminded her she had an appointment at the China National Machinery Import and Export Corporation that morning. She sat in a daze before rushing into the restroom to get herself together. She emerged just as beautiful and energetic as ever, but it was too late. I'd already seen behind the mask. Of course, she didn't give a damn what I thought about her.

I went back to taking pictures in the Square. More honestly, I went to the Square to pass time under the pretense of taking pictures. There was so much to see. People from virtually every work unit in Beijing came to voice their support. I frequently ran into people I knew. After graduation, my classmates and I had gone our separate ways. Not in our wildest dreams did we imagine our first reunion would take place under these circumstances.

One day, I ran into a group of protesters from the Chinese Academy of Social Sciences. Two of my former classmates had worked there since graduation. One was at the Institute of Foreign Literature. She was a bespectacled bookworm and in the past, didn't care at all for politics. The other worked for the Institute of Linguistics, and was a tall, attractive young woman with a knack for making men obsessive over her. At that moment, these two drastically different friends of mine marched side by side, shoulder to shoulder, with the same grave looking on their faces.

One afternoon, I came across group after group of high school students. I was surprised that the fervor had spread to the high school level. I recognized a couple young faces from my grandmother's apartment building marching under the flag of Yuetan High School. These were the same kids who'd idled in the courtyard, sucking on free popsicles last year. The free popsicles were provided by the printing factory because of last summer's record heatwave. I couldn't believe they were old enough to march in protest, let alone place demands on the leaders of the nation. Foreheads that once dripped with sweat from hide-and-seek now bore bright red bands reading: Warriors of Democracy.

Each time I returned to my office, I would hand over the fruits of my labor to Mr. Murata, who would fax his selections, six per page, back to Japan. Usually, a page of fax took under a minute to send. Lately, it took up to half an hour as scores of foreign journalists clogged the lines. I wondered if my pictures were really worth anything. The higher-ups in Japan had access to high quality, professional newspapers if they needed. But Mr. Murata kept faxing them, which indicated that I might have contributed something that I myself wasn't aware of.

Mr. Murata cared only about the slogans and banners. He never concerned himself with the portraits I shot. I met a classmate of mine at the Square who worked for the *Chinese Journal of Photography*. He invited me to submit photos for publication, and I gladly obliged. I delivered a selection of my best photographs. One appeared in print just a few days later.

The picture showed a salesman from Pecan Inc. named Zhang with his younger brother. Zhang's brother was a junior at Renmin University and joined the hunger strike. Zhang had come to the Square hoping to convince his brother to return to school. Already several days into the strike, baking in the intense heat of the May sun, Zhang's brother was half-conscious, and propped up against his elder brother's shoulder. I raised my lens, realizing they were perfectly composed in a classical triangle. It was only after publication that I realized I needed Zhang's permission. I called Zhang, and he said it was fine.

The hunger strike entered day six on May 18. Over 3500 students had been hospitalized, with 32 in critical condition. People from all walks of life, fearing for the student's safety, took to the streets, voicing their support. They decried the government's heartlessness in letting thousands of youth teeter on the brink of death.

The People's Republic of China is formally a multi-party state, though every party is all under the leadership of the Communist Party of China. Members of these parties, including celebrities and those from influential public interest groups, personally delivered letters to the high leadership, demanding that the nation's leaders put a stop to the madness.

Among the million protesters present that day, there were three groups more notable than others: Farmers from remote areas, students and teachers from the Central Party's training school, and even a Chinese Air Force sergeant in full uniform who claimed that many of his fellow soldiers were in the crowd as well.

At eleven that morning, Li Peng finally emerged from the doors of the Great Hall and announced his willingness to speak to the students in person. When news spread, the whole square roared in excitement. This was a milestone in the protests in 1989. It meant that the people's show of force could no longer be ignored.

I was at the Square when Li Peng was meeting the student representatives, and like everyone else, I was overwhelmed by joy.

The students didn't like Li Peng, not only because he was a conservative, but also because he wasn't very smart. There was a running joke at the time in China: A man tells a foreign journalist that Li Peng has an IQ of less than a hundred, and is subsequently jailed for leaking national secrets. In China, rarely would any leader speak publicly without reading from a script, so it was hard to tell who was smart and who wasn't. Li Peng earned his reputation because of his special knack for pausing precisely when he wasn't supposed to when reading scripts, creating confusion. How could a person who couldn't even read a script pull off an open, unscripted discussion? That was the suspense of the day. That evening, I went home early just to watch the meeting on TV. After dinner, I tuned in eagerly, ready for a good laugh.

Li Peng sounded like a concerned elder at first: "You're all still so young. Not even as old as my youngest child." His kindness fell on deaf ears. The kids had succeeded. They'd screamed, "Li Peng, now!" at Xinhua Gate and knelt on the steps of the People's Hall. By mounting a hunger strike, they'd finally dragged Li Peng down from his high throne. They had the attention of an entire nation, and they dispatched his platitudes without a blink. They quickly issued two demands. First, they demanded that the government recognize the protests as patriotic action, not a counterrevolutionary conspiracy. Second, they demanded that the government formally dialogue with the students and broadcast the meeting live to the public.

When pressed to reply on the spot, Li Peng spoke at a measured pace, "The issues raised by our dear students are important indeed... I feel their frustration and understand their concerns. As a member of our Party, and Premier of this great nation, I shall not hide my views, but I must not reveal them to you today."

I couldn't help but laugh. Not only was Li Peng's IQ cause for concern, but he completely lacked charisma.

The students sat expressionless. Perhaps they were too sick to laugh. I looked for familiar faces and recognized Wang Dan, Wu'erkaixi and Wang Chaohua. Wang Dan was from Peking University and had been a student leader even before Tiananmen. Wu'erkaixi was from Central University for Nationalities. An Uygur from Xinjiang Province, he rose to fame when the students tried to attack Xinhua Gate. Wang Chaohua was a female graduate student from the Chinese Academy of Social Sciences. She was the oldest of the student leaders, and appeared calmer and more thoughtful than the others. All of them had been on hunger strike for days. They looked emaciated and exhausted. Wang Chaohua spoke in a low and raspy voice. Wang Dan wore a thick coat. He probably had a fever. A student whose name I've forgotten came to the meeting dragging an IV pole with a tube leading into his arm.

Li Peng continued, "In these last few days, the city of Beijing has entered a state of virtual anarchy. I sincerely hope our dear students will consider what the true result of your actions could be."

"If society falls into chaos, it's the government's fault, not ours," Wang Dan retorted.

"The government is not going to turn a blind eye to this chaos," Li Peng replied.

An alarm rang in my head. I wondered what Li Peng was implying.

Wu'erkaixi shot back, "This isn't a matter of convincing the few of us. If one student on strike refuses to leave the square, thousands will stand by his side."

My laughter tapered off. Something was very wrong with that statement.

When the hunger strike began, we often compared the student movement to Solidarity, the Polish labor union founded a few years earlier. Solidarity had the ability to carry out a successful strike, and after reaching an agreement with the government, had equal ability to send all workers back to work. It was this kind of leadership that gave them the qualifications to negotiate with the ruling party. What about the leaders of our movement? Could they truly take charge of the situation?

Wu'erkaixi's words told a dangerous story. If the students couldn't be accurately represented by their leaders, and the end of the strike depended on the satisfaction of every student, what end could ever be in sight? What was the point of demanding a sit-down with government officials and broadcasting it to every home in the country? Maybe Li Peng was smarter than he seemed.

I sat in front of the TV in gloom.

Chapter 12

Under Martial Law

As students met with Li Peng, Cui Jian performed in the square. I was crushed to learn I'd missed it.

"What did he sing?" I asked a student.

"Every song you know, he sang."

"Even 'Starting All Over?!'"

He thought for a moment. "Why not?"

It was my favorite song of his by far, but seemed an odd choice for the occasion:

I just want to leave this place
I just want to exist in space
At the edge of this life I hover
I just want to start all over

"Don't you think it's a bit dark?" I asked. I'd first thought of the word "ominous," but pulled back a bit.

"Dark?" He was confused. "You don't even know... The whole place went crazy."

I could imagine. As soon as that guitar boomed, and those drums pounded, who would have bothered to listen to the lyrics?

"He was a funny guy, too," he continued, making an air guitar gesture. He elaborated, saying Cui Jian declared that his guitar loved the students as much as he did: "It may be at my front, but my guitar's got your back."

Once the hunger strike began, the office TV was on from the moment we got in, to the minute we left. The sound was kept muted. On the morning of May 19, I glanced over to see Zhao Ziyang in the Square preparing to make an address. I called the others. We huddled around. I grabbed the remote and turned the volume up.

The event had been recorded earlier. The speech took place under a hazy curtain of dawn. In his seven-minute address, he implored the students to think about their health and end the strike. Their young bodies, he advised, were not as strong as they might think. He reminded them that fasting caused irreparable damage, and that the students might later regret it. The students received his concern no more favorably than Li Peng's, even though Zhao was a moderate reformist.

The hunger strike put the legitimacy of the Party to the test. The Communist Party of China had been avoiding the fundamental question of whether one-party rule was legitimate. Without any checks and balances, could they deliver the utopian existence they had promised the nation? They kept their mouths shut tight whenever they were questioned on the matter.

Their strategy was to draw a parallel between parenting and governing. They appeared in the public under specific circumstances. After a flood, earthquake, or other natural disaster, Party leaders would comfort families who had lost everything, and reassure them that they were in good hands. "Do you have enough food? Enough tents? Enough clean water?" They would ask. Grief-stricken families who had never received such attention before suddenly became the subject of blatantly staged concern. They stared at the camera lens bewildered, and murmured their thanks to the Party with trembling hands and spontaneous tears. All of it was faithfully captured by the cameraman and broadcast to the whole nation. Party leaders portrayed themselves as caring patriarchs, and the students had called their bluff. Letting them starve to death in front of the whole nation would forfeit the parental status the Party had carefully cultivated for decades. They couldn't give in to their demands, which would destabilize the very foundation of the autocracy.

Neither option would do, and therefore Zhao Ziyang's speech was doomed to be devoid of any actual content. On the surface, his speech wasn't much different from Li Peng's, but if you listened carefully, you could hear different undertone. Li Peng's was murderous. Zhao Ziyang's was like a swan song.

"The channels of communication are still open," Zhao Ziyang declared. "But there is a process for such matters. Things can't simply happen with a snap of the fingers. We have rules to follow." He paused. "The entire Party is worried about you. The entire nation is on edge. This situation cannot continue. You have your whole lives ahead of you. You should live happy and healthy."

That was his way of signaling that moderate reformists had lost their power struggle with Party conservatives. His only hope to stay in power and facilitate progress would be for the students to vacate the square of their own accord.

But his plea fell on deaf ears. The students thought they had brought the elders all to their knees.

For the three of us watching in the office, Zhao couldn't have been any clearer. As we prepared to leave for the day, Mr. Murata said that if martial law was imposed, I didn't need to come to work. It was a Saturday anyway.

"What if it goes till Monday?" I asked.

He rested his head on the back of his chair, leaned back, and looked straight up at the ceiling. With what seemed to be the last of his energy, he said solemnly, "We'll talk about it then..."

But how? The closest payphone to my grandmother's apartment was blocks away at Beijing Children's Hospital. If the Party really did impose martial law, would soldiers simply let me saunter down the street to use the phone?

Early the next morning, I turned on the radio.

The city would go under martial law at 10 am.

I threw on my clothes and shot for the door. My grandmother called out, "Can't you just not go to work?"

"It doesn't start till ten. I just have to be quick."

"But how will you get back? Everything will be shut down."

"I'll be home late, but don't worry." Martial law was a good excuse to come home whenever I pleased.

The bus was more crowded than usual. I wasn't the only one hoping to get to work before ten. Passengers coming from the west side of town claimed that military trucks were already rolling in from Shijingshan and Fengtai districts, but had been surrounded by angry mobs of civilians and were stuck where they stood. All roads from the west and southwest into downtown were completely blocked.

At work, I heard from Mr. Murata that the roads from the east had been blocked by angry mobs as well. According to Zhao, every road into the city center was full of people, leaving military trucks stranded. The outer borders of city had been surrounded by soldiers, but civilians had blocked soldiers from pushing any further than the Third Ring.

We went over to the balcony to check up on things. Ten o'clock struck and nothing happened. No gunshots rang out. No military trucks lumbered down Chang'an Avenue. At noon, helicopters began to circle the Square, and the people below raised their voices in defiance. Even up on the eleventh floor, we could hear them shouting.

Up until it was time for us to go home, the military was still nowhere to be seen. Bus service had stopped, but taxis darted this way and that. It seemed that aside from public transit, the city was still functional.

Mr. Murata decided that the company would give me an extra 20 RMB to take a cab each day for as long as martial law went on. I happily took the money, but opted to walk.

The students still blanketed the Square, and seemed more vocal, more emboldened, and more scornful of a government that couldn't even follow through on its own threats. Instead of forcing them to flee, the Party had only made their numbers greater. The crowd belted out "L'Internationale" as I passed by.

Our generation were brought up singing "L'Internationale." It was ingrained in our hearts and minds. The song was born from the back-alley uprising of the Paris Commune against the French Republic; a situation not unlike the present. It seemed chosen purely out of convenience, but I had concerns. Wasn't this song closely related to communism? Karl Marx regarded the Paris Commune as an example of a "dictatorship of the proletariat."

Ever since the protests started, Mr. Murata had doubted if the students really wanted a fully functional market economy. He suspected that they wanted to erase it entirely. I had dismissed his suspicions with disdain.

On May 20th, 1989, I walked home from work again to pocket another 20 RMB. As I passed the square, "L'Internationale" rang out, again.

Rise up cursed of this world!
Rise up prisoners of the hunger!
Volcanos shake and reason thunders,
Their golden castles break asunder.
From this day time starts again,
We stand to the bitter end.
The world will change, the mighty fall.
We are nothing, and so we're all.
This is our final stand,
We fight together, hand in hand,
The Internationale will unite the human race.
This is our final stand,
We fight together, hand in hand,

The Internationale will unite the human race.

I repeated the lyrics in my mind line by line. *The Internationale will unite the human race.* Was this what they were sacrificing their lives for? Dread washed over me. What if the students succeeded? Would they take everything I owned and would own in the future?

I told myself it was just a song. It was more likely they weren't even thinking about the market economy, private property, or anything like that. Still, I felt like I parted ways with them ideologically. I began to think like Mr. Murata, even though I was basically a glorified tea girl masquerading as a secretary.

May 21st was a Sunday. My grandmother was dead set against me going to work, and handed me a shopping list instead. Recent events had brought her right back to when the entire city was besieged by the communist army in the winter of 1948. To me it was yet another overreaction, but I still decided to obey her orders. I trudged back and forth from the shops, heaving sacks of rice, flour, salt, sugar, and ten or so jars of fermented bean curd. Every time I made a trip, I ran into someone I knew. It wasn't anyone's proudest moment. Men claimed their wives harped them half to death to stock up. Women claimed their husbands had done the same. Me? I was forced by my grandma! And I was telling the truth!

My final trip to the store was imbued with a sense of hard-earned victory. I had singlehandedly prepared us for the apocalypse, but instead of the praise I deserved, my grandmother handed me two buckets, and told me to fill them with water. When I got to the washroom, there was a line. In it was a high school student I had seen in the Square a few days before. One of the vigilant "Warriors of Democracy." Waiting in line, he seemed like any other teenager, unable to keep still. Even a Warrior of Democracy was no match for the dictator at home.

Monday finally came, and with it, my chance to escape the doomsday tower and get back to work. I left at 7:30 sharp, much earlier than usual. With bus service still at a halt, and almost no families able to afford a car, the streets became the domain of cyclists.

Roads in Beijing were (and still are) separated into one section for cars, and one for bicycles. The line is marked by low steel fences set in concrete pylons. In theory they're movable, but I'd never seen them moved even once. They were simply too heavy. But that day, at the main intersection of Fuxingmen, a group of people had proven just how movable they were. Against the collective strength, steel and concrete looked as light and flexible as paper and plastic. They shoved them into the middle of the street to form a blockade.

The brute strength of a determined group of people had never scared me like that. I wondered how far they were willing to go to.

As I approached the Great Hall of the People, I saw a tall, thin, young man on a motorcycle standing with one foot on the curb, looking for something.

When his gaze caught mine, he shouted, "Hey! Wang Yuan!"

"Are you Weidong, or Weiguo?" I asked in amusement.

He let out a hearty laugh, "You tell me!"

"I'd say Weiguo. Weidong's got a wife telling him what to do now. My guess is he's at the shops."

He laughed even louder, "Right on the money!"

"What are you doing here?" I asked.

"Waiting for a friend," he said, patting the seat behind him. "We got a lot done yesterday."

"Ah I get it... the 'Flying Tigers,' eh?"

"Something like that," he replied sheepishly.

Starting the Sunday before, many motorcyclists had acted as messengers, delivering the latest on military movements from the outskirts to the city center. Their work helped coordinate plans to push the army back out into the suburbs. They gave themselves the name "Flying Tigers." The moniker was proudly displayed on flags held high by the secondary on the back of the bike, or on white banners tied across the bike itself.

The owners of motorcycles were generally shopkeepers or small-scale entrepreneurs. They were well-off, but still looked down upon by the general public. The tumult of 1989 gave this group a new sense of worth. In time of war, speed is vital, and motorcycles were the fastest means of sharing information. Riding in formation, they tore up the street with a strength and authority they had long sought and definitely deserved.

Weiguo was a "Flying Tiger!" How exciting!

But I wondered how he would feel if he knew the students wanted to do away with private property. "Thanks for your support of the students," I blurted out. "All this running around for them isn't hurting your business, is it?"

His previously jovial expression quickly changed. As usual, I hadn't chosen my words carefully. "Them," "you," I was perpetuating a boundary he had endured for years.

"What business is there right now, anyway?" he shot back. "The city is under martial law. What a disgrace! From the end of the Qing Dynasty up to the Kuomintang, Beijing has never been under martial law! Hell, even the Japanese occupation couldn't do it."

Another revelation for me. I had wondered why these locals who had never cared what the students protested about were suddenly so incensed. Weiguo's monologue helped me to connect the dots. It was a matter of self-respect for Beijing residents, who considered themselves above those from other provinces. Martial law meant the city wasn't theirs anymore. Their birthright could be taken by soldiers from Hebei, Shanxi, Henan, Shandong, Liaoning, Jiangsu, you name it.

The more he spoke, the angrier he became. Before I knew it, he'd attracted a crowd of about twenty. This was a common occurrence in those days. All it took was for one person to start speaking a bit louder than the others, and all of a sudden they were surrounded by an audience hungry for the latest developments. Seeing the gathering crowd, Weiguo became more animated and turned our private conversation into a speech for all to hear:

"True Beijing natives, there is nothing we can't do! We are heroes, not cowards! These outsiders want to occupy our city? We'll show them where to go! This is our city! Those of you who have the guts, stand up! Fight for Tiananmen! Fight for Beijing!"

While his audience was clapping, a bus appeared with a speaker mounted on top, blasting, "Rise up! Fight for Tiananmen! Fight for Beijing! Martial law is a premeditated plot and a counterrevolutionary coup!"

Coup? Isn't that the same word the government used to rebuke the protesters? I never would have called martial law a coup. The students, whose bold words had stolen away Weiguo's fans, began throwing leaflets through the window. People turned to chase the bus and fight for leaflets in the air. It was just the two of us again.

"Where're you going?" Weiguo asked me. "I'll give you a ride."

I pointed to the Beijing Hotel and replied, "I'm going to work. I'm almost there anyway. Besides, don't you Flying Tigers ride together?"

He explained that the Flying Tigers weren't tightly organized. Most of them didn't know each other. He had set a time to meet two others in front of the Great Hall, but they hadn't shown up yet.

"Motorcycles are faster than anything out there," he proudly exclaimed. "You wanna see for yourself?"

I climbed on the back, and before I'd figured out what to hold on to, we took off. I was taken by surprise and almost lost my balance. I frantically gripped a piece of metal under the seat, but still felt insecure. "Hold on to my waist!" he shouted. I tentatively circled his waist with both arms. It felt far too intimate, but I dared not let go. This was what being on a motorcycle was like? I had seen girls on the back of bikes lounging with ease, proudly waving Flying Tigers flags. Why was I terrified out of my wits? We flew past the Square. I closed my eyes, teeth clenched.

Just as I'd grown accustomed to the speed, we came to a sudden halt, and I went slamming into his back. I opened my eyes in horror as he sped up again and swerved back toward the Square.

He turned his head halfway and shouted, "Let's say hello to the students!"

He drove us straight toward a couple of parked buses, shouting, "Good morning, brothers and sisters!"

A few heads raised on each roof. It appeared that students had slept on the roofs of the buses instead of inside them. Some were startled and confused, but others quickly responded in kind. While circling the buses, Weiguo popped a wheelie, eliciting a wave of applause. Delighted, we returned to Chang'an Avenue. Hearing the wind whizzing by, I was scared to open my eyes before we suddenly halted again.

"Here we are." I heard Weiguo say.

I cautiously opened my eyes to find us at the doors to the hotel, right in front of the two large security guards who were perpetually on duty. Their job was mostly to open doors for guests arriving in cars. They rarely, if ever, had to help someone off a motorcycle. They looked on with intense curiosity as I dismounted and thanked Weiguo before heading inside.

"Was it fun?" he asked, smiling.

"You bet!" I replied, pretending to be at ease.

"Want to ride again?"

"Maybe."

"Call me when you have time."

"Sure."

He mounted his bike and sped off.

As I entered the lobby, I noticed a guy with piercing eyes and a suspicious conservative flat-top. He shot straight for the door to take down Weiguo's plate number. Another stood in the center of the lobby, staring coldly at me. I strode on, pretending to notice nothing. As the elevator closed, I pressed every button on the control panel. I'd learned from spy novels.

The next day, I got a call from Min. I thought I might never hear from her again. I was thrilled to hear her voice. She sounded angry.

"What did you do to Weiguo?"

"What are you talking about? I didn't do anything."

"He talked about you all night last night."

"I ran into him by the Square yesterday while I was walking to work and we said a few words to each other. That's all."

"Ran into him? How convenient! Stay away from Weiguo. He's got a girlfriend now."

"What are you implying? I run into people at the Square all the time. I'd run into just about everyone I've known in my life, except you. You've never even been to the Square, have you? Hiding away in the sweet cottage of your marriage?"

"Oh, I've been there," she snorted. "I just didn't run into you. By the way, I got the money you sent. I donated it to the students."

"Nice. I thank you on their behalf."

It was clear that Min and I would never be friends again. She couldn't forgive me. But I didn't feel any great sense of regret, either. She was married and I was still single. It was definitely a clear enough line to separate us.

Tens of thousands took to the streets. They scattered to the city's every corner, blocking military vehicles, and keeping them from breaching the city center. The city was at war, but under that tragic dome, there were still small incidents that kept you from fully abandoning worldly calculation.

One crisp morning, a student approached me asking for donations. I happily gave all I had on me. Feeling I had done my part, I continued on, and found two more doing the same, but I had nothing left to give as they held out the makeshift boxes with desperate hope in their eyes. I could only shake my head in embarrassment as I walked by.

After running into the same situation two days in a row, I made a plan. I would spare the 20 RMB every day for taxis I wasn't taking, with 10 on my way to work, and 10 on my way home. A cap of 1 to 2 RMB per occurrence, for an average of 10 to 20 groups I encountered every day.

This was just one example of the students' lack of coordination. Another was the increasingly sorry state of the Square. It looked more like a refugee camp than a gathering of the nation's intellectual elite. It was a garbage dump on good days, and a stinky garbage dump on rainy ones.

Nevertheless, there was an unavoidable question: Who was leading the charge in the Square? Starting in late April, I would get bombarded with flier after flier every time I walked past, each with a name of different organization emblazoned across it, claiming to be calling the shots.

There was the "Higher Education Federation for Autonomous Rule," who orchestrated some of the largest marches since the death of Hu Yaobang. There was the "Ministry of Hunger Strikes," who took over after the ambulance-ridden events began. There was "Tiananmen Defense League," which basically consisted of the same people of the "Ministry of Hunger Strikes," out with new tactics to respond to martial law. There was the "Federation for Worker's Autonomy," the name of which was a sure sign that the protests reached beyond the students. There was the "Capital Joint Conference of the People," which was founded by the city's more visible intellectuals, aiming to coordinate every group in the city.

Years later, I read Zhao Dingxin's *The Power of Tiananmen: State-Society Relations and the 1989 Beijing Student Movement*, which chronicled in painstaking detail the rise and fall of the innumerable organizations fought to lead the fight. Zhao's narrative reminded me of the days I was simply an observer who walked past the Square twice a day. Without the eye of a sociologist or an historian, I wondered if what I saw was simply anarchy. Still, every time I saw their young, hopeful eyes, my heart would melt. Who was I to judge them?

The criminals of the city might have had the same mindset.

With police virtually absent from the streets, thieves and robbers counterintuitively decided to take a break from their duties as well. From the time martial law was declared, life continued normally until that fateful June 4th morning. It was time to put everything else aside. We were all from Beijing and all in this together.

Ironically, anarchy became its own brand of order.

Military forces in the city's suburbs appeared to be in no rush to make it to the city. One after another, battalions sent to crack down on the populace were forced to retreat, heading back to base to await orders. Before long, people of Beijing had grown used to a bizarre life under half-martial law. It seemed anarchy had won, and was a great deal more civilized than the Party had led people to believe.

On the morning of May 25th, someone handed me a flyer entitled: "The Last Battle Between Darkness and Light." It was published by the Capital Joint Conference of the People. It called on citizens from every walk of life to resist martial law and continue to fight for the Square.

Democracy is a matter of life and death for the Chinese people. Now is when we win or lose; live or die. If we emerge victorious, our nation will begin its walk down the path toward a democratic future: A fair future for us all, where despots and those who seek to stand in the way of progress will never stop us. They will never silence our voice. They will never stop the march of history!

That same morning, I got a call from the hotel's front desk, saying a "Mr. Wang" wanted to see me. I wondered who on earth was running around the city on business calls at a time like this. I was met with a heavy Tianjin-tinged accent on the other end of the line, "Sis!"

It was my younger brother, Wang Yi. He was the only one in our family actually born and raised in Tianjin. When we were kids, I used to make fun of his Tianjin accent, to which he would complain, "Why? My classmates all think my Tianjin accent isn't pure enough."

He was a freshman at Yanshan University, an engineering school in the City of Qinhuangdao, Hebei province. Classes had been suspended, so he and several classmates had come to Beijing to do their part at Tiananmen. As soon as they left the train station, however, they'd gotten separated in the sea of people. Wandering the streets trying to track everyone down, he found himself in front of the Beijing Hotel. He asked for me at the front desk, but never expected it would be so easy to get me on the phone. I told him to stay where he was, let Mr. Murata know I had some personal business to take care of, and dashed out the door.

I couldn't say my brother and I were particularly close, which was the inevitable result of Chinese parents' heavy-handed preference for sons over daughters. Still, seeing him there, I felt a strange, new sense of togetherness. Under martial law, all of Beijing were brothers and sisters. Why not us?

I hadn't seen him since Chinese New Year a few months before, but he looked taller, and far more tan. By his side was a young girl who introduced herself with the surname Qin. I assumed she was his girlfriend. I asked if they were hungry, and they replied that they were famished.

I took them to the Peace Restaurant next to Dongfeng market. In those days, if a restaurant was named "peace," you could safely bet it served Western food.

As we ate, I got them up to speed on the chaos in the Square. I stressed the anarchic side of the situation to scare him out of going, but my brother had already sensed it. The minute they got off the train, they were accosted by different groups of students, each claiming to be official leaders who would whisk them off to Tiananmen by bus.

"See? That's what I mean," I sighed. "There's so many leaders, but no one really knows who's in charge."

I launched into a long and winding monologue, during which I realized how lonely and oppressed I felt. I had many criticisms of the students, but I carefully kept them from Mr. Murata and Ms. Kawashima. They were foreigners, after all. Guo Yan was nowhere to be found, and my grandmother didn't even understand what I was talking about. My brother arrived at just the right time.

"All in all, the Chinese don't know how democracy operates. Five years ago, when we protested against a lights-out policy at Peking University, I learned that autonomy was the foundation of democracy. The statement was way beyond me at the time, but now I finally get it. Democracy doesn't necessarily mean everybody will be happy, which is what the students are pursuing. Look at Solidarity in Poland! They negotiate with the government on behalf of workers. The workers in turn to adhere to the outcome, whatever it may be. What the students lack is a governing body. I know there are a couple of student activists leading the charge, but all they're doing is showing off how extreme they are. If they show one ounce of compromise, the students will immediately abandon them.

I've heard that the students have voted several times on whether or not to leave the Square, and the majority votes to stay every time. People who want to withdraw have already voted with their feet. At present, the students in the Square are mostly fresh from outside Beijing, like you guys. They'll leave in a couple days when they get bored, but there'll always be new blood coming. How can we go on like this? The students should go back to school and start preparing to build their own system of governance from scratch."

My brother replied that it was impossible. At his university, even the lowest ranks of student leadership were decided upon by teachers. There would never be a chance for students to govern themselves.

"Maybe the protests are ahead of their time," I sighed.

But will there ever be a right time? The Party will never allow any self-governing body to flourish in China, meaning democracy has no chance of coming about gradually. Demonstrators had sacrificed too much. Things were far past the point of no return. If such a fierce struggle couldn't even earn people the right to vote, their struggle would be nothing more than a few drops of rain in a scorching desert.

I thought of "The Last Battle Between Darkness and Light:"

Fellow countrymen! There is already no road back. If even one of us backs down, the enemies of democracy will prevail, and they will make sure there is hell to pay… Ten years of opening up and reform, ten years of progress, and ten years of a better life will be gone in the blink of an eye.

Although the rhetoric sounded as if it had come from the very Party it sought to dismantle, it wasn't entirely wrong. As much as I didn't want the conflict be resolved by violence, I could think of no other possible outcomes.

"So, my point is, don't stay at the Square overnight."

He had no desire to go back to school. The dorms were all empty. Who was he going to play soccer with?

"OK, so go home then. Tianjin's only an hour away. The trains run all the time."

"Fine," he conceded.

I doubted he'd actually follow my instructions. He'd never listened to me before. Since I went to the top university in the nation, and he ended up at the lowest-ranking one, he thought I was a bookworm but that he had the street smarts.

We left the restaurant and headed south down Wangfujing Street. My brother insisted we head to the Square. Knowing he wouldn't listen to me, I told him once again that he could go and have a look, but that he should leave before dark. "You need to be out of the city by nightfall. Period. If the military decides to strike, that's when they'll do it."

Not far from the restaurant was a well-known fruit shop called Si Ji Xiang. It sat at the top of a flight of stairs between a tea shop and a food mart. Every year, as soon as watermelon came into season, the shop would open a dedicated watermelon window, offering everything from a whole melon, to halves, quarters, wedges or even squares on sticks. It was before refrigerators, so people gathered in front of the shop, eating slices of watermelon to beat the heat. There was a large, rectangular box on the curb into which people could spit seeds and drop rinds. Flies circled the box, making the scene look unsanitary and unrefined. Eating watermelon on the street always looked like pigs eating at a trough to me, but that day, seeing people gathering in front of the fruit shop, I felt a sense of nostalgia. I was scared that the life I'd known was disappearing.

I asked my brother if he wanted some. He said no. I asked Miss Qin, who hadn't said a word the entire time. She knew immediately that I wanted watermelon but didn't want to eat alone. "Yeah!" she nodded. "Look at how they cut it! It's so cute! I want one!"

I bought two wedges and gave her one. We stood together at the trough spitting seeds. My brother stood in the shade of a nearby tree, looking like a bored husband who had endured an entire day's shopping. The flies buzzing around me almost brought me to tears. My longing for a more peaceful and prosaic life thrilled me. I made a silent promise to Qin: if we lived through this, I'd be taking her side whenever she and my brother got in a fight.

Chapter 13

The Hutongs

From May 25th on, I stayed away from the main thoroughfares on my way to work and stuck to the maze-like alleys of the hutongs. At first, I just wanted to avoid the chaos on the main streets, but I soon found that walking in the hutongs was fun in its own right. On the wide expanse of the city's main boulevards, there was only one possible route, while the labyrinthine alleys provided endless options.

The last time I'd cut through here was before the completion of the Second Ring. Ancient Beijing was enclosed by city walls. Modern Beijing built upon the same notion of enclosure, but exchanged city walls for freeways. My grandmother's home was one block west of the outside of the Second Ring. In elementary school, my friends and I often went to Yangmaying Worker's Club: a theater tucked inside a Hutong. After the Second Ring was built, I needed to cross under the viaduct and wait for pedestrian traffic lights. Though the distance remained the same, it took longer to get there.

In 1978, I was forced to move to Tianjin because I didn't have Beijing residency. When I went back Beijing to visit my grandmother that summer, I learned how it was to feel excluded. I didn't feel like going to Yangmaying Worker's Club anymore. It was inside the Second Ring, which safeguarded a magnificent capital city that didn't want me. If Beijing didn't want me, the very heart of that city must want me even less.

But why are the hutongs considered the essence of Beijing? Because of their central location, or because of their long history?

In 1271, Genghis Khan's grandson Kublai Khan founded the Yuan Dynasty, which became the first foreign dynasty to rule China. Kublai Khan built Khanbaliq, which is the foundation of modern Beijing. Legend has it that the Mongolians, accustomed to nomadic life, cherished their sense of direction and wanted to keep it sharp even in the city, so Khanbaliq was designed on vertical and horizontal axes.

As originally designed, neighborhoods in Khanbaliq were formed using four major streets as borders. Within every neighborhood were alleys formed by rows of traditional courtyard residences known as siheyuan. The alleys were called hutongs, or "wells" in Mongolian; a sign of their reverence for water.

In other words, hutongs, the very essence of Beijing, were born of foreign culture. But over six-hundred years of existence, they grew to become a symbol of Beijing identity, and took on a secret, insular life of their own. After 1949, Beijing saw a massive increase in population. Employees of the ever-enlarging central government, workers in new industries, and a yearly influx of college graduates all found themselves bound for Beijing. The majority of newcomers were assigned to live in new developments outside the hutong areas. These were mostly apartment buildings like the one my grandmother lived in. The vast majority of families still living in hutongs had inhabited the same courtyards for literally hundreds of years, and saw themselves as the most native of Beijing natives.

More than ten years later, I finally worked up the courage to travel the hutongs again, and found they'd grown shorter and narrower. Walls had begun to crack and crumble, and patches of paint peeled off, revealing gray brick underneath. The mortar between the bricks had eroded away here and there, leaving some areas looking rather precarious. There had been attempts to perform some hasty repairs. Some walls had been casually coated with a layer of cement that didn't match the original color, much less its structural integrity.

I was sad to see that this neighborhood had been left out of the economic boom. The march of modernity, superficial as it was, had been unable to penetrate the hutongs. The residents had every right to be angry at bureaucratic profiteers and join the student protests, but it seemed that they didn't really care. Though near civil war roiled uncontrollably just streets away, life inside the hutongs continued in tranquility and indifference. Every morning on my way to work, elderly masters sat at stone chessboards, deftly moving pieces to and fro as appreciators nodded, remarked or cheered. The hutong was the center of their universe.

The sky above the hutongs was forever framed in by four brick corners. That rectangular expanse of blue played host to ugly gray utility poles, lush green tree tops, and white pigeons descending and ascending in the air. Its leisurely atmosphere was intoxicating, and I sometimes would forget all about the barricades, abandoned buses, boarded windows, screaming, smoke, and fire on the main roads. One day, as I cut home from work via Xiyangmaying Hutong, the narrow passage unexpectedly opened up to reveal a perfectly square structure. It was the Workers' Club I'd frequented as a kid.

I was surprised to find out that the Workers' Club was out of business. It was probably because it was owned by the labor union, and the urban factories had lost out to those in the countryside. Next to the window of the abandoned box office, old posters still hung in glass cases, suspended in time. Many of them were for films I'd never even heard of.

There was *The Last Clue in the Big Case*. Set in 1942 at the height of the Asia-Pacific War, the priceless Peking Man's skull mysteriously disappears. The race is on between the invading Japanese, American special agents, Chinese archaeologists, and underground communist operatives. There was a film called *The Phantom Lover*, in which a rich merchant's daughter falls in love with an opera singer. Their love is vehemently disapproved of by her father, who hires a group of thugs to disfigure the singer's face, forcing him to shroud himself in a dark cloak and haunt his former stage. There was *The AIDS Patient*. In the 1980s, a dying foreign professor confesses to authorities that he is HIV-positive and has slept with three young Chinese women. His words spark a race against time to contain a possibly disastrous epidemic.

I was amazed that China had produced these movies purely for entertainment. When I was at Peking University, we were in the midst of a cinematic renaissance at the hands of China's Fifth Generation directors. The movement produced such notable art films as Chen Kaige's *Yellow Earth*, Zhang Junzhao's *One and Eight*, and Zhang Yimou's *Red Sorghum*. This movement, as well as Cui Jian's music, inspired me to join the ranks of the avant-garde. I was in frantic pursuit of philosophical content and painstakingly studied the language of cinema. I considered myself unworthy of even setting foot in a theater if I hadn't mastered the lingo, terms like "Mise-en-scéne," "stream of consciousness," and "auteur."

That was the mark that the Hu Yaobang era left on me. Not only I didn't enjoy art simply for fun, I would never produce art for other people's entertainment either. I would shun popularity. It was synonymous with vulgarity.

But that day, peering through the disused glass cases at the fading posters inside, I finally felt the attraction of the movies I'd always looked down upon. I knew the stories were bullshit, but I somehow still felt their pull. I wanted to know who successfully claimed that lost treasure, and if they ever found the girls who'd slept with the corrupt professor. I wanted to pass a few hours without thinking too hard. I wanted to avoid reality. It was just like eating watermelon on the street: peaceful, prosaic, and without ambition.

It was a week into martial law, but with the military reluctant to open fire, the students did as they pleased in the Square. On May 27th, the Capital Joint Conference issued a proposition for resolution, and advised that students retreat and pursue alternate methods. The document was called the "Ten Declarations" and was read aloud by Wang Dan at an evening press conference. Declaration Eight suggested students end their occupation of Tiananmen on May 30th with a massive parade, but reserve the right to return on June 20th when the People's Congress session began. It was promptly rejected by another student leader named Chai Ling, who dismissed the declarations as phony solutions dreamed up by ivory tower intellectuals.

Who truly spoke for the students in the Square? One after another, people stepped up to claim the throne, but were overthrown by more radical candidates. The Taiwanese singer Hou Dejian proposed an election in which each student got a vote, but even that was ignored.

A bewildered legion of reporters left the press conference with nothing but contradictory information. When the "Ten Declarations" were printed and distributed to every corner of the Square, Declaration Eight had been re-written in a much harsher, confrontational manner: "If the People's Congress does not hold an emergency meeting within a matter of days to address the issues at hand, student occupation will continue until at least June 20."

From May 27 to June 3, depression hit me from time to time. I was in high spirits when the first protest began. Without any improvement, that cry for change became empty noise. Now, when I thought of the protests, the first things that came to mind were the inconveniences they caused. Transportation systems were paralyzed. Groceries were difficult to get. Life was like traveling through an endless tunnel. I had wanted something to break me out of my mundane life, but now, I'd fallen into something worse. I hoped that the chaos would end soon and that life would return to normal. Still, I didn't want the students come out of this empty-handed.

How would these protests end? I'd observed the situation meticulously but had no idea what to expect. One moment, I was convinced the students would win. The next, I waited nervously for the military to strike. Both were likely. Every once in a while, one would tip the scale slightly, only to find the opposite side had done the same.

On May 27, the scales of fate continued their cruel dance when Wan Li, head of the National People's Congress, broke his silence and declared his support of martial law, which shattered the students' hopes. That evening in Hong Kong, the entertainment world rallied together to stage a massive "Concert for Democracy." Jackie Chan, Teresa Teng, Anita Mui, Hou Dejian, Lowell Lo, Roman Tam, and many more performed nonstop for twelve hours, and raised thirteen million HKD for the students' cause. On one side, you had the words of Wan Li, an extreme heavyweight among Chinese politicians. On the other, you had the people of Hong Kong: accountants, secretaries, salesmen, cashiers, taxi drivers, housewives...They may be insignificant individually but their numbers were in the millions. Could their collective voices outweigh the judgment of a single powerful man?

On May 29, I got a call from Guo Yan.

"I'm back! I just got in yesterday!" he sounded content.

"Your dad let you off the hook?" I was dubious. "I thought you had to wait till everything calmed down."

"Well, I can't just do everything my dad says. Otherwise, it'd be too late."

"Too late for what?"

"Democracy is just around the corner!" he exclaimed. "That means freedom of the press. If I don't jump on the bandwagon by the time the dust settles, I won't get a piece of the pie."

"Wow, wow, wow, what am I hearing here?" I replied. "Are you seriously that opportunistic?"

He realized his tongue had slipped and quickly tried to backtrack, saying he owed everything to his editor. With all the events of late, their staff had mostly abandoned their posts, leaving the paper paralyzed. He couldn't sit by in good conscience.

It was a terribly concocted lie. He was so devoted to his editor that he decided to hide at his daddy's house for over three weeks? Give me a break.

Still, I was interested in why exactly he thought the students would win. He answered as if it were the most obvious answer under the sun, "Do you even need to ask? Come on. The people will never side with the Party."

"I don't know... Mr. Murata says the opposite."

"What the hell does a Japanese guy know?" he scoffed.

He told me he was on his way to report on something at the Central Academy of Fine Arts and asked if I wanted to go. Some students were crafting their own version of the Statue of Liberty and planned to install it at Tiananmen Square that night. I immediately refused, and not in the kindest manner. He tried to sweet-talk me into changing my mind. I heard him out. It never hurts to hear how you're the best thing that ever happened to someone, even if you know it's not true. But if you listen to a lie long enough, you'll simply start to believe it. I was half dazed when suddenly a woman's voice took over the line. "She said she didn't want to go. Stop wasting your time."

The line clicked dead. Guo Yan had hung up in a hurry. I held the receiver in front of my face and stared at it, unable to process what just happened. Yang at the front desk had warned me that big brother was eavesdropping on our calls, and he was right.

It took me a few minutes to recover. Although I'd always hated the state police, I didn't resent this specific policewoman. She sounded like some idle woman from our neighborhood, nosy and big-mouthed. Most of the time, she was simply annoying, but occasionally she saved someone's day.

Still, Guo Yan had piqued my interest. After work, I headed to the Central Academy of Fine Arts. The school was one-mile north of Wangfujing, in a hutong named Xiaowei. As I got closer to the gates of the school, the mass of people grew impenetrable. Bicyclists angrily rang their bells, attempting to break through the wall of bodies. For residents of the hutong, the whole spectacle was yet another unwelcome disturbance from the outside world. They just wanted to get home.

Dusk settled in. "Excuse me! Excuse me!" Someone called out. Four flatbed rickshaws slowly wheeled out of the gates with large cloths covering each vehicle. Someone from the crowd yanked one off, revealing a snow-white form underneath. The flashes of cameras instantly turned the evening to broad daylight. Someone next to me explained that the statue was over ten meters tall, and no one vehicle was big enough to move it. The students had to cut it into pieces and reassemble it on arrival.

The rickshaws carrying the parts of the statue slowly made a turn into another hutong, then onto Wangfujing Street with a thousand flashbulbs' leading the way. With a larger street came a larger crowd, and the four carts crawled forward at a snail's pace.

From time to time, the cloths covering the statue were ripped away. I tried my best to roll with the agitated mass of people, getting glimpses of a leg, a torso, a head, and something resembling a torch. The air of the night felt boiling. The overall atmosphere was quite upbeat, but I had the feeling I was in a funeral procession, following the carts on which Lady Liberty lay, murdered and chopped into pieces. But when I looked around, all I saw were ecstatic faces. All I heard were shouts of joy. It was only me who was mourning.

It wasn't until 11 at night that the statue finally reached the Square, where a massive scaffold lay in wait. Tens of thousands of people surrounded the scaffold in eager anticipation. The statue was made of a porous plastic, and the students pleaded with the crowd to stop smoking near the assembly site, and to stop taking flash photos, as the bulbs produced heat.

I might as well head home since I wasn't going to get close to it. I walked as fast as I could. I made it back ten minutes short of midnight to find my grandmother sitting feebly on her bed, with her back against the wall as if she needed it to stay upright.

"You can't stay out this late," she groaned. "You're going to give me a heart attack."

"Some stuff came up at the last minute...Besides, it's not even midnight."

An anguished look fell over her face, toiling over her next words. "From this day on, you're home every night by seven. Otherwise, you don't live here anymore."

I never imagined she could be so resolute.

"Fine," I blurted out before thinking it through. As soon as the word left my lips, I remembered my Japanese classes. It would start on June 1, from six to eight. Today was already the 29th, technically the 30th. How was I going to find a place to live in one day?

I tossed and turned in the dark, unable to clear my head. I'd registered long before the hunger strikes. Tiananmen was a warzone now. There was no way a school right next to it would continue classes. I should go ask them tomorrow. I sighed. This battle had gone on long enough. I couldn't live like this anymore.

The assembly of Statue of Liberty continued through to noon the next day, after which the exhausted creators held a brief ceremony to honor its completion. They randomly chose a man and woman from the crowd to pull the rope and finally unveil it. The moment the curtain dropped, fearless roars of "Long live democracy!" thundered forth from the crowd. The Statue of Liberty was situated on the invisible central axis running through Tiananmen Square, staring straight across Chang'an Avenue at the massive portrait of Mao Zedong on Tiananmen Tower. The sight of the Statue of Liberty greatly uplifted the students' spirits.

Fundraisers in Hong Kong purchased the protesters a massive number of tents. The students organized them in neat, color-coded rows throughout the Square. Almost overnight, the garbage-laden occupation camp turned into a gleaming, multicolored playground. The spacious tents provided much-needed shelter from Beijing's scorching May temperatures.

The tents just came in in time. On the night of May 30, fierce winds and rain pummeled Beijing, but with the tents now in place, students fared quite well. They frolicked and chatted the night away like they were at a slumber party. Neither blazing sun nor pouring rain could drive them away.

June 1 was International Children's Day. Every year, the Party arranged for members of the Young Pioneers of China to travel to Tiananmen for a large ceremony during which they would take an oath. This year, with the square occupied by students, the ceremony was cancelled. With no school, parents took their kids to see the new Statue of Liberty, just like it was a normal day of field trip.

After Hu Yaobang's passing, it seemed all party decrees would be announced on weekends. On Friday, June 2, Mr. Murata grimly predicted that the Party would take the Square by force on the weekend. But "force" was too vague. Canon's head office wanted a straight answer: Would the Chinese military turn guns on its own people?

I felt it was a likely outcome, but surely they would only use rubber bullets. At least that's what people were saying.

"I doubt it," Mr. Murata said.

"Why not?"

"I don't think China has time to import them. Western countries have weapons embargoes on China."

"You mean China doesn't manufacture rubber bullets? It can't be harder than making real ones!" I exclaimed.

"Rubber bullets are made to scare and disperse. If a country sees regular problems with riots or civil unrest, they would stock up on rubber ones. But China's never had this problem before."

Panic washed over me. "They're gonna use real bullets? That can't be true!"

"Personally, I still don't think they'll use their guns," Mr. Murata said calmly. "They'll probably do what they did during the last mass protests in 1976. Water hoses and wooden clubs did the trick then. I don't see why they wouldn't now."

I breathed a sigh of relief. Mr. Murata knew so much about Chinese history.

That afternoon, Ms. Kawashima handed me several boxes of documents for shredding. In and of itself, it was nothing out of the ordinary. Our office shredded documents at regular intervals throughout the year. Still, something felt off, as if she was preparing for the worst. Would Chinese soldiers burst into the hotel and search every foreigner's office?

It turned out my Japanese class was canceled indefinitely. I had more time to figure out if I wanted to live with my grandmother or not.

The shredder hummed, tearing the documents into thin strips. Before long, the trash can overflowed, which meant a trip to the dumpster at the end of the hall. The cavernous hallway made the normally imperceptible sound of my feet thunderous. Most offices in the hotel had been closed for at least a week. If any room showed signs of life, it was most likely occupied by foreign journalists.

The last box was filled with the pictures I'd taken. All the victories and defeats I'd worked so hard to capture. These glimpses of history were to go into the shredder. I was unable to accept it. I saved as many as I could and slipped them into my bag when Ms. Kawashima's back was turned.

No matter how gloomy of a day it was, there was always one thing that made me happy. Each floor of the hotel had a public restroom, and each was equipped with a scale. I decided to weigh myself for the first time in months, and I found that I was under a hundred and twenty pounds. It was a goal that had eluded me since the day I'd stopped growing taller. It had to be the result of trekking to and from work everyday.

That afternoon, Mr. Murata waited until the last possible second to fax his assessment of the situation to the head office in Japan. The machine let out a long, steady tone, and a sigh marking the end of an era it too had grown too weary to endure. Mr. Murata turned to me and told me that I wouldn't need to come in tomorrow. I wanted to ask about the week after, but held my tongue. If I'd learned anything from recent events, it was that no one could predict anything.

As I passed the Square on my way home, I noticed the Monument to the People's Heroes had again become the center of attention. A crowd had gathered around a small group of men with a banner reading *You Leave Us No Choice!*

It had to mean escalation of conflict. But how much further could they go past starving themselves to death? There were rumors of students who had been calling for self-immolation. My heart pounded fiercely.

Many years later, I learned that historians had named the people holding the banner the "Four Gentlemen." They were Liu Xiaobo, a teacher from Beijing Normal University; Hou Dejian, a Taiwanese singer; Zhou Duo, a manager at the Stone Group in Beijing; and Gao Xin, the former editor-in-chief of Beijing Normal University's school newspaper. They entered Tiananmen Square at four o'clock on the afternoon of June 2, declaring a seventy-two-hour hunger strike.

From the moment the protests began, influential members of the intellectual community tried to offer guidance and assistance by acting as intermediaries between the students and the Party. The students, however, ignored the offer and were suspicious of the motives behind it. As the conflict continued to spiral downward, Liu Xiaobo realized that if he wanted to gain the students' trust, he had to join them.

He resolved to find some like-minded writers and scholars to start a hunger strike of their own. In the end, he found three allies.

I was stumbling my way through the crowd toward the monument when one of the men began to sing. I was too far away to see who it was, but through the distorted speakers, I heard a Taiwanese twang to his voice. The song was "Descendants of the Dragon," written and composed by Hou Dejian. I assumed the singer was probably Hou himself. The crowd joined in and sang along. I breathed a sigh of relief. No one would burn themselves today.

When Hou stopped to catch his breath, Liu Xiaobo stepped up and gave a speech. He claimed that both the students and the government had done their fair share of escalating the crisis, while proudly praising their own resolve:

We will not allow hatred to poison our wisdom, for we have no enemies.

Twenty years later, as he faced his fourth prison sentence for political dissidence, Liu Xiaobo read his essay "I Have No Enemies" in court. It was proof that for two decades, the words he spoke that afternoon at Tiananmen had never left the recesses of his heart. But in the moment it was far from what the masses wanted to hear. They quickly drowned him out, chanting for the return of Hou Dejian.

I lost interest and wandered off. In those days, many speakers were positioned throughout the square. Each had a limited reach, and messages clashed with each other. From where I stood, I could hear two accounts from two different speakers, both shouting the same thing: soldiers were on their way.

The military has already deployed squads of soldiers to clear the square...

They are entering the city by truck or on foot, in uniform or undercover, but they are coming..

...From all directions...

Every student, every teacher, every resident of Beijing, take to the streets and keep them at bay!

Now is the time... The last stand.

The broadcast was intended to raise alarm, but it only served to confuse. "By truck or by foot?" "In uniform or undercover?" "From what direction?" I shrugged in disapproval and wandered off seeking a calmer speaker. I ended up at the Federation for Worker's Autonomy:

All students and citizens of Beijing, please report to the Federation tent to collect your weapons. Cleavers, batons, chains, bamboo rods, and other modes of self-defense will be distributed on a first-come, first-serve basis.

They definitely sounded more clear and concise than the students, but if I walked over to their tent, would they really just hand me a weapon? How could they be sure I wasn't an undercover soldier? I started to feel unsafe.

I exited the Square and crossed Chang'an Avenue. I saw a bus parked in the middle of the street to block the military vehicles. A young man in his twenties slashed the rear tires with a knife before darting around to the other side. The bus sank to the ground like an exhausted horse.

At Xinhua Gate, students and citizens gathered in front of the tightly sealed gates, which were guarded by several hundred members of the People's Liberation Army. Both sides stood in complete silence.

Near Liubukou, I saw yet another bus-turned-barricade, this time with tires intact. Several young people who appeared to be college students stood on the roof, screaming through megaphones. *They are closer. Soldiers have entered the western suburbs.* Walking several steps, I saw another bus lying across the road, smeared with soot. At a construction site next to Xidan Street, a crowd of people stole bricks and rebar, arming themselves for war.

Running along Xidan for a short while, I dashed into the first hutong I could find. As always, the hutongs were an inside world that kept out of the fanning flames of battle. People would only fan their charcoal to cook dinner inside their serene, ramshackle walls. Players and enthusiasts, each balancing a bowl and chopsticks in one hand, surrounded stone chessboards in the alleys. The smell of each family's signature dishes wafted through the air.

Turning the corner, I was back at the entrance to Xiyangmaying.

My childhood heaven, the Workers' Club, was just steps away. I relaxed. I was only 15 minutes away from home.

I noticed a group of people gathered around a utility pole, each with a look more grave than the next. Clearly something unusual had happened.

I stayed on the perimeter, standing on my tiptoes to catch a glimpse. It was a smashed package of hardtack. There was no brand on the package, which meant it was military issue. Volunteers had canvassed the area for clues, leading them here, where they'd found a mysterious triangle drawn in chalk on the pole. One after another, residents were called forth to claim responsibility, or at least take a guess as to how it got there.

"I didn't draw that...My kid didn't either," one mumbled.

"We don't even have chalk," another replied.

"Next in line. Take a look, please," someone called out.

People in front started looking back. My heart jumped. I quickly peeled away and slipped into another hutong.

"Why bother? We all know what it is...some mark from a military scout!" I heard one man shout. "We all need to be vigilant. Who's seen any strangers here lately?"

I took off running as fast as my legs could carry me, all the way to the traffic lights under the Second Ring. Once crossed the Second Ring, my grandmother's home was steps away. Panting and shaking, I gulped and gasped in an effort to catch my breath.

Chapter 14

Tonight is the Night

Since I'd moved in with my grandmother in June, 1988, I spent almost every weekend and holiday at the office. On the morning of June 3, I woke up knowing instinctively that I would stay home. I'd been so fierce and defiant, but when history actually reached a turning point, I became a coward.

I was definitely afraid of physical violence at the hands of the military. They had guns, batons, tanks, you name it. Still, if I died or got hurt standing up to martial law, I could call myself a hero. But what if I got hit by a random falling brick? What if I was killed by wayward Molotov cocktail? There was no glory in becoming collateral damage.

One of the beauties of living in a metropolis was the gift of anonymity. But the day before, when the hutong residents warned one another of strangers, I got scared. I was a stranger carrying piles of suspicious photos. If they searched me, I had no proof of what side I was on. They might think I was spying for the government. Martial law had sent Beijing decades back, and downgraded a networked major city into isolated feudal strongholds. I decided to hole up and leave the braver souls to face their destiny.

My grandmother sat on her bed, busy with her needlework. Occasionally, she'd pause, gently set her needle in a ball of thread, and get up to look out the window. After a few seconds, she'd whisper as quietly as a church mouse, "Come here... come here... quick!"

I went over to join her, peering out to the street below. She pinched my arm, and pointed to the base of a tree. I peeked through the thick branches and leaves, and caught a glimpse of a young man looking around in a suspicious manner before darting into the cover of another tree. He was in a white shirt and green pants with a green canvas bag over his shoulder.

Rumor had it that the army had been sent to infiltrate the city in small, clandestine groups. Not wanting to be spotted, they carried their uniform jackets in canvas bags, leaving them in white shirts and green pants.

"Do you think... Is it..." she shuddered.

"Most likely," I whispered.

"Don't leave the house!" she implored.

I murmured my compliance, before returning to bed with a wave of shame. She still regarded me as a brave and curious soul.

Meanwhile, inside of the six-story, L-shaped fortress, light started to pour in the hallways again, as neighbors began to open their doors. After nearly a decade of groping our separate ways in darkness, grave threat from the outside world pressured us to open up and unite.

In the shared kitchen, fires burned all day long. With few able to go outside, there was all the time in the world to make complicated dishes. It also served as a makeshift newsroom where everyone could stop by and learn the latest.

The Xue family that lived next to the stairwell had been arguing since breakfast. Mr. Xue's aunt was sick at Fuxing Hospital. He wanted to visit her. Mrs. Xue didn't want to go because the hospital was close to Muxidi, an area that had fallen into chaos the day before. "Bullets don't care who they kill," she stressed. Mr. Xue didn't disagree. But his aunt was getting out of the hospital tomorrow. What if the military didn't strike today? They would lose their last chance to visit her and she would bear a grudge forever.

At first, I thought nothing of the aunt. She was just another part of their extended family. But as the argument unfolded, a clearer portrait of the aunt in question began to appear. Mr. Xue's mother had passed away when he was young, leaving her sister—Mr. Xue's aunt—to raise him. She was about 5'8", and slight as a branch with an angular, resolute face. She was basically the diametric opposite of my short, stocky grandmother. But what was it that they had in common? There had to be something. Finally it came to mind: Liberation Feet.

I remembered everything now. I was in elementary school. The Xues had a baby and the aunt came to help take care of the newborn. Holding her smelly bundle of joy, she struck up a conversation with my grandmother in the hall, marveling at her shoes, "I love your shoes! Where'd you get 'em from?"

"I made them myself," my grandmother proudly proclaimed. "I can make you a pair if you want."

"That'd be amazing! thanks!"

Yeah, that was definitely her. The box of memory had been prized open. Somehow, digging out that old woman from the depths of my memory cheered me up.

But why hadn't I seen her lately? I realized Grandma had been making fewer shoes than she normally did. She was still doing needlework, but rarely shoes. Some companies had revived the tradition of making shoes for ladies with Liberation Feet. My mother often asked my grandmother if she wanted a pair from a famous shoemaker in Tianjin. My grandmother always said no. According to her, the word for "shoes" and the word for "evil" were homonyms, and it was wrong for a daughter to give the gift of evil to her mother. I assumed that my grandmother just didn't want to bother her. If that really was her reasoning, wasn't it equally wrong for her to be making evil for herself and for friends? Either way, now that people could buy specialty shoes at stores, they stopped asking my grandmother to make them. That was why I hadn't seen Mr. Xue's aunt any more.

Around noon, footsteps drifted down the hall, getting closer, then stopped by the turning point of the L-shaped hall. Mrs. Xue called out her doorway, "Little Chen! You're back! What's the scene at Muxidi?"

Upon hearing the question, people poured out of their rooms. Before you knew it, Chen and Mrs. Xue were tightly surrounded.

I didn't know Chen very well. She looked like she was in her late twenties or early thirties. She must have moved in during the ten years I was absent. She was thin and nimble, with bright eyes full of life. She seemed to be on her way to the men's washroom to fill a bucket with water when she was suddenly thrust into the spotlight, which she loved.

She answered in an almost happy tone of voice, "It's crazy. It's chaos. If you don't absolutely need to go there, stay away. All the bricks have been torn out of the sidewalks and thrown at soldiers. Someone tried to put one in my hand, but I refused. How am I supposed to throw a brick that far? What if I hit someone on our side by mistake?" She giggled.

"Yeah, yeah!" The audience nodded eagerly, "Then what?"

"Then I got the hell out of there." Enjoying her time in the spotlight, she took a deep breath and continued, "Oh yeah! Last night, a Jeep lost control and plowed into a crowd on the sidewalk. It killed three people. The students blocked the truck in and found a bunch of helmets, guns, and knives inside. They took 'em all out and spread them across the hood. If you really want to see, they might still be there."

Suddenly, a man stepped forward from the crowd and shouted in her face: "You're still standing around here fucking gossiping? Our kid's gonna starve to death!"

Her audience stared on, slightly embarrassed. Mrs. Xue stepped forward, "Don't be mad at her. I asked her."

The man's demeanor softened somewhat, but he continued, "You know what this idiot did?" He yelled, pointing to Chen. "She strapped a three-year-old to the back of a bike and took him to that war zone. All she cares about is poking her nose where it doesn't belong. She calls herself a mother? She doesn't give a shit if our kid gets killed."

The crowd started wondering if Chen was too much.

"Next time, just let me know," Mrs. Xue grabbed Chen's hand and shook it firmly. "I can look after your kid. It's no problem."

Chen stormed off into the men's restroom, and her audience silently dispersed. Water rashed angrily onto the bottom of her bucket. The sound softened as the water level rose.

I heard Chen's slippers shuffle into the distance. It was my turn to get water. Kettle in hand, I ran into Uncle Li coming the other direction. He asked incredulously, "You're home?"

His incredulity felt like a performance. He was emphasizing something. I simply uttered "Yeah," hoping that would be the end of it. However, my cue went directly over his head. "I've never seen you home in broad daylight before! Your grandmother always talks about how busy you are at that Japanese company. You don't even get Sundays off, do you?"

"Yeah, that was before. But today, you know," I muttered dispassionately. I wondered if he really didn't know why I was home. Every factory in Beijing had stopped production and let its workers stay home. It was a war zone outside. I thought for a second and decided to get out of the conversation, "I don't feel well today."

He nodded and set me free.

Ever since I'd missed Min's wedding, I tried my best to avoid Uncle Li, which he responded to with increasing enthusiasm. He would fumble around for random topics, seemingly just to thwart my attempt to flee. I couldn't shake the feeling that his rambling conversations were part of a patient, careful mission to expose me somehow. Maybe I was just being paranoid, but I'd heard more than a couple rumors about him. It was said that behind his outwardly friendly demeanor lay the dark heart hungry for revenge.

Maybe he knew I'd broken my promise to be Min's bridesmaid, or maybe he never really approved of Min getting married and felt I was an accomplice to the crime. I was guilty of the first charge, but definitely not the second.

I carried the kettle back down the hall, where our portable stove was positioned outside the door of our apartment. It was old-fashioned and required perfect timing to light a match with your left hand, and simultaneously turn the gas knob with your right. Turn it early, you'd release too much gas; Turn it too late, you'd waste a match. Either way, the head of the household would scold me for throwing money down the drain. I was nervous. It'd been ten-plus years since I'd last had to light it and I had only a split second to get it right. Somehow, without a whiff of gas in the air, nor a speck of ash on the ground, the blue flame came out on the first try. I still belonged.

Somewhere between dusk and evening, the calm in the hallway was shattered by a loud scream, the sound of a foot chase, and the thud of human flesh on the concrete. Terror swept the air. Had soldiers smashed their way in? People shot out their doors to find a young man attempting to get away while his parents clung to him for dear life. The old couples' knees dragged on the floor. The young man managed to shake his mother off, who screamed as she hit the floor. The father let go of his son to tend to his wife, and the young man bolted for the stairwell. His path was blocked. People on the lower floor had heard the commotion and flooded the hallway. He gripped the rails, preparing to jump before being overpowered by two large middle-aged men.

"Let me...go!" he screamed, fighting.

It was Qiao. He was around my age. We played together when we were little. We rarely spoke after we'd grown up, but I knew he was one of only two young people in our building who'd chosen self-employment. Factory workers all had the same dream for their children: go to college and get a government-assigned job. If that didn't work, the kids could replace their parents at the factory as their parents retired.

Qiao loved to dance, but after failing for three consecutive years to get into Beijing Dance Academy, he decided to buck the system and work for himself, mostly as a backup dancer at large concerts.

He was a handsome, lithe young man, who walked as only a dancer could. It was like his feet never touched the ground. He sported long bangs that he would gently toss to one side to see who he was speaking to. Lots of people didn't like him, reading his mannerisms as annoying affectations.

He looked like a fallen angel now. His long, lean limbs were firmly trapped by his much larger keepers as his long bangs danced to and fro. They delivered him back to his home. His parents padlocked the door from outside. He proceeded to beat and kick the door with a great deal of ferocity. A neighbor pushed a love seat across their doorway, providing a blockade and a place for the old couple to rest. They huddled together, trembling.

Another neighbor asked if they were hurt, or if they needed to go to the hospital. They insisted they were fine.

"What on earth was all that about?" Someone finally asked.

"It's that damn martial law," his mother replied, sobbing.

It all started with Fei Xiang. Fei Xiang was born Kris Phillips in Taiwan to an American father and a Chinese mother. He rose to fame as a pop star in 1987 at the age of 27. Following a performance on China Central TV's annual Chinese New Year Gala, he skyrocketed to popularity throughout mainland China. In 1989, he'd planned a nationwide tour, and was in need of dozens of dancers. Qiao made it through auditions, and had been rehearsing for over six months. He took it very seriously. This was his big break. The tour was scheduled to open in Beijing on May 19. No one could possibly have imagined that the date would be met with a citywide lockdown.

Fearing for his safety, his parents forbade him from going. They figured the concert would surely be canceled anyway. It turned out that martial law didn't dissuade Fei Xiang fans. Even if public transportation was shut down, they still managed to get to the stadium. The show went off without a hitch, and was a perfect start to the nationwide tour that followed, but Qiao was fired immediately.

"Ever since he lost that job, he hasn't been right in the head. He's been talking to himself," his mother said. "Just now, he heard something on the radio, then all of a sudden he went crazy and said he had to get to Tiananmen."

"It was that Emergency Announcement," someone offered.

Since 6:30pm, the radio and TV had started broadcasting an "Emergency Announcement" non-stop. Almost everyone's radio made the same sound. When Qiao's mother fell silent, we heard the announcement more clearly:

All city residents, be advised. Stay in your homes. Avoid public places. Avoid Tiananmen Square. Workers in mass industry, do not leave your posts. All others are to remain at home for your own safety.

Qiao's father muttered, "Is there any way you can turn it down a bit?"

The radio fell silent. The father bowed to the crowd, his hands outstretched in gratitude.

"Thank you everyone. I'm sorry to have caused all this trouble. Please don't worry about us. Thank you all. Thank you so much."

Qiao was continuing to attack the door, but it seemed he was running out of steam.

My grandmother asked what all the racket was about and I told her every last detail. She said in a hushed voice, "That family's always been weird. I hear he's not really the father's son."

It was true that the father and the son didn't really look like each other, but that sounded like a stretch. I wanted to ask what else my grandmother knew, but I stopped myself. Digging through other people's dirty laundry was never a hobby of mine, and I refused to let my confinement change me.

The sky had gone black. White smoke poured out of the chimney at the children's hospital. The smoke from the children's hospital was usually odorless. Why did it smell like fireworks? Perhaps the smell drifted in from a distance? I looked to the southwest, toward Muxidi. With so many buildings in the way, I couldn't see. Still, I occasionally heard faint explosions, brakes screeching, and distant shouts. Underneath my window, the street was deadly silent.

My grandfather was listening to his radio as always. The quiet made the static-tinged stream of Peking Opera stand out even more.

My grandfather retired in 1980 when I was living with my parents in Tianjin. I remember overhearing my parents discussing my grandfather's options. He'd started his career at the railway industry before 1949, and his residency registration had been tied to the Ministry of Railways ever since. It was a corporate account, and when his retirement came he needed to find somewhere to dock his residence registration. Of course, he could only choose a place where his family had already settled.

My mother was worried that my grandmother might not want her husband back. It turned out that my mother's worry was unnecessary. Grandma accepted her husband, but not without pointing out, time and time again, that just because she'd chosen to stay in Beijing and had never left he could easily register in Beijing as well. She finally got the triumph and closure she had been waiting for almost forty years.

When I moved in last year, it was the beginning of me getting to know my grandfather. I only had vague memories of him from my childhood. He returned home twice a year for two weeks. He seemed cold and intimidating. As an adult, I wasn't afraid of him. But he was still cold, not only to me, but to my grandmother. It was probably because he spoke so little. My grandmother and grandfather lived in two separate rooms that connected. He spent all his day in his room, only coming out for lunch and dinner. He loved to listen to the radio and always did so at a deafening volume because of his hearing problems. Static-warped voices always drifted over to our part of the house, even with his door closed. When he came out, he brought his radio to the dinning table. When my grandmother nagged him about something, she didn't even get a raised eyebrow in return.

At dinner, he dutifully wolfed down his portion, and then took his leave. He never said one word more than was absolutely necessary. His lips moved so imperceptibly that it was always a struggle to even make out what he said.

He was listening to *Farewell My Concubine*, a classic Peking opera adapted from a true story. In about 200 BC, two warlords, Liu Bang and Xiang Yu, were vying for power. Faced with likely defeat, on the eve of their showdown, Xiang Yu sank into a deep depression. His concubine Miss Yu committed suicide in hopes of eliminating any distraction from her lover's mind.

I'd never really taken a liking to Peking Opera. The stories made no sense to me. Why would Miss Yu want to kill herself? If she'd already decided to die, the least she could do would be to go into battle and take an enemy with her. Maybe she could have made the difference between victory and defeat. But this was clearly not how Peking Opera worked. Miss Yu wasn't Wonder Woman.

In the opera, as her lover lays sleeping in their tent, Miss Yu slips out into the light of a full moon, singing as she walks:

My sleeping king, my love, my dear,
I take my leave, for when I'm near,
Your heart rests on our love, not war.
Jade moons alight, forevermore.

I listened as Miss Yu's voice drifted high and low. I imagined her hips swaying with each step. I didn't understand what kind of catharsis an audience got from this kind of story, but who was I to judge? This art form had existed for longer than I'd been alive. People must have their reasons.

June 3 was a moonless night. I envisioned a soft glow lighting

Miss Yu's way as the faint sound of shouting reverberated across the horizon. A light murmur followed. For a moment, I couldn't tell what universe I was in. I gathered myself and listened intently. I was certain I heard more shouts and tires screeching. In the distance, the sky was tinted purple. The column of smoke from the hospital wasn't white any more, but was stained a light orange at its tip from the fading day. The air smelled more of gunpowder.

The military was coming. My grandfather cranked up the radio.

Around 9:30 pm, after most people had shut their doors for the night, a woman's scream shattered the silence on the floor. We finally had an excuse and poured into the hall.

Qiao's mother stood in front of her door, dazed, as if she'd seen a ghost.

Her son had escaped.

"How'd he get out?" someone asked, pointing at the padlock and loveseat still blocking the way.

"I don't know. We've been sitting here the whole time. After a while it was too quiet, so I went to check on him, and the place is empty."

Some guessed he'd simply jumped out the window. His mother rushed downstairs. A group of neighbors were hot on her heels, half of them still in pajamas. They went out and searched the area underneath Qiao family's window, then expanded their search almost to Yuetan Park. They found nothing. Not a drop of blood, nor a piece of cloth. Even if a hundred-plus pound man had actually managed to jump from a third-story window unscathed, there was no way he'd be able to avoid leaving a footprint in the ground.

He had to have climbed out and over to the makeshift kitchen next door before escaping down the stairs. It sounded impossible. There was never a moment when that kitchen was empty, but people could've been so preoccupied with cooking or gossiping that they might not have even noticed.

His mother was flanked by two women. She made a sudden break from their grasp, and in a flash, she was already halfway down the street. Her two guardians gave chase, and soon succeeded in retrieving her. The rest of the crowd caught up and formed a circle around her to keep her contained.

"Let me go! Let me go! Let me die with him!" she shrieked, choking on her own tears.

"How are you even going to find him? You don't even know if he went to Muxidi or Tiananmen." That was true. We were a mile from Muxidi, and three from Tiananmen. Both the possible destinations.

"Come on, calm down. Think of his father...don't throw your life away and leave him all alone..." someone said, as if Qiao had already died.

Someone remembered the balcony on the roof: "We can see all of Chang'an Avenue from up there."

"Nah, that thing was sealed off long ago."

"With what? A couple pieces of wood?"

I had almost forgotten about the balcony. It was the neighborhood children's favorite place to play hide-and-seek before I started elementary school. One day, we caught a man and woman having an intimate moment up there. The man threatened us not to speak of it, but apparently some of us did, and the balcony was soon declared off limits.

Around ten o'clock, the street lights suddenly shut off, plunging the entire area into darkness. Panicked whispers rippled through the crowd as we gazed toward the direction of Chang'an Avenue, which seemed even brighter in comparison.

We were facing Yuetan Street. On the south side of it, a crowd had gathered at a flowerbed next to an apartment building. The lights from Chang'an Avenue bathed them in an eerie glow. The crowd seemed strangely petrified, like ghosts too scared to haunt.

The man next to me, Mr. Sun, took out a cigarette and offered the pack around. I took a sudden step back, accidentally stepping on the toes of the person behind me. I turned around to apologize, and saw it was Chen, her child fast asleep on her back.

The sound of a radio drifted out the window of an unknown apartment.

All city residents, be advised. Stay in your homes...

"Shut that damn thing off!" A cry rose from our crowd.

The radio fell silent and a deathly quiet settled over us. Unable to see clearly, we jumped at every gust of wind. No one even dared to speak. Even Mrs. Qiao stopped crying.

A scream arose from across the street, "Down with fascists!"

"Freedom belongs to the people!" we shouted back.

The shouting awoke Chen's baby son and he began to cry.

Our chants came from the 1967 Albanian film *Triumph Over Death*, which rose to popularity in China in 1969. Based on a true story, the film depicts a pair of female guerillas fight against fascists. Told from multiple interwoven perspectives in a complex plot structure, it was unlike any film China had produced at the time. As a result, it required repeated viewings to finally make sense. Over and over, those two phrases were drilled into our mind. After dinner on any given day, it wasn't uncommon to hear two kids ask each other:

"Down with fascists. Wanna go play in Yuetan Park?"

"Freedom belongs to the people. Hold on, lemme go to the bathroom first."

We shouted on and on as our voices grew hoarse, as if our collective voices could exorcise the quiet demons that lay in wait.

Chen, unable to calm her child, retreated inside. Clearly not wanting to leave, she looked back at Chang'an Avenue three times each step.

I heard a soft popping sound like bubbles at the top of a glass of Coke. Once...twice...three times. I looked at those around me, and the grave concentration on their faces told me I wasn't the only one who'd heard it. A minute later, it stopped as suddenly as it started.

I heard it again, only louder. This time, it wasn't a glass of Coke but a case of the stuff dumped into a scalding pot. Before we could even determine what we were hearing, it ceased again.

Days later we learned why the gunshots had come in bursts.

Soldiers coming from the west had been thwarted by blockades at Muxidi, and by ten o'clock, had been ordered to open fire. The opening salvos took down the front line, and those still standing rushed to their aid, creating small gaps, and enabling the soldiers to advance. As soon as the wounded were rushed from the scene, those remaining reorganized, hurling bricks and Molotov cocktails at the soldiers, who fired again. Overall, the civilians were losing ground, and the soldiers were advancing. Each burst of fire brought the army roughly ten meters closer to Tiananmen.

Far from the frontlines, we just heard the gunshots growing louder. By the time the army had reached a position near us, the shots sounded like the crackle of beans in a hot frying pan. The soldiers were directly south of us at the intersection of Nanlishi Road and Chang'an Avenue.

"They're here!" Someone screamed from atop the balcony, sending some of those down on the street into a panicked race inside.

"It sounds like rubber bullets!" Mr. Sun claimed, trying to calm us.

"So what? Rubber bullets make this OK? This is fucking fascism!"

Just then, someone else yelled, "Look! That's gunpowder."

We raised our heads to see a dark orange cloud rising through the night air.

"I think they're real," someone murmured. "I smell gunpowder."

I was wondering if I should go back inside. At that very moment, a black dot appeared on the horizon, barreling toward us. Then came another. And another... The dots grew larger and became rickshaws. They seemed like a cloud of black bats bursting out of a dark sky.

The first stopped at our corner, and the driver shouted for directions to the Children's Hospital. The main entrance was right down the street, but at this hour only the emergency clinic, hidden down a side alley, was open. We started answering, but our sentences were fragmented, confusing the driver. Mr. Sun bolted into action, racing forward and waving for the driver to follow. The first rickshaw disappeared down a small back street with the remaining ones not far behind.

In the dark, it was impossible to tell just how wounded the people in the rickshaws were, but it didn't look like the work of rubber bullets.

More shots rang out, but the sound was growing softer. Soldiers had broken through Nanlishi Road on their way to Tiananmen. They marched along Chang'an Avenue, further east, passing us by. Everyone felt dejected and resigned.

Mr. Sun returned, running across the intersection with the agility and precision of a soldier.

"So? Are they rubber bullets?" someone asked, anxiously.

"They're fucking real," he shook his head.

An unexpected roar of laughter erupted through the crowd. His detractors patted him on the shoulder, chiding, "What did I tell you? They're not gonna use rubber. Metal ones are way cheaper!"

"When the hell did you tell me that?" Mr. Sun angrily retorted. "You fucking liar."

They went back and forth like a group of gamblers reviewing their games.

In any event, we had our answer. Someone let out a yawn. It was late. One after another, we filed back into the building. Suddenly Qiao's mother screamed out:

"Qiao!"

Her voice had become more and more hoarse as the day went on, but the sound of her crying out for her son still had the power to drill through granite. I turned around to see her security detail had dwindled to one.

As she bolted across the street, I rushed over and joined the woman trying to hold her in check. I thought she was losing it again. She twisted around like a trapped animal, pleading with her captors.

"Let me go!" she shouted. "I saw him. It's him! Trust me!"

I surveyed the other side of the street where the group of people was still gathered around the flowerbed. All I could make out was shadows. How could she tell who was who?

"Qiao!" She cried again. This time, it was a cry of excitement, like a child who had found their adversary in a game of hide-and-seek. "I see you! Come out! It's alright!"

The flowerbed was the center of the garden. Several people, probably residents of the building next to it, sat at its edge. As her voice trailed, a solitary figure rose and began to walk towards us, crossing the street in a strange slow pace. It was Qiao, gliding, floating. His mother charged through the darkness, arms outstretched until she could touch the stained front of Qiao's shirt.

Her hands flailed wildly across his chest as Qiao walked on as if feeling nothing.

"It's not his blood!" his mother suddenly cried. "It's not his blood!"

Chapter 15

In under a Week

The next morning, Radio Beijing reported the Tiananmen Massacre.

Years later, a friend of mine told me that as he listened to the broadcast, he pulled his curtains tight and hid in the pitch black of his room. Rumor had it soldiers would open fire on any sign of life. Even a flick of a light switch could get you killed. He kept his radio as low as possible.

This is Radio Beijing. Never forget June 3, 1989: the most tragic event in the history of the nation's capital.

Radio Beijing was a shortwave station. Its signal was easily scrambled by electronic interferences. Machines in neighboring factories, streetcars, combustion engines, and even desk lamps could distort the signal. But that morning, the city lay in darkness, and nearly all modern conveniences stopped functioning. The sound of Radio Beijing was crystal clear.

Tears rolled down my friend's face.

I missed the broadcast. Gunshots continued until two in the morning, before a silence fell heavily upon the city. Exhausted, I couldn't help but doze off in the embrace of the blackout.

On any other morning, the crack of dawn would've brought with it the growing clamor of street cleaners, breakfast stalls, newspaper vendors, and bicycle bells. But on June 4, the street might as well have been a long-abandoned film set. Even if there were a few people, they didn't dare make a sound. No one wanted to declare to the world that they were alive. Being alive was a fact you better keep to yourself.

I slept till noon and awoke to see my grandmother perched on her bed, sewing away. I walked over to the window and saw that soldiers had taken the nearby intersection. They stood in pairs, back to back, in full uniform. Sun glinted off their guns and helmets. Unbelievable.

I dragged myself down the hall to the kitchen, basin in hand. People were gathered around the long, rectangular sink, arguing over the death toll. I took my time washing my face and brushing my teeth while listening intently. There were two stories. The first version of events was that the fight lasted through the night and ended with every student killed. Auntie Zhao, Min's mother, held fast to this story, and described the gore in vivid detail as if she'd seen it herself.

"Bodies were piled over bodies like a mountain. Blood rushed toward the drains like a river galloping toward the sea." She smacked her lips.

The second version was that the majority of students left the Square in peace. The ubiquitous Chen backed this story. She claimed to have seen thousands of students marching west past Sanlihe this morning. In their tattered clothes, they looked gaunt and malnourished. Heads were bowed in defeat. Last time she'd seen a crowd like that was in 1976 when refugees from earthquake-stricken areas evacuated toward the cities.

Chen's version was far more credible. Sanlihe was only a mile and a half west of our neighborhood. It was well within reason for Chen to trek over for peek.

"You've gotta be kidding me! Those brats are alive?" a middle-aged man shouted.

"They're miserable, but they're alive," Chen confirmed.

"I don't believe it! It's not fair!" someone else chimed in.

I rarely spoke up in the public kitchen. Everyone in the room was my senior, and in Chinese culture, seniority means superiority. Even so, it was shocking to find that these people didn't even want the students to escape alive.

"What do you mean?" I said, surprising myself. "Don't you want the students to live?"

"I saw it with my own eyes," Chen claimed. "Though I don't believe it either. Civilians were protecting the students, right? The military was butchering its way through every civilian in its path, right? You tell me. Why, when they finally reach the Square, would they simply let the brats go?"

Auntie Zhao chimed in, "Like I said, they all died! There's no way they lived through that."

"But I saw it with my own eyes," Chen insisted.

"It's possible that the government just let the students go," Xue contemplated. "They're still kids. I always said it wasn't worth defending the students."

"What the hell? People paid the ultimate price and the students just get off scot free?"

"We don't know for sure," another smirked. "It's almost graduation. Maybe the only job they can get'll be hard labor in the countryside."

I could feel someone glaring at me as they spoke. Thanks to my grandma, the whole building knew I'd gone to Peking University. Plus, my sympathy toward the students alone made me stand out. I hastily ran a wet rag across my face before heading out.

At least I'd gotten some useful information out. Last night, people had thrown bricks at soldiers out of every tall building on Chang'an Avenue. Therefore, soldiers had started shooting at every open window. This morning, at Muxidi, a senior Party leader's son-in-law had been shot to death through a window when he turned on a light to brush his teeth. I faithfully relayed the message to my grandmother, who hurriedly shut our window. The June heat was growing more insufferable by the minute. Thank god we could leave the door open, bringing cool, and foul crosswinds from the men's restroom down the hall.

The last time we had to close our windows and hide in the corners. It was in 1972 when Richard Nixon visited China. The neighborhood registration officer passed orders door to door, threatening that snipers would shoot anyone who dared poke their head out a window. Seventeen years later, life seemed to have come back around. Nixon's visit opened China's doors to the world. Would those doors close in the wake of the crackdown?

As evening descended, my grandmother paced through the apartment, evaluating our chance of making it through the night. She decided my cot was too dangerous, as it directly faced the window, placing me in the line of fire. She declared I should sleep with her, and that I should take the spot closer to the wall. It seemed unnecessary, but I was touched. She put my safety before hers.

Moonlight shone through the thin curtain, casting a pale glow over my empty cot and part of the bed closest to the window. Supposedly, anywhere the light reached, a bullet could too. I told her to slide further from the window. She pushed herself into me, holding my shoulders.

She hadn't held me like this since I was twelve. She did it often when I was little, especially when I had a fever. Steeped in Chinese tradition, my grandmother knew every trick to torture a fever away: scraping the skin to bring "bad blood" to the surface, pinching the pressure point between the thumb and index finger... Every painful technique somehow made another pain disappear. Every time she administered one of her cures, I would scream like a stuck pig. Somehow, her cures always worked. When she thought I'd had enough and stopped torturing me, my illness magically alleviated. Still, I hated her for it. My body would be drenched in sweat, and my face wet with tears. I turned on my side, refusing to lay eyes on her. She would stroke my head, move down my shoulders, trace down to my arms and back. Her gentle, hypnotic touch would lull me to sleep.

I couldn't remember the last time we had been this close. It almost felt uncomfortable. I held her wrists and found the skin around them looser than I remembered. I placed her hands back on her chest. She let out a contented groan and drifted off to sleep.

She was lonely.

Who wasn't?

At seven o'clock on the evening of June 4, I turned on China Central Television news. The hosts, Du Xian and Zhang Hongmin, were dressed in black, looking solemn. Du Xian began reading a script that denounced counterrevolutionary riots and claimed military forces had emerged victorious. Du Xian's eyes welled with tears.

The hosts' silent protest had caught authorities off guard. Du Xian's reading lasted only a minute before the director cut them off. The screen went black. Du Xian's bleak voice continued over a blank screen with rolling captions.

The next day, Du Xian and Zhang Hongmin had disappeared and were replaced by Li Ruiying and Xue Fei. Xue Fei also mourned publicly, and he too was fired. Another host quickly replaced him. There were always more people willing to do dirty jobs.

It only took a couple days for the media to pull a 180, changing from expressing condolences for the fallen civilians to lashing out against their crimes. They accused the civilians of creating illegal blockades, surrounding and attacking military forces, beating soldiers with fists and bricks. A soldier was slaughtered and his body was hung from an overpass, lit on fire. Two more had been kidnapped upon release from the hospital and remained missing. Looters ran rampant throughout stores in Xidan, beating anyone who stood in their way.

If you say a lie enough times, it becomes truth. People's criticism of the government began to die under the weight of propaganda. They started to wonder if those dead civilians were actually innocent. Images of the soldier's charred body hanging from Chongwenmen overpass played ad infinitum on the news. A commentator screamed in furious condemnation:

It's not enough that they murdered this innocent soldier...They then felt the need to show off their handiwork, burning him and hanging him from a bridge for all to see.

In the public kitchen, hatred for the government was definitely cooling.

"These thugs have gone too far! They are sick! Sick in the head," someone said.

When the phrase "sick in the head" was brought up, the conversation turned to Qiao. "Do you think he could do something like this?"

His mother stood up abruptly, screaming that not only had her son not hurt a soul, but had taken it upon himself to help carry the wounded to the hospital.

June 7, at 11:00 in the evening, my grandmother and I were tucked in bed in a bit tighter than I would have preferred. Suddenly, I heard footsteps from the street, getting louder as they approached the building. Someone called out, "Stop! Stay where you are!" The footsteps made it just below our window when I heard a gunshot, and a body hitting the ground. A woman screamed. Several more shots rang out. I'd never heard gunfire that close.

My face and my grandmother's were centimeters away from each other. Neither of us dared utter a word, much less move a muscle. I gripped her hands tightly. Then came the sound of more footsteps... more shouts...more screams, and a woman's cries of pain. Had someone really got shot? A few minutes later, the street was silent again.

For a long time, we remained motionless like animals who'd narrowly escaped a chase. Perhaps hunters were still lurking.

I thought of Guo Yan. Was he at the Square when it all happened? It was likely, given his plan to take advantage of the media frenzy.

Was he still alive?

It was the first time I didn't question whether or not I loved him. Love felt like a trivial consideration compared to simply staying alive. I didn't love him anymore, but I still wanted him to live. I didn't want anyone dead, not even that poor soldier. His body burned until it shriveled up like overcooked pork. No one deserved that. But if Guo Yan was alive, he was probably scuttling around the city like a rat, digging up anything he could to fabricate heroic stories of the Liberation Army. What a shameless way to live. I had to find out how Guo Yan was doing. I had to know that he was alive and suffering.

Daylight came for the fifth time since the massacre. There was a strange buzzing outside. It was faint at first, like a swarm of mosquitoes, then grew to sound like a cloud of flies.

I needed to get to the restroom and opened our door. I peered down the hall to see several people standing outside the door to the restroom. Chen's face lit up as she saw me:

"Did you hear that last night? They killed a woman."

"I heard the gunshots, but I didn't know she died."

A look of disbelief came across her face. "You didn't see it?"

I said nothing.

"Come on, come on. Let's see go it!" She brushed past me on her way to our front door, poking her head inside. "Auntie!" she smiled to my grandmother, "good morning! Aye, your house is the best spot in the hall!"

My grandmother stammered, "Y–yeah, it's not bad."

"Can I look out your window for a minute? I'll be gone before you know it!"

Pure terror came over my grandmother's face. She turned white and shot out of the room like a bullet. We stood in the hall, shoulder to shoulder. Chen was followed by several other onlookers, all of whom bowed to my grandmother out of a mix of embarrassment and excitement.

Chen pushed the wooden-framed windows out into the open air, letting in a dense torrent of voices. My grandmother clutched her chest, looking as if she might faint. I rushed her to her bed, but she forced herself to sit upright since guests were present. None of them noticed her pale, sweat-soaked face.

"Let's go to the street and take a closer look," decided Chen. "We can't see anything from here, it's just a sea of heads."

Her followers were hesitant. Soldiers were on duty only a couple of meters away.

"With that many people down there, I'm sure it's fine," someone murmured.

"Let's find out!" Chen exclaimed, turning to me.

"My grandmother's not feeling well," I replied. Finally, everyone noticed the state my grandmother was in. "Auntie, we're so sorry to have bothered you. Please, rest up!" They ushered themselves out as quickly as they came.

The house was ours again, I walked over to close the window, when I glanced down to see the sea of heads Chen had described. The body was probably up against the wall below our window.

It wasn't long before our hall's reconnaissance team returned with findings. It was a young male factory worker who had gotten off late and was mistaken for a troublemaker.

The young man's tragic fate freed many residents from their homes. Even the most timid people who didn't even step out for food went to see the dead body. One after the other, daredevils returned unscathed, marveling at how friendly and pleasant the soldiers had become since last night's execution.

"The soldiers were actually really nice."

"Did you see the guy in the roundabout? He smiled at me."

It turned out the dead man was married, but he'd been having an affair with a nurse who worked the night shift at the Children's Hospital. Troops stopped them as they snuck back to her place. In the late '80s, if police saw a man and woman walking hand-in-hand in the middle of the night, they might ask to see their ID. If they suspected you were having an affair, you'd be taken to the police station and the leader of your work unit would be informed. He must have been scared, and took off running. The story made sense. A normal night shift worker wouldn't have run.

"What a pity. Why did he have to run? Is losing face really worse than death?"

"Hard to say. Maybe his wife is a tigress."

Everyone agreed it was the young man's bad luck.

Around noon, someone came to collect the body and the turmoil downstairs finally died down.

I took advantage of my grandmother's afternoon nap to leave the apartment. If she woke up and found I wasn't there, I could say I'd gone to the bathroom. I made my way straight out the front door of our building. What I saw on the street looked like any other day at first glance. The only difference was that the pedestrians looked like sleepwalkers.

I walked to the payphone near the alley leading to the back entrance of Children's Hospital. Countless wounded people had been carried in this same door on the night of June 3. After struggling attempts to open the narrow door, I squeezed into the booth and dialed the Metropark Lido Hotel, where Mr. Murata lived.

I told the operator the room number I wanted to ring. She asked who I was and "may I ask what this is concerning?" I'd called Mr. Murata many times before at his hotel, but this was the first time the operator wanted to know about my business.

The hold music was a simple, eight-bar loop over and over. When Mr. Murata picked up the receiver, the music was replaced by a heavy buzz. The monitoring equipment had been turned on.

I cleared my throat, "Hello? It's me! Wang! How have you been?"

"I'm well, thanks for asking!" His reply sounded enthusiastic, but still a bit broken.

"When are we headed back to work?" I asked.

"Monday," he replied, "but call me Sunday to confirm."

A massive weight lifted from my shoulders. Mr. Murata was still in Beijing. I still had a job.

I tried my best to close the door behind me, but it hung haphazardly in its frame like a kid's first carpentry project.

I saw Qiao walking in my direction. Our eyes met, and I saw that he'd returned to normal. His thousand-yard stare had been replaced by a lucid expression. "Hey, Wang Yan. Where you going?"

The name "Wang Yan" instantly brought back my childhood memory. I said as casually as when we were little.

"Nowhere, just making a call. You?"

"I'm heading to the hospital."

I remembered his mother shouting about him carrying a wounded man there in the heat of battle.

"Was that guy your friend?" I asked.

"Nah," he replied. "I'd never met him before that night. He had a super nice camera I'd never seen before and he let me mess around with it. Right as I was handing it back to him, he got hit. It could've easily been me. There were rumors that they were specifically targeting people with cameras."

I remembered the two incidents in which my camera had nearly been stolen. It seemed that in any time of violence, a camera was the enemy.

Though we had never done more than exchanging pleasantries in the past, he asked if I wanted to go with him. I thought for a moment and decided to come along.

We made our way down the alley to the rear entrance. We walked through the gates and found a notice posted on the wall to our right. A small crowd had gathered. It was a list of the dead.

Since June 4, countless families had begun to comb the city's hospitals looking for lost loved ones. Staff had found it necessary to post lists of the deceased. If the name of the person they were looking for tragically appeared, there was nothing left to do but claim the body at the morgue. If not, it was on to the next hospital.

I wanted to ask the name of Qiao's friend, but I was afraid to make a sound. There were several people standing before us, eyes glued to the notice. I could feel the anxiety from the back of their heads.

Qiao held his breath as well. He read the list from beginning to end, then again just to be sure. Without a word, he pulled my arm and we left, exiting the main gate in silence.

"You have some time?" he asked, once we were out on the street.

"Yeah, sure."

We sat down near one of the small flowerbeds next to the entrance. He took out a pack of cigarettes and offered me one. I didn't smoke, but I took it anyway. He smoked nearly halfway of his before saying, "I wanna go find him. You coming?"

"Are you sure he's still there?"

"He must be there. His name isn't on the list."

"Do you know his name?"

"I just know his last name is Guo. The list didn't have any Guos on it."

Panic ran through me. I put my cigarette out in the dirt.

"Sorry, I've got something to do," I said abruptly.

I ran back to the phone. In the back of my mind, I knew it was only a slim chance it was Guo Yan, but it gave me an excuse to call. Guo Yan had given me the number for the phone in the security room at his gated community. I had never called. Guo Yan said never to call unless it was an absolute emergency.

An old woman answered the phone. A moment later, I heard her shout into the courtyard through a megaphone: "Building 16, room 501, Guo Yan, you have a phone call."

Then silence. I heard the woman drop back into her chair, flip through the paper, and occasionally exchange pleasantries with passing residents.

The sound of footsteps grew louder, echoing as they entered the small, concrete room. "Auntie Liu, is someone looking for Guo Yan?" It was a young woman's voice.

"Yeah," Auntie Liu replied.

"He's taking a nap."

"Well, you answer it then."

The phone bumped against the desk. The young woman raised it to her ear, sounding like she'd received too many calls on her husband's behalf. "Hello? Who's looking for Guo Yan?"

Her gentle voice smashed all my fantasies about Guo Yan. I painfully realized that there was nothing real between us. As the guns rang out, a man only made sense if I could hold him in my arms. Otherwise, we are both empty words to each other. I hung up without a word.

It seemed like a miracle that life in Beijing had more or less returned to normal in less than a week. Charred military transports were pulled from the roads. Concrete pylons were now neatly returned to their rightful places. Shops, both small and large, opened their doors again, bringing the city back to life.

Chinese people have a tendency to bestow legitimacy to the victors. If you won, you chose how history would be written. If you lost, what was once called courage would be seen as recklessness, and righteousness became stubbornness. The fascists we'd cursed were now praised. "Go up against the Party? Yeah, right," people scoffed.

On Sunday, I ventured out again to call Mr. Murata, but the payphone was out of service. On my way home, I ran into Uncle Li. His face warmed, "Wang Yan! You don't look so hot. You OK?"

"I'm fine. Do you know where I can find a payphone?"

"You've been off work for what, a week now? Is your boss still in China?"

"I hope so. Last time I checked..."

He didn't wait for me to finish. "Min's always talking about how busy you are, and how you make so much money." The smile never left his eyes.

I felt there was a "but" coming.

"No way. I'm just a secretary."

"You're not just any secretary. You're a secretary for a foreigner," he said, looking over my head. "But you can't depend on foreigners, can you? One minute they're here, the next they're gone. And then what?"

He tilted his head slightly and narrowed his eyes. He acted casual, but was watching my every move.

He was upset because I'd missed Min's wedding. He felt I'd broken my promise out of arrogance.

I knew I was in the wrong, and I felt apologetic, but this was between Min and me. He wasn't entitled to any sort of revenge. However, he'd been patiently waiting for a chance to belittle me.

It just so happened that I'd had current affairs on my mind a lot lately, so I had my answers ready.

"Then what? Which way do *you* think China's going to go?" I asked. "Do you really think China's going to regress 17 years? Do you think you could handle being separated from your father again? Do you think Auntie Zhao and your two children are going to lose their Beijing residency? If you really believe those things are going to happen, then you can gloat."

He froze. I smiled and walked inside.

On Monday, I hadn't received word either way and decided to head to work. On the street, I could feel just how badly people wanted things to go back to how they were. A few were still madly searching hospitals for loved ones. It was said that one mother stumbled across her son's rotting corpse in a hospital garage a month after he'd passed. He was only recognizable by his belongings. But those unfortunate few could be easily overlooked. For most, the chaos of the past two months was nothing more than a bad dream. All they had to do was wake up and embrace a new morning.

From the moment the protests began, my world had revolved around Tiananmen Square. To a Japanese person, it was only a small part of a much larger picture. Since 1989, there was only one thing on any Japanese citizen's mind: consumption tax. Prime Minister Noboru Takeshita successfully instituted a 3% consumption tax after a series of hard-fought negotiations, but he was soon forced to resign following an insider-trading scandal. On June 3, Sosuke Uno was sworn in as the seventy-fifth prime minister of Japan, inheriting a broken government.

The four of us, Mr. Murata, Ms. Kawashima, Zhao, and I, sat together in the same room again.

"Japan changed prime ministers on June 3?" I couldn't believe it.

"Mm hmm," Mr. Murata replied.

Sosuke Uno stepped into office on the morning of June 3, and Tiananmen Massacre happened that evening. He barely had a moment to assess the situation. The next day, George Bush Sr., issued a statement declaring economic sanctions against China. Mr. Uno only condemned the Chinese government's use of weapons against its own people.

On June 6, nearly twelve hundred employees of Sanwa Bank, Sumitomo Bank, Nippon Life, Panasonic, Seibu Department Stores, Mitsukoshi Limited, and others fled back to Japan. The next day, Chinese military forces attacked Japan's Diplomatic Residence Compound and three Japanese consuls' homes were attached, scaring away nearly eighteen-hundred more Japanese.

Canon had requested that their employees do the same, but Mr. Murata and Ms. Kawashima resolved to stay. "We're even staying despite Mr. Murata's favorite bar closing down," Ms. Kawashima said with a wink. Clearly it was less the cocktails, but more the waitresses. I couldn't have cared less. There was nothing in the world left to laugh about, but I thought it best to play along. It really meant the world to me that they stayed behind. The least I could do was pretend Ms. Kawashima was funny.

Lunchtime came, and Mr. Murata suggested we all head downstairs to the hotel's Chinese restaurant—his treat. At the touch of a button, the elevator whisked us off to the first floor without stopping. We marched into a vast, empty dining hall, where a dozen idle waitresses suddenly snapped to attention, bowing as we walked in.

The massive hall was able to seat three hundred, but currently held only one Western couple. They were quietly eating near the window as tanks rumbled down an otherwise empty Chang'an Avenue.

As we took our seats and picked up our menus, Mr. Murata told us to each order our favorite dish. He'd never been considerate like this before. Normally he just ordered for everyone. Although Mr. Murata was putting on his best front, his voice had the tenor of a swan song. Any meal could be our last together.

Simply by chance, I opened my menu right to shark fin stew.

I had a classmate in elementary school whose last name was Huang. An aunt on his father's side lived in America, but his father had cut off all communication with her when anti-American sentiment reached a fever pitch in the '50s. In the '70s, following in Nixon's footsteps, Huang's aunt visited China for the first time in well over two decades. She stayed at the Beijing Hotel and invited her brother and her nephew to lunch at the hotel's restaurant.

She ordered many delicacies, among them, a steaming bowl of noodles and shredded pork. When the noodles were placed on the table, her eyes lit up, "I've been dreaming of this for so many years."

Huang was ecstatic too. Pork was his favorite. At a time when meat was rationed, a ten-year-old boy could never get enough. But even in all his excitement, he was too self-conscious to eat the shredded pork for fear of appearing greedy. Instead, he declared war on the noodles. These were not normal noodles. They were oddly short, slippery, and really hard to pick up with chopsticks. Each translucent strand only made his longing for meat stronger. He cleared through every last noodle as fast as he could to quell his craving for that mouthwatering pork.

His aunt was dumbfounded. She gathered herself up and remarked, bemusedly, at how much her nephew apparently loved eating shark fin. It was then that his father realized, with no shortage of embarrassment, that his son had devoured a bowl of shark fin by mistake.

According to Huang, his father had planned to ask her to take his son to America, hoping he'd have a better life, but after the shark fin incident, they simply said their thanks and left.

Though I'd never tasted shark fin, a wave of nostalgia overtook me. My strong feeling wasn't about the delicacy itself, really. It was about the end of an era. To me, Huang's aunt symbolized the start of reform and opening up. Now that China was threatening to close its doors, I'd better taste that legendary shark fin before it was too late.

"I'll have the shark fin soup," I said.

Zhao scoffed. "Shark fin? Are you serious? It doesn't even taste like anything!"

I blushed, "I wanna try it. What're you getting then, genius?"

He ordered duck in consommé.

The waitress left and we chatted over steaming cups of tea. Another line of tanks rumbled by, or maybe the ones from a few minutes ago simply made another pass. Either way, these were on our side of the street and rattled all the china in the dining room as their treads tore up the pavement. The Western couple at the window could hardly look away. One of them whipped out a camera. I could tell by the way he moved that he wasn't a journalist. Surely they were tourists; two of the very few who'd stayed behind out of pure curiosity.

Just then, the tanks stopped dead in their tracks and one swung its turret directly into the dining room. A waitress let out a terrified scream and the dish she was carrying went crashing onto the carpet. Her dress was covered in what was to be the couple's lunch. All of us ducked under our tables.

The seconds passed like hours. Finally, the china above our heads began to clatter again. The tanks were on their way. A young man, apparently the manager, came to our table, bent to meet our gaze, and assured us we were safe.

As I climbed out, I saw a look of shame on Mr. Murata's face. He was our leader, but he had cowered in fear like everyone else. The manager apologized and informed us that both the shark fin soup and duck were slow-cooked dishes which had to be ordered two days in advance. The restaurant had been a ghost town for days, and was down to just the basics. "If you'd like some Yangzhou fried rice..."

"Actually, that's perfect," I replied. "Maybe it's a good sign. If I can't eat shark fin, that means Mr. Murata can't leave, right?"

Mr. Murata smiled.

Chapter 16

Force Majeure

When Bush Sr. imposed trade sanctions, seven European countries followed suit. Simultaneously, World Bank, Asian Development Bank, and countless others froze China's lines of credit, bringing trade to standstill.

The Beijing Hotel became a ghost town. Long-term commercial leases took a dive and tourist stays were near zero. Some staff worried about the future, while others were happy that their cleaning duties had been reduced to an hour per day. Yang was the latter. Whenever I called the service desk and got a busy signal, I would go out to find a service clerk in person. Most of the time, I would find Yang slouched behind the service desk, listening to the phone with a distant look on his face, occasionally mumbling, "Uh, huh" with a slight nod.

My job still included mailing advertising materials to potential customers. Armed with my trusty stamp holder, I slipped into the empty elevator. The pre-recorded female voice gently announced "going down," just as it always did, but the "n" seemed to reverberate endlessly, as if the elevator were dragging me down into a bottomless pit.

In its heyday, the lobby had been the hub of the hotel. Just out of the elevator was a bustling sea of people. Businessmen in crisp white shirts scuttled from one client to the next. Tourists, accompanied by a near-constant squeak of sneakers, were herded onto buses. Backpackers pointed at maps while bellhops struggled to keep up with what was being asked. Foreign journalists waited out front for their drivers.

Today, the lobby was empty except for one stout man lounging on couch. His sharp eyes darted around, and the newspaper in front of his face looked like a prop. In a far corner of the lobby, two more men stood next to the "Employees Only" sign by the back door. They were most likely National Security, but who or what were they spying on?

In Mid-June, I needed to cash a check at Bank of China. I called a taxis lined up outside. On hearing where I was headed, the man made no attempt to hide his annoyance. He'd probably been waiting at least an hour hoping for a fare to the airport, not some girl too lazy to walk a couple of blocks.

Though the bank was only blocks away, I didn't feel safe walking back with a bag of cash. I reassured him in a fawning tone, "Can you wait for me and bring me back?" Round-trip plus waiting was always more profitable than a one-way trip.

Placated, he switched the meter on. The trip was embarrassingly short. We were there in less than five minutes. I reminded him to just keep the meter running.

I climbed the bank's neoclassical steps and went in the heavy front door flanked by six towering, stone pillars. I was the only customer.

The hall felt cavernous. Every step echoed off the high ceiling.

A woman I knew sat behind the window. She was in her thirties and kept her naturally curly hair impeccably cut. We'd always exchange pleasantries. One day, as she cashed a check for me, a tall, slender foreign man sauntered over and told me in English how beautiful I was. I thanked him. The teller warned me in Chinese, "Be careful. That guy's been standing around in here for an hour. He says the same thing to every girl." I smiled. From then on, I felt like we were allies.

But today, I didn't even get a comment about the weather. It was as if she'd never seen me before. I handed her the check and uttered, "I'd like to cash this please." She silently took it and produced a bound stack of cash, tore the seal and fed it into a cash-counter. Finally, she picked them up and bound them again, sliding the stack through the window.

My driver was less than thrilled, "Already? Great..." He hadn't had time to finish a cigarette.

On our way back, we stopped at a red light on the east side of the Square. Our car was the only one at the intersection. I thought back to when I was a little girl sitting on the front steps of my grandmother's building, watching the traffic lights click back and forth on empty streets.

"Fucking Bush!" the driver suddenly growled. "Who does he think he's punishing? Asshole thinks he's punishing China's government, but all he's doing is ruining our lives!"

"I'm not sure we can put it all on the sanctions," I rebutted. "There are tanks roaming the streets. Who wants to visit China under martial law?"

"Nah...people still wanna come. Hell, they probably wanna come even more just to see what all the fuss is about. Americans love China. It's their fucking president that demonizes us." His declaration sounded straight out of propaganda.

The light turned green and he stepped on the gas, heaving a massive sigh, "It's already the 15th, but I haven't even made one-sixth of my rent. I owe the taxi company two thousand a month!" He was in a very different position from Yang, who received his monthly salary no matter what.

Just hours after the blood of the innocent spilled through the streets of Beijing, Solidarity scored a major victory in Poland. One side of the world cried out of rage, the other out of joy.

I kept wondering if our failure inspired their success. Up until Poland's June 3 election, polls had shown the Communist Party in the lead. That same night, the Chinese Communist Party turned its guns on its own people. Solidarity swept Poland and shocked the world. Communism in Poland was dead. Could it be coincidence?

Every communist regime is built upon the premise that the government represents the downtrodden and the oppressed. When China's communist rulers butchered their own people, did other communist nations not learn anything? I read the news of Poland with a mix of joy and jealousy. I had no idea my anguish would peak five months later when the Berlin Wall fell.

Warrants were issued for the arrests of 21 student leaders. Their images were looped on state television, printed in newspapers, and plastered on walls all over the city. Scores of activists were arrested. Some went into hiding. Fang Lizhi and his wife Li Shuxian snuck into the American Embassy, seeking asylum, leading to yet another international incident. The US Embassy was considered American soil. The Chinese government had no authority. China, however, vowed not to let them slip so easily.

Fang Lizhi was an astrophysicist. In 1984, he became vice president of the University of Science and Technology of China. The 1986 movement that spread through Beijing schools had, in fact, begun with Fang Lizhi. On December 4, 1986, he addressed the students at a mass assembly, saying "Democracy isn't 'handed down' from above. It's fought for from the bottom up!"

In spring of 1987, after the fall of Hu Yaobang, Fang Lizhi was removed from his position and demoted to a research position at the Beijing Observatory. A few months before the passing of Hu Yaobang, Fang wrote "China's Despair and China's Hope," an essay published in Hong Kong. It's English translation by Perry Link appeared in the *New York Review of Books*.

"China's Despair and China's Hope" addressed the Party head-on. It argued that China's transition to a market economy couldn't take place without establishing democracy. That essay became my very heart and soul. I admired Professor Fang and regarded him as one of very few in China who prescribed the right medicine for China's problems.

Fang and Li remained in the US Embassy until June 25, 1990, when Chinese authorities allowed them to board a U.S. Air Force C-135 transport plane to Britain. For the entire year they spent in hiding, the diplomatic district was heavily patrolled. Ms. Kawashima's residence, the Yong'an Apartments, was within the diplomatic district. It wasn't uncommon for Zhao to be stopped for inspection when he drove in the vicinity alone, but he'd never been stopped when Ms. Kawashima or Mr. Murata was with him, which was interesting.

One evening, he was ordered to open his trunk for a canine search. Everyone has their weakness, and strapping, six-foot-tall Zhao's weakness was dogs. He trembled as they eyed the car and its driver. The next day, he ranted, "Your teachers are crooks. They sent students to their deaths, then go running for the embassy."

Fang Lizhi wasn't my teacher, but Li Shuxian, was an assistant professor at the Department of Physics at Peking University, and could be considered a teacher of mine in a peripheral sense. "First of all, it was the government that sent soldiers to kill the students, not the teachers. Second, are they supposed to just throw their lives away too? They have as much of a right to protect themselves as anyone else!"

I felt somewhat obligated to defend them, but deep in the recesses of my heart I felt betrayed by Fang and Li.

It was as if China was a home ruled by an abusive father. Our neighbors simply locked their doors, hoping that our father's hands would ache with regret if we just stayed isolated long enough. The older brother who promised to get us out had left us behind. Our family became a lesson for other families to learn from. They'd sit at the table, speaking civilly about how to be a happy family again.

I walked the hall between the east and central wings of the Beijing Hotel. The already spacious passage felt endless. I passed the coffee shop where Guo Yan and I had talked. On the table we'd sat at, there was a vase of plastic flowers. On Chang'an Avenue, a line of tanks happened by, leaving the plastic petals quivering.

Even in desert, water sometimes springs forth.

On June 11, seventeen-year-old Michael Chang, an American-born Taiwanese tennis player, came from obscurity to win the French Open, becoming the youngest men's champion in Grand Slam history. In his victory speech, he declared, "God bless each and every one of you, especially China."

Those few simple words sent a crack ripping across our obsidian sky. I was still connected to a world where human beings existed despite the machinations of a tyrannical government. Sadly, most of China never heard him. Government censors scrubbed his message from the face of the earth.

Our office plunged into a strange silence. One day, the phone rang, and I picked up the receiver, eager to greet. "Canon Beijing, what can I do for you?"

"It's me," said a calmly bemused voice on the other end. It was Zhi Hua.

"Where are you?" I asked.

"I'm at home. In Tianjin."

"When're you coming back?"

"Fall semester, if there's a school to come back to."

"Of course there will be," I said reassuringly. "If I make it out to Tianjin, I'll let you know."

"Sounds good."

She hung up. Long-distance calls were expensive, and every word meant money. She had said more than she needed to say. She wanted to make sure I was OK, and she knew I wanted to know she was OK. My life meant something to someone. This thought lifted my mood considerably.

Red terror continued to propagate. Images of student leaders on the run flashed endlessly across television screens. Military forces patrolled city streets, simply to remind people who was in control. Economic growth slowed to a halt. Inflation, previously soaring, finally began to settle, bringing down the prices of goods. An export-driven economy with nowhere to export to was a terrifying proposition, but to the average person, it felt long overdue. Never mind the tremendous wave of unemployment that was sure to follow, seafood, without a foreign port to go to, cost half what it did yesterday. The intoxicating aromas of fish stews and fried shrimp wafted down the halls of my grandma's apartment at all hours of the day. I could finally buy the silk pajamas I'd coveted for months in the hotel gift shop. A third off and I could just pay RMB instead of dealing with that pesky foreign exchange nonsense? Sold. I'd deal with tomorrow when it came.

Once an oracle for all things Chinese, Mr. Murata's fortune telling skills had taken a turn since the nation fell to chaos. He had been positive that the government would never open fire. As the opening shots rang out through the June 3 sky, I thought Mr. Murata's career in China would be history. About this, I, too, was wrong. The city was in the midst of civil war. The streets held more soldiers than citizens. Who would headquarters find to replace him? It would probably be far easier to just let him continue his job. Ironically, Mr. Murata's position was more secure than ever.

Ms. Kawashima wasn't going anywhere either. Zhao told me that she'd been assigned to Beijing because she'd pissed the wrong person off back home in the first place, and in Mr. Murata she'd found pretty much the only Canon boss who would work with her. Besides, she received plenty in stipends for living in a foreign country. It was a far higher income than what she'd received in Japan.

As televisions outside China were flooded with images of

blood-soaked streets, foreigners who dared to stay behind were treated like gods by China's government. As long as you weren't a foreign journalist who asked the wrong questions, or a misguided humanitarian attempting to harbor student leaders, China would welcome you with enthusiastic arms. People like Mr. Murata and Ms. Kawashima were fawned over, since they were there simply to keep the wheels of commerce rolling.

Endless calls began to pour in from Dalian's Economic and Technological Development Zone, before delegations began to appear in person. They were doing everything they could to ensure that Canon continued constructing their assembly plant in Dalian. The investment was worth billions of Yen, and would create five thousand jobs. Plus, it would boom other industries, like import-export services.

Usually placed on harbor-adjacent land for the sake of logistics, Economic and Technological Development Zones are areas in which foreign companies enjoy a multitude of preferential treatment and policies. The wildly slashed taxes, coupled with discounted prices on land were too much for Canon to resist. Though Japan had announced sanctions against the Chinese government, private industry was free to do as it pleased. But the protests at Tiananmen, and the government's brazen display of force had understandably left the company wondering whether it wanted to invest in a country so unstable. The higher-ups in Tokyo needed to be reassured, and the assurance of officials in Dalian wasn't enough.

In recent years, Mr. Murata had established relationships with numerous members of China's elite, but recently he had upped his efforts. He and Ms. Kawashima went out to lunch for business almost every day. One day, just before lunch, a man entered the office unannounced. He couldn't have been more than 5'4", with a long nose that made him somewhat look like a Westerner. His sudden appearance jolted Mr. Murata from his seat. He made a beeline for the man, shook his hand enthusiastically, and exclaimed, "Mr. Yang!

What a pleasant surprise!"

The unexpected guest took a seat on the sofa, and Mr. Murata set about showing him the latest cameras Canon had to offer. There wasn't a person who'd ever been to our office that wouldn't kill for a chance to get their hands on the latest Canon cameras. Mr. Yang, however, remained stone-faced. He listened quietly, occasionally picking up a camera and inspecting it for a bit before setting it back on the table.

"I'm curating a photo exhibition," he stated. "If you have any interest..."

"Of course!" Mr. Murata said eagerly. "When is it?"

"You doing anything right now?" Mr. Yang asked.

"Nothing that can't wait."

"Then let's go." Mr. Yang stood up.

Mr. Murata told Zhao to bring the car around. Mr. Yang protested emotionlessly, "No need for all that, just come in my car."

With that, he simply walked out. Mr. Murata and Ms. Kawashima were hot on his heels. As he passed, Mr. Murata asked me to cancel his lunch appointment using whatever excuse I could find.

I waited until they were out of earshot before asking Zhao who on earth Mr. Yang was.

"He's the head of the Chinese Photographers Association," Zhao replied.

A few days later, Mr. Murata handed me a pile of papers and instructed me draw up a press release. The Chinese Photographers Association was organizing a photography competition, and Canon had assumed the role of official sponsor.

Zhao leaned over to me and whispered, "Remember that photography guy with the big nose? Figured it out. He's Yang Shangkun's son."

Yang Shangkun was one of the Eight Immortals of the Communist Party, and vice-chairman of the Central Military Committee. His younger brother, Yang Baibing, was secretary-general of the Military

Committee and commander-in-chief of the operations upholding martial law. In other words, the order to "clear the Square" came straight from Yang Baibing.

Canon was in contact with the commander-in-chief of the massacre. I felt betrayed again. A much bigger betrayal than that of the professors did to me. Sure, I hadn't stood with the students, but I had a basic understanding of what justice should be. It didn't matter how badly organized the protests were, or how naïve the students' demands. They didn't deserve to die.

My face stayed sullen for days. Mr. Murata noticed before anyone else and tried to cheer me up by reminding me that Japan needed China as much as China needed Japan. The two countries may have their disagreements, but in the end, their economies were inseparable. Neither country would benefit from China going down.

"Ms. Wang, if Canon were to leave China today, where would you work?"

"I'd go back to Pecan."

"Pecan is a joint-venture between Founder Group and Canon. If Canon is forced out, there's no Pecan."

"OK, then I'll go back to Founder."

"You think Founder would survive? Their only customers are corporations, government offices, schools, and newspapers. After Zhao Ziyang's failed attempt to break the price ceiling, those entities have severely limited their spending. Founder was already in trouble before the protests, as far as I know."

"Well, whatever, I'll teach at Peking University. I still have school work permit."

"Oh really?" he exclaimed, genuinely puzzled by my confidence.

"You think you're actually a Peking University staff member? Come on. That's just a title they gave you so you could get a job with Founder Group. If China returned to a planned economy tomorrow, and Founder went under, no one at that school would recognize your status."

"OK, so what then? They'll just throw me out in the street?"

"Oh, Ms. Wang," He chided, "that mentality of yours really is the product of a planned economy."

There was nothing more to argue about. I knew what he meant. If the country went back to its old ways, there was an entire generation left stuck between two opposing economic systems. We were the sacrificial lambs for the failed experiment.

I wanted China to become a free market just as much as he did. I hoped Canon would never leave. I wanted to wear dazzling business suits with matching shoes like Ms. Kawashima. I wanted a house, a car...But did that really mean I had to make good with filth like the Yangs?

I quelled my concerns by convincing myself that the photographer had nothing to do with the Party's violent oppression. It wasn't his fault he was the nephew of the man who pulled the trigger.

He was of less consequence than his father and uncle, just as I was less important than Mr. Murata and Ms. Kawashima. All I could do was refill Mr. Yang's tea during his visits. All I could do was write a press release about the upcoming competition. If I didn't want to, there were a thousand in line who would be more than happy to.

I worked hard to convince myself I was unimportant. I was a mere speck of dust under the starry sky. If I didn't consider myself responsible for the tragedy or its aftermath, I could go about my work free of guilt. But thinking myself inconsequential didn't lift the weight from my heart, it only made me more indignant and resentful. I'd always felt under pressure living in this country. Its oppression was intended to mold me into a tiny screw to be installed in the great machine of dictatorship. It was intended to make me negligible as a person. And now, it had succeeded.

No, I told myself. *I'm going to be human.* I'm going to take responsibility. I don't know what and how yet, but I must take responsibility for something. I'll find something only I can do. I'll identify some change only I can make. I will be of consequence.

"Don't worry," said Mr. Murata. "In time, truth and justice will win out, but for now, there's never been a better time to do business in China. The government has no choice but to repair relations with the West, and it's willing to do just about anything to make that happen."

A few days later, he explained the dilemma to me, "China makes Western countries nervous because only one man calls the shots here. Who gave the order to quell the student rebellion? Deng Xiaoping. Who gave the order to reform and open up the entire country? Deng Xiaoping. Do America and its allies want Deng Xiaoping to step down? Not really. The whole Tiananmen incident represents the sheer magnitude of the power struggle between Deng Xiaoping and his adversaries. If those adversaries rise to power, it would completely throw the whole train in reverse."

"Do you mean Bush prefers Deng Xiaoping over his opponents?"

"I guess so."

"Then why the sanctions?"

"They have to at least look like they're in line with the principles of democracy."

"So, what you're saying is..."

"If the West has no choice but to accept the unfathomable idea that China is a dictatorship with a booming free economy, they will. And by the time they do so, Canon will already be miles ahead. It'll take America and its allies years to catch up."

I had nothing to say.

"But don't worry. Democracy will come along, as long as Chinese people continue to amass wealth. If one day, China had a middle class of 10 million people, it would only be a matter of time until democracy came about. Imagine 10 million well-educated, hardworking people just like you."

I felt flattered.

Our office was scheduled to move to the new China World Trade

Center by January 1, 1990. It was supposed to be Beijing's first world class, state-of-the-art commercial complex, containing five office towers, two apartment buildings, two hotels, and a shopping center. The office towers alone had over 3.4 million square feet of space. From the moment I first came to Canon, Mr. Murata had promised that just one more year, and we'd finally have a real office. One with no bed marks in the carpet, no bathtub in the bathroom, and a massive open workspace behind tall glass doors with the Canon logo proudly engraved on them. There'd be a meeting room with an electronic whiteboard and projector. Everything would be custom made and imported from Japan.

"Take a look at this catalogue. I want to show you the chairs I ordered for the meeting room. They look nice, right? I'll let you in on a secret: they're really not that comfortable. People fall asleep in meetings if the chairs are too cozy," he said with glee.

We laughed and we were as excited. I imagined I'd wear smart business suits like the models in the Canon catalogs, and deftly give customers presentations on Canon's latest and greatest.

In mid-August, a sales representative from the CWTC paid a visit to Mr. Murata. The company was a joint-venture between a domestic partner and the Guo brothers from Malaysia. The sales offices were run by the foreign side, and mainly staffed by Singaporean and Malaysian Chinese employees. Fluent in both Chinese and English, their every word had been thoroughly rehearsed.

"Mr. Murata, I regret to inform you that due to force majeure, completion of the China World Trade Center will be delayed by at least six months."

"What do you mean by force majeure?"

"Unforeseeable circumstances."

"I know that. I'm just not sure what unforeseeable circumstances you're referring to."

"It's a rather well-known event. I'm sure you understand what I'm refering to."

Mr. Murata did not.

With no other choice, the representative slowly and methodically explained:

"Mr. Murata, the bulk of construction was completed in May, but during the unfortunate incident back in June, several panes of glass were damaged by...martial law enforcement. Each piece is imported from France, and made to order. We've pressed the factory for replacements, but due to the trade embargo, things have been a bit tricky. We sincerely apologize for the inconvenience."

Mr. Murata was speechless.

A few hours later, Mr. Murata, Ms. Kawashima, and I piled into Zhao's car and headed to the construction site about four miles away. Today, Bejing's Central Business District easily rivals Manhattan or Ginza, but in 1989 it was a wild frontier. Once populated by long-abandoned factories, the district hugged the city's Third Ring, outside of which was little but overgrown grasslands.

I'd memorized every inch of that building from the brochures. Our thirty-three story, glass-encased home would be one of the tallest buildings in Beijing, second only to the Jingguang Center. Jingguang Center was skinny and awkward looking, though of record height. The World Trade Center, in comparison, looked grandiose and dignified because its architects had found a better balance between its height and width.

Zhao brought the car to a stop, and I found myself face to face with the building of my dreams. Everything was exactly what I had hoped it would be. On its thousands of panes of glass, blue skies, white clouds, and the nearby Third Ring combined to form a kaleidoscope of colors, with occasional dark spots disrupting its otherwise perfect exterior.

The dark spots on its façade were panes of glass that had been removed. According to the sales representative, they'd been shattered by bullets. Soldiers had shot at open windows because they'd perceived a threat, but why would they shoot up a glass wall? This was vandalism.

Mr. Murata crossed his arms and inspected the building itself, the surrounding area, and the vehicles that flitted in and out of the construction site. His investigation complete, he announced his assessment: The broken glass was an excuse.

While the exterior had indeed been completed, the interior was another matter. Electrical and plumbing were infinitely more time consuming, especially for Chinese workers who were inexperienced with a project of this size. The workers were far behind schedule, and the company was facing a slew of contract violations. Like a gift from the gods, Tiananmen massacre became their excuse.

"Look there," Mr. Murata pointed to the building. "Curved panes of glass like that have to be custom ordered for sure, because each pane is shaped differently according to its position. But it really only effects the few offices they're in front of. It has nothing to do with the overall safety and function of the building. Why would they need to postpone the move-in for six months? They're throwing away half a year's rent for an entire building this size? I don't believe that for a second."

I sported my wild guess, "Maybe those holes did some critical damage? What if the air pressure inside isn't safe?"

"Then they'd cover up the holes with whatever they had handy. Why leave them like that? It's for us to see, that's why."

"Why don't we go in?" I suggested. "Maybe they're in there right now, putting the final touches on things."

"You can't just walk into a construction site. You need to make an appointment. And I guarantee they wouldn't allow it. You've seen how good they are at excuses," said Mr. Murata.

He was right. They denied his request.

And little did we know the Beijing Hotel would turn cutthroat when renegotiating our lease. They raised our rent by fifty percent. The hotel figured that Canon wasn't going anywhere in the short term. They had to milk those extra six months as much as they could.

"What a bunch of crooks!" Mr. Murata exclaimed, his face was crimson with rage.

"Force majeure," "unforeseeable circumstances," "It's well known..." Everyone could see right through those empty phrases, but there wasn't a thing anyone could do about it. China had entered a new era where outright lies could effectively stop further questioning, and things wouldn't stop getting worse if you stopped pursuing the truth. Doing that could set off a chain of events far beyond anyone's imagination. For almost thirty years, the sight of that towering glass building had been stuck in my mind, same with the black holes that littered its otherwise gleaming surface. Those weren't any ordinary black holes. They were seeds that could grow into massive chasms that would suck in any object, or any amount of light.

Chapter 17

Goodbye, Grandma

In June, I got a call from a college classmate I hadn't seen in months. His name was Lian. He worked for a paper founded by the All-China Federation of Returned Overseas Chinese. He asked if we could meet. I suggested Yuetan Park, as it was about midway between my grandmother's apartment and his office.

At 6pm, I stood at the park's north gate watching one of the gardeners tidy up. There was nothing interesting about him. I just needed to look somewhere. Suddenly, he turned to me and his eyes shot daggers from under his massive straw hat. I felt uncomfortable and wondered if I'd stared too long. The city was still on edge, and you didn't just stare at someone without reason. I quickly turned my gaze to the steady current of cyclists on the street, though I couldn't keep from stealing glances at that gardener. Was there something off about him, or was it just me? It was almost 6:30. Since when did gardeners work night shifts?

Finally, I saw Lian far off in the river of bicycles. Back in school, he was president of the Chinese Department Student Union, and was known as a stalwart crusader for his fellow students. He looked to his left, then his right, and flashed me a small grin. I briskly turned and headed into the park as he struggled to keep up.

As he lifted his slight frame off his bike, it seemed that the events of recent months had knocked him down to size a bit. Perhaps it had done the same to me.

Lian had always been a vivacious, charismatic character, but the Lian who stood before me was a broken man. His face had gone gray with worry and exhaustion. I asked if the events at Tiananmen had affected him badly. "Of course they have," he answered. "Who haven't they affected?" His work unit had begun forcing its staff to write detailed reports of their whereabouts from April 15 on, down to the hour. At first it seemed a simple enough task. He'd been to Tiananmen, but only a handful of times, each at the request of his editor-in-chief. What was wrong with that?

But there's something wrong with anything, if you look at it hard enough. Suppose one of his coworkers claimed to have seen him in the square on a certain day, while he failed to mention it in his own report. No one would believe he'd simply forgotten. For the past month, he'd been walking a fine line, attempting to stay away from traps and avoid entrapping others. It was exhausting, having to trust blindly in others without coordinating anything.

In the end, he was cleared of any suspicion, but was still instructed to hand over any documents having to do with Tiananmen. He had collected many flyers and pamphlets sent out by various student organizations. Those were precious documents, and he planned to write a book after all this was over, but he had nowhere to hide them. With three to a room in the dorms, privacy was a myth. So, he thought of me.

He pointed at the back of his bike, then he produced a manila envelope nearly bursting at the seams. I took his precious cargo solemnly and marched home.

Soon, it was my turn to be subject to review. Little to my knowledge, Pecan Inc. had already been undergoing political review since mid-June. The entirety of Pecan's Chinese staff was made up of Peking

University graduates, which out them at the top of the government's hit-list. The only reason I'd been left out until late July was simply that I'd been overlooked.

"Several meetings have been held here," the HR person called me, chuckling. "Pecan was just about to announce that the company was in the clear, until we remembered you." I was to report to the company's headquarters in Zhongguancun the following afternoon.

At lunch, the next day, I left the Beijing Hotel on an empty stomach, and set out for Pecan headquarters. I took the #103 trolley, in hopes that it would buy me a few minutes as it wove through the old part of the city.

I was in the midst of an intense internal debate. Should I tell them about my multiple trips to the Square, and the pictures I'd taken for Canon? Unlike Lian, there was no one to check my story against. Mr. Murata and Ms. Kawashima were Japanese, and therefore off the hook. Zhao worked for FESCO, and had no obligation to answer to Pecan.

I'd only made one mistake. It was the photo I'd published in the *Chinese Journal of Photography*, on which a salesman from Pecan named Zhang and his younger brother appeared.

In and of itself, the photo wasn't really an issue, but in post-Tiananmen China, everyone had to prepare for the worst. They would ask if I'd only been to the Square the one time. It would seem odd that I just happened upon an old classmate the one time I'd gone to the Square. Plus, where were the other thirty-five shots from that roll? The whole thing was one endless ball of string. The more they pulled, the more would unravel. I would have no choice but to come clean about the photographs and faxes to Tokyo.

I needed to keep my mouth shut. But what if Zhang had already told them everything? On the other hand, if Zhang had said nothing, my confession would drag him down. It was a typical prisoner's dilemma.

The trolley was a smart choice. Since it went through the densely populated old city, each of its stops was only a couple hundred yards from the last, and the trolley never even got up to speed before it had to slow down again. Due to its low efficiency, it was hardly the most popular line in the city. I could actually sit by a window.

A month had gone by, and the drab olive of military garb had become part of the landscape. Soldiers were no longer coldly patrolling the streets, machine guns in hand. They had woven themselves into the fabric of the city with friendly gestures. Near Beihai Park, several soldiers swept the sidewalk. At an intersection close to Baita Temple, another helped an old woman across the street. They all wore huge inviting smiles. They were bending over backwards to win back the community they had set about butchering only a month before.

Beijing had bought the narrative that its residents raised rod and stone against a peace-loving military, and we were now reliant on that same military for a sense of normalcy.

Should I or should I not confess about the picture?

I hated myself for not using a pseudonym. My classmate at the journal had even asked if I was sure I wanted to use my real name.

"Why not?" I asked. "I want people know it's my work."

I could see my father, shaking his head with scorn. *I told you this would happen.* He would have said.

I thought of Teresa in Milan Kundera's *The Unbearable Lightness of Being*. She bravely captures the seething crowds of the Prague Spring, and passes the film off to foreign reporters. Later, when her photos are published abroad, the secret police use them as evidence in their efforts to cleanse her country of dissidents. The book may have been set in late '60s Czechoslovakia, but my reality and that of the book seemed to merge into one another.

Around two in the afternoon, I arrived at the Pecan offices outside the east wall of Peking University. The neighborhood, Zhongguancun, was an odd mix of residential and commercial buildings that hosted a cluster of high-tech companies backed by nearby universities. The area had become known as "China's Silicon Valley," but after the crackdown, it was a ghost town. Some heads of companies had fled the country after assisting the students in various ways.

I'd gone over my options a million times. With neither option particularly preferable, I decided to stay put and see how things played out. I opened the towering glass double-doors and wandered into the main hall. The mid-afternoon sun was swallowed up by the dusky, lightless room. Against the wall was a display of the company's latest computers and printers. A meeting was taking place in the middle of the hall. Each employee struggled to force a look of interest. I saw Zhang. He was looking at me too, but he looked away as soon as I looked at him. Was he pretending we hadn't met? Or had he already spilled his guts and felt too ashamed to look me in the eye? I found an empty chair, took out my notebook, and like everyone else in the room, I pretended to take notes.

During a break, I ran into Zhang in the tea room. "Wang Yuan!" he exclaimed, as if seeing a long-lost friend. "What're you doing here? You never come out here! Those Japanese...they're strict, huh?"

"You said it. They really know how to exploit a worker."

"Last time you called, you said something about a newspaper? Which one was it again?"

I took the cue, "Ahh, yeah, I was asking on behalf of an old classmate. He's an editor, and the paper he works for was looking to upgrade their systems. I was gonna send his business your way, but with all the investigations, everyone's busy answering questions. Who knows when things'll get back to normal?"

"No worries, just remember me when the time comes! I'm their man!" he smiled.

The assistant manager, who happened to be in the finance department next door, overheard our conversation. As I passed by, he flagged me down, "Ms. Wang! You work on the Japanese side. I'll bet you know about all kinds of customers we never hear of. If you have any leads, you'll let us know, right?"

"Sure thing!" I answered.

And that was the extent of the investigation. I returned to the hotel, wrote my hour-by-hour account of my whereabouts, then faxed it over. The matter was settled. I was off the hook. I chalked it up to my quick wit and superior intellect. Only later in life did I realize it was pure dumb luck. Just because they were given an order to shoot, didn't mean everyone actually tried to hit their target. I was lucky that leadership at Pecan didn't seem at all enthusiastic about knowing every detail of everyone's life.

One evening towards the end of July, I sat at the desk in my grandmother's apartment and opened the lower left-hand drawer to find my bag was missing. The bag held Lian's documents, all the pictures I had made off with, and a copy of the *Chinese Journal of Photography* I wished had never existed. In a panic, I flung open every drawer in the desk. It was nowhere to be seen. I tore through my grandmother's dresser. Nothing.

I stood in the middle of the apartment, eyes darting left and right. My grandmother sat on her bed, pretending to mind her own business. It wasn't like her. Usually, I couldn't look around for even a full minute without her asking what I was doing.

"Did you see my backpack?" I asked her.

She thought for a moment, using a sewing needle to scratch her head, before ambling out, "Ahh yeah, I forgot to tell you. Lu Hua came by today. She had too much stuff to carry when she left, so I let her use it."

"What about all the stuff that was inside?"

"The stuff inside?" she blinked, looking perplexed.

"Yeah. Papers. My papers," I was near the end of my patience.

"Was it anything important?"

"Yes, they're important. Why else would I care?"

"Aye, what would I know? I can't even read."

"Where'd you put 'em?!" I was an ant in a frying pan, and the oil was starting to bubble.

"I thought it was waste paper. I sold it to the recycling guy," she replied casually.

"What?! Waste paper?!"

Everything went black. "What the hell could that even be worth? A few cents? Do you need money? Why didn't you ask me for it?" I screamed.

"Aye," she sighed. "You know I can't read."

She'd always been ashamed of the fact she couldn't read. Now she was wielding that fact like a weapon. I was indignant, and done with being polite, "You couldn't wait till I got back? Or do you not know how to read a clock either?"

She hung her head. I could see my words had hurt her.

"OK, I get it. If I do anything, I need to ask you," she declared as she mechanically climbed down from her bed. She headed for my desk, opened one of the drawers, and pulled out a small rectangular package about the size of a box of matchsticks.

"What's this?"

My face flushed red with both embarrassment and rage. It was a box of condoms.

"Who the hell are you to go through my bag?!" I screamed.

"Hmm? Did I do something wrong?" she asked, smirking. "At least, I didn't sell everything."

She opened the box, took out a clear, plastic pouch, and held it up to the light for further examination with a strange sarcastic smile across her face. "So what is it then? In all my years, I've never seen anything quite like it. I guess I haven't seen it all!"

It was quite possible she'd never used one, but she knew damn well what it was. I ran out of the house, and headed for the office, where I laid awake all night on the couch. I knew I could never go back, but where could I go? I'd have to rent my own place, which couldn't happen overnight. That left me only one option: the Pecan employee dorms. When morning came, I called the company to see what was available. All of their double rooms were occupied. My only option was to pay for a double room but live there alone. If a suitable roommate came, we could split it fifty-fifty.

"I'll take it. I'll move my things in tonight."

On my way to my grandmother's to collect my things after work, I couldn't help but wonder if I was overreacting. Yes, she'd humiliated me with the condoms, but the condoms were mine. If I thought there was nothing wrong with me to having premarital sex, I wouldn't feel humiliated. What exactly went wrong here?

Why she had to go about it like that? She knew she was in the wrong for selling off the contents of the bag. The condoms were her strategy to fend off my accusations. She assumed that when I was confronted with evidence of sexual activity, I would be at a loss for words, and wouldn't be in a position to comment on her behavior. It was straight out of the Party's playbook. Whenever the Communist Party wanted to bring down a political opponent, they first described him as a person without morality living a depraved life. After all they had put her through, she was no better than them. That was why I couldn't live with her together any more.

I'd made up my mind to leave. Still, I couldn't help but hope I'd return to a sobbing mess, wracked with grief over my disappearance, like every other time I'd been late. But this time, nothing. Her eyes were dry as a bone as she looked right at me, emotionless. I had to make the first move, "I've just come back for my things."

"Mmm, if it's too much for one trip, you can always leave some here and get it later."

"The second I'm out the door, you're gonna sell everything that's not bolted down."

She shrugged, showing no desire to start a new battle. Her refusal to stoop to my level only made me seem more irrational and desperate.

I left my key, and dragged my two suitcases into the dark hallway. She put down her sewing, walked me to the door, and turned on the light outside it. My heart ached. That light was the only difference I'd made for her during my stay. I didn't look back, but I knew she was watching me. After I rounded the bend in the hall, she turned the light off. And with that, I was gone.

In early September, I received a call from Lu Hua. She was in town to meet with a folk art and handicraft store at Wangfujing. Knowing I wasn't far, she called to see if I was free for lunch. I knew Lu Hua wasn't the type for Western food, so I suggested we go to Donglaishun, a traditional hot pot restaurant, my treat.

As I read the menu, it struck me that it wasn't quite as traditional as I'd remembered. According to legend, hot pot was invented by Mongolians with limited ingredients out on the prairie. At a traditional hot pot restaurant, the food on the menu was strictly lamb, rice noodles, cabbage and tofu. My jaw dropped when I saw the seafood on the menu. It was a sure indicator of influence from cuisines of southern provinces.

The waitress quickly recommended prawns as the daily special. I thought I'd misheard her when she told us the price. "How can they be that cheap?"

"Originally, the prawns were all headed overseas, but as I'm sure you know, most orders from foreign buyers have been cancelled."

Lu Hua sighed. No doubt her business was feeling the pinch as well.

"Then we'll have the prawns, as well as the lamb, rice noodles, cabbage and tofu."

The waitress brought out a pot of broth, and returned with our bowls of dipping sauce. That's the great thing about hot pot: you never have to wait for the chef to cook your food.

Through the mists of our steaming cauldron, I asked how business had been. She sighed again, "I don't really wanna talk about it."

"OK then, let's eat!"

Well into the meal, she suddenly blurted out, "I was intending to take *you* out today. I want to apologize."

"Apologize? For what?"

"If I hadn't borrowed your bag, your grandmother never would have found all that stuff. She asked me if I thought it was dangerous, and I couldn't lie to her. I told her that nothing good could come of it. You know that's true. Still, I should never have opened my big mouth. As soon as I said that, she burned all of it."

"She burned it? She told me she sold it for recycling!"

"Aye, there I go again. I need to learn when to shut my mouth."

"That's OK," I replied. "Burned...sold...what's the difference?"

The ends may have been the same, but the means couldn't have been more different. If she admitted she'd burned them, I would've immediately known she'd destroyed them on purpose. If she sold them, she could pretend she didn't know what she was selling. Maybe she cared about me more than I'd initially thought. Maybe she'd never wanted me to go.

"I stayed with her last night," Lu Hua said, interrupting my train of thought. "She talked about you the whole time. She misses you. You should go see her when you have a chance."

"I'll try."

"Do you think you'll ever move back in?" she asked.

That was a good question. My new living arrangement meant I spent three hours a day just getting to and from work. It was definitely true that life with my grandma was way easier. But there was also the downside: even if we forgave each other and I ended up moving back in, I'd live in constant agitation, fearing that she'd simply set fire to anything of mine she didn't understand. What kind of life was that? Besides, it had taken me 23 years but I was finally free. I could do whatever I wanted in my own home. There was no looking back.

I shook my head.

"Well, if you're not going to, I think I'm gonna move in," she replied. "I can look after her. If anything major happens, I' can let you know."

"You're gonna live with her?!" I asked, unable to hide my shock. "What about your business?"

"Import-export is pretty much impossible at the moment. All factories have stopped production. I'm better off just moving here and finding a job."

She picked up a prawn and studied it, before setting it back down. "I can't eat that," she declared. "Now that I know it came from a canceled foreign order, I just can't."

I couldn't shake the feeling Lu Hua had engineered my falling out with my grandmother.

Still, I didn't want to be too hard on her. Her business had been struggling, and my job was as stable as they got.

After lunch, Lu Hua asked if she could get some more Canon brochures. Even if China's import-export industry was frozen in place, she still wanted to keep up with the rest of the world. On our way back, we passed the entrance to a hutong. A crowd had gathered to watch a soldier try and back a massive military truck through two trees with only inches of clearance on either side.

The crowd silently took pleasure in the soldier's frustration. "Ah, he's from the countryside," someone muttered. When the poor guy misjudged the gap and slammed the truck into the trees, the crowd came to life. "I told you," someone hissed, "he has to be from the countryside."

They laughed, clicking their tongues in disapproval.

When we finally reached a less crowded area, Lu Hua suddenly grabbed me by the shoulders, and asked in an anxious whisper, "Did they really kill people?"

No one who lived in the city would ask such a question. Lu Hua lived three hours away by bus. It saddened me that truth couldn't overcome even a distance that small. I didn't know how to respond. A simple "yes" wouldn't justify the gravity of events. After a struggle, I answered as directly as she'd asked, "Yeah. Of course."

I felt she only half believed me. "If you don't believe me, ask my grandmother. They killed someone right underneath her window. Or go to Dabeiyao and look at the World Trade Center. Our company can't move into our new offices because soldiers shot out a bunch of windows."

We passed soldier after soldier, undercover cop after undercover cop, until we reached the Beijing Hotel's barren lobby.

As we rode the elevator to the eleventh floor, Lu Hua was quite verbal about her enchantment with the hotel's opulence. I accepted the praise with casual grace, though she'd secretly scratched my ego right where it itched. I opened the door to the office and poked my head in to see who was around. I had no desire to introduce Lu Hua to anyone. The plan was for me to sneak in, grab her a couple of brochures, and sent her on her way.

To my surprise, I opened the door to find a cake on the living room table, which Ms. Kawashima was happily dividing into slices. Mr. Murata called out, "Ms. Wang! You got back just in time! Get in here! Have some cake!"

I looked back at Lu Hua.

"Bring your friend! Come on in!"

We went in together, when I noticed someone else in the room in addition to our usual four, a man who looked familiar. It took me a moment to recognize him as the man from headquarters that Ms. Kawashima swooned over. The one who looked like an older version of Hideki Saijo. I should have remembered his name, but my brain refused to function.

It must have been his birthday. I would have known if it were one of ours.

"Whose birthday is it?" I asked gleefully, hoping that someone would say his name.

"No one's," Mr. Murata explained, "Canon just broke ground on the Dalian factory! We're celebrating!"

"That's amazing! Congratulations!" Lu Hua blurted out as Ms. Kawashima handed her a piece of cake.

"You have room for that?" I asked.

"Either way, I'll give it my best shot!" she exclaimed with a huge smile.

"Ahh, see? That's the attitude! I like her!" Mr. Murata proclaimed, giving her a thumbs up.

What was it with everyone? First my grandmother, now my boss? Was there a single person who didn't like her more than me? I ate my cake like a sulking child.

That afternoon, I stole away to the public bathroom on our floor and stepped on the scale. I had gained five pounds in three months.

The China World Trade Center, Beijing, China.
Photo by Prasit Rodphan

Chapter 18

The Ringside Seat

I'd moved into a dorm building that Pecan leased from Peking University's affiliated middle school. The middle school was tucked away in a modest-looking hutong, overshadowed by the nearby Haidian Theater.

New school years usually started in September, but as early as August 10, students lugging suitcases began appearing on buses as I was heading home from work. School was starting early to make up for classes missed in May and June, which meant Zhi Hua must be back as well. I wanted to look her up, but somehow found myself in no hurry. The middle school was about a mile and a half from Peking University, and getting home had turned into a grueling, two-hour ordeal. I wasn't eager to add another thirty-minute walk. It was only ten minutes by bike, but I hadn't owned a bike in years.

With a room of my own, I didn't have to head to the office on Sundays anymore, but having total freedom severely dampened my sense of urgency. Every Sunday morning, I had the same debate with myself. I never could decide whether I'd get more done in ten hours at home, or six at the office with four spent commuting. No matter which option I chose, I wished I'd done the opposite when evening rolled around.

One Sunday in September, the conflict raged on as always. I decided to stay home, but a couple hours later I regretted it. I emerged from the front door of the dorm and stood facing an empty football field. The students who headed home on weekends wouldn't be back until after dinner that night.

Since June, I hadn't stared at a vast open space. Now, gazing down that seemingly endless field, I felt as if my soul came untethered and went soaring up to the heavens like a balloon cut loose. Fall is the best season in Beijing. The cloudless sky was as clear as a pane of freshly-cleaned glass. My head was spinning. I thought of Zhi Hua. I had to see her. Today.

We agreed to meet at the campus convenience store. It was on the middle of a path between my old dorm, Building 31, and the Triangle. We each bought a yogurt and sat at a small table near a window.

It had been almost six months since we'd seen each other. There were plenty of other things we could have talked about, but it wasn't long before the conversation quickly turned to the morning of June 4. Zhi Hua said that that morning, students who had occupied the Square began returning to campus with news of bloodshed. Rumors began to circulate that soldiers would soon strike the school itself, and arrest anyone in their path, regardless of involvement in the protests. It sounded like a mass execution of the student population. The school's administration was paralyzed. The staff was in no position to guarantee anyone's safety, though nothing could stop teachers from protecting any student they could. The entirety of the student body decided they had no choice but to flee. Zhi Hua followed suit. But there was a problem. Beijing Train Station was right next to Tiananmen, and there was no way they could get around the checkpoints.

In the end, they figured out a route that would bypass the Beijing Station. Almost every passenger on the train was a student. All of them wanted the same thing: to get out of the city alive. When the train's whistle wailed, they breathed a collective sigh of relief.

Someone started singing "L'Internationale," and before long, the entire car joined in.

"'L'Internationale'...Can you believe it?" she asked with a bitter smile.

Of course I believed it.

Voices echoed through the car as they left the gray shades of Beijing for the vast emptiness of the North China Plain. Along the tracks, an old country road came in and out of sight.

"It's a tank!" someone shouted, sending waves of terror through the train. Most ducked for cover, while a few peered outside. It wasn't a tank at all, but merely tracks that one had left in the asphalt. Everyone stopped singing, as if they wanted to swallow up every word they had uttered.

It was years later that I realized what Zhi Hua's story meant. Most of the students on that train were nowhere near the Square when the massacre happened, but even seeing tracks left by a tank was terrifying. From then on, images, written words, even pronunciations of tanks would trigger nightmares. The incident had hijacked our brains. Our generation would never raise our voices in protest again. Not in twenty years, not in thirty years, not in our lifetimes.

I looked out the window toward the path running to Building 31. The window was spotless, except for a spider weaving a web in a far corner.

"It feels like a hundred years ago," I sighed.

"Yeah," Zhi Hua sighed in kind. "Let's not talk about it anymore."

I agreed. My yogurt was gone but I still sucked at the straw mindlessly.

After a brief silence, Zhi Hua said, "I want to go to America."

"I thought you always wanted to go to America."

"Yeah, but now I can't wait. I'm applying as soon as I can."

Her master's was a three-year program. She wouldn't be finished until 1991. It didn't make sense to apply now.

"We can study for the TOEFL and GRE together. We can keep

each other on track," she suggested stridently.

I agreed without hesitation.

But hesitation came knocking later that evening. If I wanted to register for the TOEFL or GRE, I needed permission from my employer's HR department. I might as well broadcast to the whole company that I was planning to leave. What kind of boss kept employees who weren't going to stick around? Even if Mr. Murata somehow didn't fire me, what would happen if I got no offers from America? I'd be the laughingstock of the company.

Zhi Hua had a similar problem. After the Tiananmen incident, the school stopped giving permits for the exams. It was clear they were afraid of students fleeing overseas en masse. Her parents had managed to get her a permit through their connections in Tianjin. Since it was issued in Tianjin, she had to take the test there.

We started out in the same boat, but at the first sign of storm, I chose to stay onshore. Zhi Hua, however, persevered. From then on, she continued to overcome her fair share of obstacles while mine seemed to overtake me. Our roads in life would never again intertwine.

On the morning Zhi Hua took the TOEFL, a feeling of unease crept over me. I arrived at the hotel early, headed to the post office downstairs, and sent her a telegram wishing her good luck. She probably wouldn't get it until she got home. Besides, it might have only served as a distraction.

The telegram did nothing to ease my restlessness. I still needed to do something more provocative. I sat down and wrote a letter to Guo Yan's wife.

It was short and sweet:

A few months ago, I had an affair with your husband.

I left it unsigned.

I knew their address, but I also knew Guo Yan would recognize my handwriting, so I had Zhao write the envelope for me. With my masterpiece complete, I made a second trip to the post office.

One day passed, two days, three...Time went on and I still hadn't heard a thing. Did the letter simply disappear into thin air? Could she really not care?

Two weeks later, Guo Yan finally called, "You really did your good deed for the day, didn't you?"

"Huh? I don't know what you're talking about," I said demurely.

"I know it was you who wrote that letter. You think you're smart not signing it, but I know it was you."

I kept silent.

"I really misjudged you. I thought you were a decent person. I never would have expected this from you. And getting a man to write the address? Genius, I have to admit. I handed her the fucking letter myself, joking that some stud must have written her a love letter."

I couldn't help but chuckle.

"I really was fucking blind, wasn't I? You're a fucking devil!" he screamed before he hung up the phone.

I was satisfied. His wife would never let him forget about me.

I'd missed my chance to take the TOEFL with Zhi Hua, but that didn't mean I had abandoned my American dream. I had taken the exam before as a senior in college, and I'd scored pretty high. That score would be valid for three years. As long as I could do well on the GRE, I'd catch up.

Then October came, and with it, more distractions. The Dalian factory opened, and two new FESCO employees joined our team. Both were recent graduates of the Department of Japanese at the Beijing Foreign Language Institute. One was a young man with the last name Gu, and the other, a woman named Liao. As the company welcomed new employees, Mr. Murata welcomed a new woman into his life. He got married.

His marital status was supposed to have nothing to do with his work, but he changed noticeably. Before, he would disappear the second he got off work and whisk his girlfriend off to any number of romantic restaurants. After he sealed the deal, he often got the entire office to work overtime before treating us to dinner. Ms. Kawashima explained that in Japan, if a married man came home immediately after work, he would be met with his wife's scorn. It signified he had no real importance within the company. No married Japanese man would ever dare come home early, or even on time. Instead, they either sat in the office counting the ceiling tiles, or opted to go for dinner and drinks with coworkers in the same predicament. I'd never heard anything so ridiculous in my life. Ms. Kawashima agreed, and said she had no intention of marrying a Japanese man for that exact reason.

At least twice a week, Mr. Murata's predicament became all of ours. If someone was in town from Tokyo, Hong Kong, or Dalian, we would all go out to dinner in the name of treating our guest. If there wasn't anyone in town, Mr. Murata would call up anyone who had something to do with Canon.

In every seemingly ridiculous situation, there is always something that ends up making sense. It turned out Mr. Murata's constant parade of dinners actually benefitted the company. Over the course of conversation, the unexpected would occasionally come up, like new developments surrounding the unending problem of "wet goods:" a term I'd never heard before it floated across the table one evening.

In 1980s in China, the southeast coast was home to a massive smuggling industry. Large ships would come from abroad loaded with products sealed in plastic bags, which smugglers would throw into the shallows. Small skiffs would head out from land, collect the parcels, and take them to shore, hence the name "wet goods." It later became an umbrella term for any and all goods smuggled in to avoid tariffs. In the late '80s, no small number of Canon products on the Chinese market were smuggled. The main office in Tokyo couldn't say the exact number.

One evening, Mr. Murata called up Mr. Sun, the manager of Canon's designated repair shop two streets over, and invited him to wine and dine. Over dinner, Mr. Murata asked how many people had brought in cameras for repair last month, and how many had a warranty card in their name? Based on Mr. Sun's answers, Mr. Murata could piece together a rough picture of just how rampant smuggling problem had become. It proved that Chinese ownership of Canon cameras was far greater than official exports. It was said that these numbers were crucial to the headquarters' decision to open one more plant in China.

I'd been at Canon for over a year, but my Japanese hadn't gotten any better. Ms. Liao's arrival meant I had a personal translator who could hear any juicy tidbits exchanged between Mr. Murata and Ms. Kawashima. Mr. Gu, however, had no enthusiasm our gossip. He wore immaculate, striped shirts, and perched haughtily in his chair, shooting us the occasional standoffish glance.

"What are you wearing?" I asked. "I love the print."

"This?" he replied, pointing to his shirt. "You don't know Junko Koshino?"

The next time he wore a similar shirt, I commented, "More Junko Koshino! I love it!"

He shook his head, as if saying one cannot make a carving from rotten wood. I guess it wasn't Junko Koshino. It looked same to me.

One day, Ms. Liao told me she'd overheard Mr. Murata and Ms. Kawashima talking about the annual budget. Mr. Murata said that we hadn't reached even 70% of our spending goal for the past 10 months, and if we couldn't find a way to spend money faster, who knows what paltry sum the head office would allot us next year?

Ms. Kawashima placed blame squarely on the Tiananmen protests, to which Mr. Murata replied, "By the end of the year, no one will even remember that. All they'll think is that we don't need much money to run this office!"

"Well, let's take the office out for karaoke then," Ms. Kawashima suggested.

There was a lot to unpack, but the detail Ms. Liao stressed was: "We're going to karaoke soon. You'd better start practicing."

In 1989, karaoke was high-end entertainment only found at four- or five-star hotels. December came, and just as Ms. Liao had forecast, we started going to karaoke after dinner. The first time we went, I was petrified and didn't go near the mic. By our third visit, I'd gathered up the courage to give it a try.

Karaoke never ended before eleven, which was well past the end of bus service. I needed to take a cab each time. Dinner and karaoke were on the company's dime, but how I got home was up to me. We always went out to the eastern part of Beijing, where most foreign companies and embassies were clustered. It cost me at least 20 RMB to get back to my dorm on the other side of town.

In early 1990, China's Ministry of Education announced another new regulation: any graduates who planned to study abroad before working in China for at least six years had to pay a "cultivation fee" to get the necessary papers. This move was intended to curb China's massive loss of educated workers after the Tiananmen crackdown. The fee was calculated by the number of years of higher education a person received. With a four-year degree, the fee was 10,000 RMB. With a master's, you paid an additional 12,000 RMB. 10,000 RMB in 1990 could sustain an average family for five years. My parents only made five hundred a month combined. I made that much myself, but it would still take twenty months of living on the street without food before my fee could be paid.

Each time, as I exited through some hotel's shiny automatic doors into the chilly night, a wave of regret came crashing down on me. What was I doing with my life? I was wasting time I should spend studying. I was wasting money I should be saving to buy my freedom. As my cab whisked me away down the long, empty streets, I watched each occasional flicker of life as it disappeared into the void.

On January 11, 1990, martial law was officially lifted. It had been so long. I honestly didn't even notice it anymore. I felt more puzzled than relieved. When in the last six months had martial law effected me? On all those cab rides home after karaoke, had I been under someone's watchful eye every time?

At some point in the spring, Guo Yan called to tell me that he and his wife had separated.

"Ha! Again?"

"It's for real this time. We've started our divorce paperwork. We just can't hand it in yet."

According to him, it was just a matter of time. His wife's work unit was going to assign housing to its employees, but only married couples were eligible. The two had no choice but to remain married on paper until the apartment was in her name. For the time being, she still appeared to live with Guo Yan, but he'd been kicked out since he was, as he put it, "the guilty party."

"Guilty party." He took great care to emphasize that phrase, as if to remind me of my part in the crime.

He was studying at the Party Cadre School. He'd be staying there for the next six months.

"Study hard," I replied coldly. "After you graduate, I bet you'll make editor-in-chief at your newspaper."

"Nah, it's not even for that. I just needed somewhere to stay, and the school had an opening. I gotta say, it's pretty nice. Everyone gets their own room. You should come see me sometime."

"You get a whole room all to yourself? Wow! Have nice dreams!"

In March, I heard Zhi Hua had been accepted to Cornell. The news settled over me like a chill on a winter day. It was the first time I didn't feel even a shred of happiness for the success of a friend. I felt excruciating envy. It wasn't only because I wanted what she'd earned. It was also because she'd had the discipline to do the impossible, step by step, exactly as she had planned. I just sat back and did nothing.

One evening, I drank a bit more than I should have at a company dinner. I thought of her in my cab home. I was puzzled by her persistence and my complete lack of it. I slouched and stared out the window for a moment before realizing something: Zhi Hua was a literary scholar. After the Tiananmen Massacre, Chinese academia fell under the Party's tight control again. If the Party asked her to pronounce my name as "yuan", she wouldn't dare point out the character even had another pronunciation. Her entire academic career would be at stake if she stayed in China. But that wasn't the case for me. I was in the private sector. I lived more comfortably and freely than most citizens. Why would I give that up?

Sure, America was great, but the only way for me to get there would be to pursue a PhD. If I chose that path, who knows how many years I'd stay ensconced in the idealistic world of the academy? In China, I had a ringside seat, but in America, the best I could hope for was to watch from the nosebleeds. In that drunken haze, this was how I rationalized my decision to stay put.

If Zhi Hua wanted to go to Cornell, she'd have to withdraw from Peking University—a decision that seemed risky. If her plans to head for America fell through, she would end up without a master's. But she wasn't afraid of burning bridges. In April, as the first spring flowers opened their petals to the sun, her application to withdraw was approved. Her next step was to move back to Tianjin, where she would apply for her passport. The day before she was set to leave, she asked me if I knew of anywhere that had a VCR she could use. She'd borrowed a copy of the movie, *The Unbearable Lightness of Being*.

"What's the rush?" I asked. "In a few months, you'll be in America. You can watch whatever you want."

"I got it for you," she replied. "I know it was adapted from your favorite book."

I tried to think of a person who might have a VCR. The only one I could think of was Guo Yan.

I called and asked if he had access to one. He said his school had a rec center with a VCR and anything else we could use, even karaoke. "You can come by anytime," he said.

"Are you sure they'll let us watch it there?" I asked.

"Of course. They don't care. The Party's not as uptight as you think. Besides, if we're gonna guide the minds of the people, we have to know the minds we're guiding, right? Anything the people like to watch, we need to watch too."

When evening came, Zhi Hua and I took a bus to the Central Party Cadre School. From the street, it looked no different from a normal university, but this school was only for Party workers and propagandists to study Marxism and other communist theories. That was why the school's students were mostly in their 30s. There was a giant stone standing guard at the school entrance. On it were six gilded characters which read: "Central Party Cadre School of the Communist Party of China." The characters had originally been written by Jiang Zemin, who'd been hand-picked by Deng Xiaoping to replace Zhao Ziyang after the Tiananmen Massacre. It was said Deng was a great appreciator of Jiang's style of governance. In particular, he praised the way Jiang had quelled the attempted uprising at Shanghai's *World Economic Herald* without spilling a single drop of blood.

Gao Yan gave me detailed instructions on how to get to the rec room. When we arrived, we found a woman in her late 30s waiting for us. She introduced herself as Wei. Guo Yan and the others had gone to attend a lecture at Qinghua University and would arrive in half an hour. She was here to help us set up. Zhi Hua tried the tape in the player. It worked fine. Wei suggested we get more chairs out of the storage room in case we drew a crowd.

I felt a tap on my shoulder as I was carrying a chair into the rec room. I turned and found Guo Yan smiling back at me. I'd imagined what it would be like meeting him again. What if I saw him on the street, or riding a bus, in a theater, a bookstore? Each scenario had played out in my mind in full color, but when the moment came, I'd lost the ability to feel. Everything around me turned black and white.

I stared at him for a while before saying, "Ah. How come you're shorter now?"

"That's all you have to say to me?" he grimaced.

I thought I'd simply said the truth. Every time I revisited a place, it always felt smaller. I guess that was because I was still growing. But even if it was true, I didn't have to say it out loud. It was at that moment I realized I had a serious character flaw. In all of my past relationships, the only thing I'd been looking for was proof that I'd grown up. That was the fundamental conflict between my grandmother and me. She still wanted me to be the 12-year-old who'd cried her heart out when I learned I'd have to leave her care, but all I wanted was to show her that I'd grown to become a woman of the world. That's why my grandmother preferred Lu Hua to me. Suddenly, I understood. I put the chair down and held out my hand to Guo Yan.

"Nice seeing you again."

"Same here."

He took my hand and shook it. It was more than a friendly shake. Lust coursed through my arm and ran toward my heart, but it wasn't strong enough to be insuppressible.

We snuck outside to a small garden. I asked him how work was going.

"Good, I suppose." He didn't look very enthusiastic.

I decided to try and cheer him up. "I'm sure you'll get promoted after you graduate."

"Probably," he thought for a moment. "But what's the point? I've lost faith in the Party."

I understood why he felt that way. The nation had sunk into widespread depression after the Tiananmen Massacre. Everything was different after June 3. The freedom of speech we'd gained in the '80s, though scant, disappeared completely. That's why Zhi Hua had to flee to the States. But she was young, and spoke English. Guo Yan wouldn't be able to flee no matter how depressed he was.

"I was worried about you," I said, looking him in the eye. "I thought you might be at the Square that night. I called your house, but your wife answered."

"I knew that was you," he said. "I should have told you I was okay."

I felt tears welling up. "Do you know why I wrote that letter?"

"I know," he said calmly. "It was my fault not letting you know I was safe. Still..." he shrugged.

"I apologize."

"It's okay. My marriage wasn't working. It would've ended with or without you." He turned to me and grabbed me by the shoulders. I wiped away my tears, finally feeling somewhat absolved.

"I have a question," I said.

"Shoot." He looked at me expectantly.

"What happened in the Square between June 3 and June 4? If you were really there, what really happened?"

"I know what you're asking." He pulled me closer. "I didn't see anything close to a massacre. There were gunshots. Maybe a couple students got hurt or killed, but most withdrew peacefully."

"Really? Are you sure?"

"No, the Square is vast, and there was a lot going on," he paused, and sighed. "Don't ask me that kind of question, please."

"Why?"

"I haven't told anybody but you and her that I was in the Square that night. I don't want to become a witness for either side. I'd get attacked no matter what I say."

"But I saw casualties at Muxidi. I saw blood on my friend's shirt."

"Yeah. Whatever."

I stared at him, shocked by his indifference.

Guo Yan clearly had his share of grudges too. "Is that the only thing you wanted to ask me?"

309

I hesitated. Did I want to ask if he'd submitted his divorce papers? Did I want to ask if we could get back together?

"Let me think about it."

"Take your time," he said, letting go of me.

We went back inside and I introduced him to Zhi Hua. I hadn't told Zhi Hua about the affair. As far as she knew, he was just a friend. Guo Yan certainly knew a lot about her, which he made painfully obvious in the familiar way he spoke. Zhi Hua was certainly surprised. I could feel her eyes burning holes into the back of my head.

The movie was entirely in English with no subtitles. One person piped up: "What are they saying? How are we supposed to watch this?"

I didn't understand it either, but I'd at least read the book. I tried my best to recall the plot from memory and serve as a makeshift interpreter. It was a sad book and the film was no different. At the end, when Sabina receives a letter informing her that Thomas and Teresa had died, I couldn't help but cry. I choked so hard that I couldn't continue translating. Everyone stared at me, wondering what the woman was holding, and how it could have this effect.

I refused Guo Yan's offer to walk us to the bus station. As Zhi Hua and I left the Party School, I suddenly understood why I'd chosen to watch the movie there. I could've found another place. I only came here because I wanted closure with Guo Yan.

Now I'd gotten it. I'd decided to part ways, but I didn't feel any lighter. Nor did I feel the soaring sense of determination I'd expected. I felt skeptical and sad.

Zhi Hua and I took the same bus home. She'd get off at the south gate of Peking University, and I'd get off two stops later. It would be our last moment together for the next several years. I tried to say something meaningful, but everything that came out of my mouth felt forced. It was late. The bus raced along the empty street, and in no time, we'd arrived at the south gate. I watched her get off the bus. I thought of how in middle school, she left Tianjin for Qinhuangdao without telling me. At least I got to bid her farewell this time. But did saying goodbye really change anything? It was such an empty gesture. The bus started again and we waved mechanically in each other's direction.

From now on, I was alone. No friendships, no love, no grandmother. For better or worse, this was the choice I'd made. At a time when personal freedom was so limited, I'd managed to free myself from all personal attachments. I hadn't finished growing up, but I was close. I was determined to cover that last mile without any guidance, interruption, or accompaniment.

I took out my portable audio player and began playing Cui Jian. It was another April, another cruel season. Compared to last year, I felt I understood him more:

I just want to leave this place.
I just want to exist in space.
At the edge of this life I hover.
I just want to start all over.

Chapter 19

The Fleeting Nineties

When I think of my life in 1989, it's like film shot on a shaky hand-held camera and played back in slow motion. I can recall events day by day, even hour by hour. I can see myself clearly in every frame. But life picked up speed after 1990. Each year passed like a month, or even a week. Before I knew it, the 90s had come to an end.

For the first half of the nineties, I was only concerned with one question: between me and Zhi Hua, who'd chosen the right path in life?

Zhi Hua left in September, 1990. Since her departure, I went to the service desk every day to see if I'd received any mail from America. I knew if she sent a letter, it wouldn't come before October. She wouldn't write me the second she got there, and it took about two weeks for mail to travel across the Pacific. Even so, I couldn't help myself.

Canon Beijing was scheduled to move to the China World Trade Tower on Oct, 2. On the day of the move, Ms. Kawashima sent me over to the new office to ensure everything was in order while the rest of the staff packed things up. As I passed the service desk, it occurred to me that I should say goodbye to Yang. Though ultimately

I thought the ritual meaningless, many people out there think it a social norm. I stopped, found Yang, and said goodbye. He answered that I was always welcome at the hotel and handed me a letter.

"Is this the letter you've been expecting?"

It was from America and had Zhi Hua's handwriting on the envelope. It was thick and heavy. I put it in my coat pocket for safekeeping. I'd need time to savor every word.

I entered the magnificent lobby of the China World Trade Center. Everything inside seemed aglow. Each company's name was carefully engraved on a massive gray matte directory. There were famous companies from around the globe: Japan, America, Hong Kong, England, France, Italy, Finland...The list went on.

There was Canon. Suite 1403.

Up on the fourteenth floor, the elevator doors opened to a sea of people scurrying back and forth. Workers rushing to finish up collided with movers, who again collided with delivery boys with bright yellow DHL logos on their breast pockets. I headed straight for the bathroom and turned on the faucet. The water was running. Great. I unlocked the door to Canon Beijing and turned on the light switches. The ceiling lights came on. Great. I took out the phone I'd brought with me, and plugged it into a jack. Nothing. I tried another. Still nothing. This was exactly what Ms. Kawashima had feared, and the very reason I was here.

The customer service office sent a phone technician in hopes of solving the problem. After removing a white plate from the wall and poring through the wiring inside, he announced, "Well, here's your problem. The line's connected all wrong. That's the electrician's job."

He set out in search of an electrician, leaving the metal plate on the floor. Curious, I peeked into the exposed space, which was stuffed with a massive tangle of wires. Thick and thin, red, yellow, blue, and green. It was the exact opposite of my dorm which had a solitary cable that ran in through the wall from a meter outside, and snaked across my ceiling, where it powered the only light in the room. It was amazing. This office's walls, as white and bright as could be, had not a single exposed wire in sight. Instead, just behind that façade lay a complex nervous system of unimaginable proportions.

As I waited for the electrician to arrive, I sat in a corner and opened Zhi Hua's letter, which was three pages long, double-sided. She told me lots of details about her new life, where she was living, what food she was eating. "Do you know Americans have a kind of chocolate you can drink?" she asked. Of course I didn't know. What else? Was there anything about America you didn't like?

Her only complaint was that Cornell was in the middle of nowhere. It was so quiet she could hear her shoes bend each blade of grass as she walked.

I read her letter over and over to the point that I almost knew it by heart. I walked casually over to the edge of the office where there was a wall of glass stretching from floor to ceiling. The panoramic view reminded me of a scene from *Wall Street*, in which Charlie Sheen leans on the railing of a balcony overlooking Manhattan. The only difference was that my version of Manhattan was still a massive expanse of factories. From the fourteenth floor, it was a sea of wide, flat rectangles with drab yellow and gray roofs. I had no idea that in ten years, all this would disappear and Jianwai SOHO, one of the most expensive neighborhoods in Beijing, would rise in its place. In terms of which country had more going on, I'd definitely made the right decision.

I always saw our move to the China World Trade Tower as my formal entrance into the world of professionals, but I failed to foresee that that world would pass me by. Without knowing it, our office had been losing its foothold.

The Canon Beijing office was a transitional liaison office established when no foreign companies were allowed to manufacture or sell in China. Ultimately, we weren't responsible for anything important. 1989 saw the opening of the Dalian plant, then one in Tianjin, one in Guangzhou, then Suzhou. The Dalian factory manufactured printer cartridges, and answered directly to Canon's printer department back in Japan. Tianjin stuck to cameras, and had their own higher-ups to report to as well. With clear-cut management structures already in place, what was our office supposed to do? The final blow came when foreign manufacturers acquired the right to manage their own import and export. Our office had lost its reason to exist. In its place came Canon China Co., Ltd: a fully functional business overseeing research, manufacturing, marketing, sales and service.

Thus, the curtain fell on Canon Beijing, as well as on FESCO and FEC.

Mr. Murata and Ms. Kawashima had basically been needed solely for their language skills. The company felt they didn't have what it took to lead Canon China. They parachuted in an MBA from a prestigious US business school, but he didn't speak Chinese. Mr. Murata or Ms. Kawashima could've acted as his interpreter if they'd chosen to, but they didn't want to be subordinate to the new boss, and returned to headquarters in Tokyo. Ms. Liao became the new boss' interpreter and secretary. I had to prepare tea for both of them, even though she was one year my junior. I didn't like doing it, and always did so with a long face. One day, Ms. Liao asked me jokingly, "You're not going to poison me, are you?" I knew it was a joke, but it still shocked me. I chose to leave before either the new boss fired me, or Ms. Liao persuaded him to.

I found a job at a small Hong Kong company of about thirty or forty employees. The business acted as a sales agent for foreign engineering machinery. Salesmen made up roughly half of our staff. Each had his own defining characteristic. There was the joker, who overflowed with tall tales and saccharine flattery. The office fashion plate was always decked out in the latest business attire, and produced a brush every ten minutes or so to ensure not a single thread was out of place.

It had the dynamic, exciting feel of a startup. It was nothing like that gigantic, bureaucratic camera company. It was full of characters and stories, which certainly helped with my writing. I instantly felt at home.

I was hired as secretary to the general manager. My desk was right outside his office. Anyone who wanted to see him had to talk to me first. I may have looked important, but I didn't have any real responsibility. If someone called the GM, the call would go to me before I transferred it to him. If he wasn't in, I would take a message. That was all.

One day, the GM gave me a list and asked me to invite everyone on it to a meeting in his office. Two minutes before the meeting, a department head who wasn't on the list showed up. I tried to explain that she hadn't been invited, but she brushed me aside, walked right in and slammed the door in my face. After much hesitation, I sheepishly pushed the door open to find everyone sat solemnly around the conference table. The boss looked up and said to me coldly, "Why did you forget to inform her? You are not needed here."

The boss had tried to use me to marginalize her, but I wasn't cut out for it. The next day, I tried to apologize, but he wouldn't give me the chance. I was on high alert for days until an important customer came to visit. When I brought tea for the client, the GM introduced me to his guest: "This is my secretary. She graduated from Peking University." I was relieved that I had value after all.

Personal computers were still well out of my price range in the early '90s. I often stayed at the office after hours to write on the company's computer. One evening, as I was typing away in the empty office, the sales manager suddenly emerged from nowhere, clearly not expecting to see me.

"What are you doing here?!" he barked.

I figured he wasn't happy with me using company property to write stories, but instead of the verbal lashing I'd expected, he coldly asked who'd instructed me to sit here. It was a strange question, and my fear quickly became curiosity as I noticed a stranger behind him. The stranger pulled a black baseball cap down over his eyes and quickly ran out the door. I suspected I was in the wrong place at the wrong time, and decided to come clean, explaining that I was just writing a story. "A story, huh?" He walked around my desk and checked the screen suspiciously, before laughing out of both relief and derision. He looked me dead in the eye and told me grimly that if I'd heard anything, it wouldn't appear in my stories if I knew what was good for me.

"I didn't hear a thing!" I assured him. He was already long gone, rushing off to join the mysterious man waiting outside the door.

I realized our office's ordinary façade could be hiding any number of dirty secrets. What those secrets were, I had no idea.

I stumbled through the next year in a haze. At the year-end celebration dinner, after wine and food, a colleague asked me when I was going abroad. I was stunned by the question.

"Why do you think I'm planning to do that?"

"I dunno. It's just a feeling."

After repeated questioning, he explained it from a management standpoint. There seemed to be no real need for a secretary whose only duty was answering the phone. Anyone in my position would feel insecure unless they were going abroad and didn't care.

If I wanted to survive at this company, I needed to devote a lot of time to knowing who I was dealing with. I should've gone out with my colleagues. The company held employee gatherings almost daily. If I'd chosen to participate, I wouldn't have had to cook dinner for myself at all. But those things didn't interest me. Every day after work, I wanted the office empty so I could write.

Another year passed and the company's influence in the industry expanded along with its market share. There was no need to pay for someone who brought nothing to the table. I was laid off.

I'd been expecting this day, but when it came, it still felt painful. I decided that when I looked for my next job, I had to find a viable career path. I wasn't going to be a secretary again. I just wasn't good with people. I stayed home for two months and hunted through employment ads.

At the end of my second month, an ad seeking a public relations manager for a members-only club caught my attention. Although the phrase "public relations" sounded like I'd still have to deal with people, what the company really needed was a writer. Plus, the concept of a members-only club was practically unheard of in China at the time, which even further piqued my interest.

The job turned out to be a perfect fit. The company bought half-page ads in economic and business-related papers, and I produced articles to fill them. I educated the general public on the perks of members-only clubs, and the VIP lifestyle as a whole.

The company was a joint venture between the Chinese Sports Commission and a renowned Malaysian club chain. I traveled with club members out to Malaysia to visit sister clubs, before writing sumptuous travel pieces describing the experience in all its exclusive, opulent glory.

The PR department was made up of two people: myself, and a girl named Yang. Though I was technically her supervisor, I never told her what to do. She was in good with one of the heads of the Sports Commission. Just how good, I couldn't really say, but I had heard it enough times to know it was probably true. One day, she pointed out that the company had a separate budget set aside for promotional activities, and suggested we hire someone to organize sports and gaming competitions that could double as promotional opportunities for the club. Of course, she had just the people in mind.

Before long, I met with Mr. Zhu, general manager of a local advertising company, to hammer out plans for a combination tennis and bridge tournament. Tennis and bridge, not coincidentally, were the favorite games of party elite. Upon learning that Party officials would be in attendance, nouveau-riche prospective club members flooded our office with registration forms. Our office ran ads in major papers before the tournament, and ran reports, results, and gorgeous photos after, all with the club's logo prominently on display. My job was done, and I had done a darn good one at that.

Several days later, Yang asked quite casually, "So how much of a kickback did you get?"

"There was supposed to be a kickback?" I asked, gobsmacked. "No one offered me a penny!"

"We spent a hundred thousand. Each of us should get at least ten thousand!"

"Really?" I didn't know how to respond.

"Well you'd better go ask for it. Those are the rules. Even if you don't take the money, everyone will think you did."

I had no choice but to give Zhu a call, hemming and hawing about a kickback I still wasn't sure even existed. Unfazed and seemingly delighted, Zhu appeared at the coffee shop below our office almost instantly, and handed me two envelopes with ten thousand RMB in each. I gave both to Yang, who insisted I keep one. I tried to resist, but eventually faltered.

By then, I'd moved to Dingfuzhuang, about six miles east of the World Trade Center, where I shared a two-bedroom apartment with a colleague from the club. I stuffed the envelope into my backpack, slung it over my shoulder, and headed home. I was on edge the entire way. I glanced over my shoulder from time to time. I opened the front door to our apartment, tiptoed into my room, and locked the door behind me immediately. I pulled out the envelope and counted the notes with a mix of joy, fear, and bewilderment.

I ran through the whole sequence of events in my mind, and it suddenly dawned on me that Yang had planned this all along. With the green light from her friend at the Sports Commission, she sent me on the errand of putting all the pieces in place. I remained blissfully unaware of what I was actually up to. She'd gotten what she wanted, and her hands had stayed clean. I'd been played. I hated myself for my greed and stupidity. How could I have become so corrupt, so fast?

I was terrified for what could come. I needed to leave.

After I quit that third job, I went through a long period of unemployment. The white-collar world was growing more and more specific by the day. Everyone needed one thing they did better than anyone else. Maybe it was speaking Japanese, being a sales wizard, or mastering international trade relations. What was my specialty? Nothing.

The only thing I did well was writing stories. In 1995, I'd already been publishing work for two years. Some stories wound up in anthologies like *The Best Short Stories of the Year*. Still, I couldn't feed myself on publishing fees. I needed a job, but I was twenty-nine with no skills that stood out in the job market. New waves of easily moldable recruits were flooding the marketplace. As far as anyone in human resources was concerned, I was obsolete.

It was hard not to feel obsolete in other ways, either. Most people my age were already married. Zhi Hua was not only married, but had already passed her exams to become a doctoral candidate. While writing her dissertation, she discovered she was pregnant. Conflicted as to whether or not to keep it, she wrote me a letter asking for advice. Was she serious? She sounded like a queen asking a beggar whether she should have steak or lamb for dinner. Jealous and enraged, I sent her a two-page reply telling her to keep it. "If nothing else," I told her, "bringing a child into the world would be a real contribution to society. Your dissertation? Apart from gathering dust on a shelf, what change will it make in the world?"

Though our relationship never really healed, I went to see my grandmother once a month. One day, as I got off the bus on Nanlishi Road, I heard a woman call my name. I turned to see Ms. Chen, the omnipresent neighbor who'd brought us news in June of 1989.

"Long time no see!" she bellowed warmly. "You're always coming to see your grandmother by yourself. You never bring your kid with you! She misses her great-granddaughter!"

"I don't have a kid. She misses who?"

"Eh? Did I remember wrong? I could have sworn she said you had a daughter!"

The younger generation in my grandmother's apartment building probably all had kids. Seeing them scurrying back and forth with children in tow surely made my grandmother envious. She didn't have a great-granddaughter of her own to parade around, so she made one up. Furious and humiliated, I got right on the next bus home.

I'd fallen behind in every facet of my life. I lacked a career, a husband, wealth, everything. What had gone wrong? I pondered long and hard, and in the end, I realized I never knew what I wanted. I was just a young person with rebellious impulses.

For me, the 1980s were a golden age in which I'd committed my biggest act of rebellion so far: I transferred majors. My friends saw me as independent and full of purpose, when in reality I was just up against whatever path my parents chose for me. I had no direction of my own.

Rebellion is easy if your goal is simply to go against the mainstream. After the Tiananmen Incident, political life seemed to close down as the economic sector opened up. Companies blossomed, markets expanded, and new jobs emerged. A thriving economy full of options made it difficult to decide what to rebel against. For the first half of the 1990s, I lived in bewilderment, not knowing what to fight for or what to invest in.

I admitted defeat and decided to head to America. I had my ill-gotten gains, which would last me about a year as I prepared for my TOEFL and GRE exams. What I'd do when I got there, I had no idea, but America was a land of opportunity, or so it was said. I could start anew. Besides, even if I had to make a living washing dishes, at least I'd be doing it where no one knew me. There would be no ubiquitous neighbors to stop me on the street.

I went to night school to study English twice a week, and crammed

English words in my head all day long. But a life without working bred wild thoughts, and eventually, anxiety and insecurity crept in. Hearing the siren of a distant fire engine, I'd see terrible visions of everything I owned reduced to ash. Only after I rushed home to check on my building could I believe things were just fine, at least for now.

In 1997, I was offered a scholarship by the Department of East Asia Studies at the University of Oregon. When I received the offer letter, I thought of Zhi Hua. Our controversy had come to an end. She'd clearly taken the right path.

It seemed there was one last obstacle in front of me. In the summer of 1990, right as Zhi Hua was about to apply for her passport, the Ministry of Public Security put forth another new policy. The gist of it was this: if you don't have relatives abroad, don't even bother applying. This was the final hoop Zhi Hua had to jump through.

Digging through her genealogy, she found a second cousin in America. That cousin's grandfather had emigrated to America in the 1940s, and had become estranged from his family. Zhi Hua and her cousin had never met, nor did they have any documents proving they were related. All he could provide was a signed affidavit and a copy of his American passport, which turned out to be enough. We began to joke that the country was no better guarded by the Party than by the philosophers at the school's south gate.

Zhi Hua assured me that when the time came for me to apply, her cousin would be happy to be mine as well. But I figured that if Zhi Hua had become an American citizen, surely she could pose as my cousin. Before writing to ask her status, I learned that the rule had been abolished two years ago. It had something to do with US President Bill Clinton's decision to allow China's most favored nation status to be renewed unconditionally. I didn't have a clue how these two things were connected, and I had no intention to find out.

Now that I had the right to apply for a passport with or without a relative abroad, I could submit my application without bothering

Zhi Hua. I got my passport. I then applied for a F-1 visa at the US Embassy, and got that too. The only thing left for me to do was buy a plane ticket. Still, the Party's inconsistency puzzled me.

Here's the facts: Since February 1, 1980, China had enjoyed most favored nation status, which came with perks like lower tariffs and higher import quotas. MFN status was subject to review once a year. If a country had a record of restricting freedom of emigration or violating human rights, MFN status could be rescinded. After the Tiananmen Massacre, whether China's MFN status could be extended for one year caused no small amount of controversy in the US Congress.

The U.S. Senate Committee on Finance met on June 20, 1990 to determine whether China would retain its MFN status. Unable to overlook China's brutal human rights violations, the meeting was rife with condemnation and fierce debate.

Senator Daniel Patrick Moynihan from New York stated:

> There is nothing more poignant about the American symbols than when those Chinese students brought the Statue of Liberty into Tiananmen Square. We owe them something. And we owe them at least not continuing to give 'most favored nation' status to approve, in effect, what happened there.

Those in favor of China retaining its status argued that China's human rights violations were undisputed, but keeping China open to the outside world would improve its human rights situation. An isolated China would benefit neither the world, nor the Chinese people. Senator Max Baucus from Montana urged committee members to "remember [that] the positive changes we saw in China in the 1980s were closely linked to expanding economic ties to the West. If economic ties to the West are broken, the incentive for progress will be gone."

Xiaoxia Gong, a Chinese history student studying at Harvard at the time, stated:

The Chinese communist regime has a history of political repressions. The Tiananmen Square Massacre in June, 1989, was only one of many heinous crimes the Chinese regime has committed against its own people. However, the critical difference of this crime with previous ones is that it was committed in front of the world. Therefore, we should make every effort to keep China's doors open...MFN status for China constitutes one of the most important components of keeping China's doors open. Private entrepreneurs are the most ardent supporters of freedom and democracy. MFN removal would harm China's budding private and quasi-private enterprises.

China did anything they could to preserve their MFN status. In accordance with the Jackson-Vanik amendment to the Trade Act of 1974, MFN status couldn't be granted to Communist countries if they restricted freedom of emigration or violated human rights in other ways. The Tiananmen Massacre was a done deal. The only thing the Party could do to improve its image was preserve freedom of emigration, which they were very reluctant to do. That's why the bogus regulation. They didn't care if you had blood ties in the US, they only cared if you knew people living abroad. Knowing someone meant you had the ability to expose the Party's emigration restrictions.

When Zhi Hua left in the early 90s, I thought we'd be separated forever, like the characters in the North Korean film *The Destiny of Kim Kyi and Yin Kyi*. Kim Kyi and Yin Kyi are twins raised apart from childhood. Kim Kyi grows up in socialist North Korea, and Yin Kyi in capitalist South Korea. Their fates are vastly different, as should be expected from a propaganda film. It turned out that my life was nothing like Kim Kyi's, nor Yin Kyi's. My life was more intertwined with Zhi Hua's than I'd imagined. We'd entered the time of globalization.

I got my passport and visa in the summer of 1997. Before I left, I looked up pretty much everyone I'd ever known and said goodbye. I finally had an accomplishment to speak of, and I wanted everyone to know.

I had a friend named Lao Xin. He'd graduated from Capital Normal University with a degree in literature. We'd met at a gathering for young authors in 1990, when he was teaching Chinese at a community college. Two years later, he and some friends opened a restaurant. Our authors group had decided to meet for dinner one evening. Seeing him racing around the restaurant playing chef one second and host the next, someone at the table let out a massive sigh. "How could you have strayed so far from your literary ambition? Is your life just about money now? What a waste!" Lao Xin bit his tongue and went about his business. It wasn't until some time later that he had a moment to join us. After regaling us with the latest talk from the restaurant industry, he turned suddenly toward his critics:

"Let me tell you the real difference between a chef and an author. A chef can eat at his own restaurant for the rest of his life, while an author can't just read his own books for the rest of his life. That's the only difference, in my eyes."

Chuckles rippled across the table. Lao Xin kept a poker face.

I saw him twice a year at best, but I kept seeing new restaurants bearing his logo popping up all across town. He'd turned his restaurant into a franchising company. In our little circle of struggling writers, some felt happy for him while others bemoaned the world losing another writer. However, Lao Xin claimed he'd never intended to write professionally.

"Then why did you major in literature?" I asked.

"Reading classics in college made me realize I don't have what it takes," he answered plainly.

By his logic, there were two possible reasons why I hadn't given up on becoming a writer yet: either I hadn't read enough to be intimidated, or I was arrogant enough to think I could produce a masterpiece.

"Why do you want to be a writer, then?" he asked.

I explained that for me, writing was a way of finding my uniqueness.

He was surprised by my answer. "You don't know if you're unique or not?"

"I know I'm unique. I firmly believe that. I just don't know how," I answered.

My answer was spontaneous. After I'd said it, I realized that that was exactly what I had been doing. From an early age, I'd thought I was different, but I'd never figured out exactly how. Writing was my effort to define myself. Eventually, writing itself became the goal.

"That's interesting," he nodded.

In July of 1997, I stopped by his restaurant and found he looked thinner than I remembered. I asked what was wrong, and learned his wife had left him.

"Why? What happened?"

"She said life with me was boring."

There was no doubt that Lao Xin was a workaholic and devoted very little time to his family. But was he boring? Never. He was one of the most quick-witted and humorous people I'd ever known. I liked talking with him. It stimulated my thinking and provoked deeper thoughts than I would have thought by myself. If his wife didn't want him, maybe my chance had come.

We began to see each other just about every day. Everything about Lao Xin was just as great as I'd imagined. I was madly in love with him. Before we knew it, summer came to an end, so did my time in China. As much as I cared about him, he wasn't worth throwing my dream away for. I said my goodbyes, and headed to America alone.

Not long after I arrived, Lao Xin got a B-1 visa and flew to Los Angeles, where he took care of some business then drove 14 hours up Eugene, Oregon. Wanting nothing to do with dorm life, we rented a two-bedroom apartment in a wooded area far away from campus. Each day, he drove me to school and back. But just like our time in Beijing, our days together in Eugene were numbered. A B-1 visa lasted three months at most. He had to return to Beijing in November.

In his absence, I had no idea how to spend a day. All my classmates lived in the dorms, while I was all by myself, far off in the hills. His car was still parked in the driveway, but I didn't know how to drive. When he was here, he was my whole world. When he left, I felt isolated.

The apartment was on the upper floor of a two-story building, directly above the home of the property manager and his family. They had a hot tub in the courtyard. The second they were done with their homework each day, the kids would head straight for the tub. The sound of the engine, coupled with the bubbling water and the kids' squeals of joy, reminded me of a Chinese idiom. "A boiling life" is its literal translation. It refers to an exciting and passionate life lived to its fullest potential.

Thanksgiving arrived. The property manager and his family were preparing their camper for a vacation out of the city. It was a dinosaur of a vehicle that spent most of its life idle in their driveway. Lao Xin used to joke that Henry Ford himself had built it with his own two hands.

At noon the day before Thanksgiving, the manager laid his tools out on the ground, and set about tuning up the camper as I read a book by my window. He was out there for hours, and this time of year, it was dark by 4 pm. They weren't going anywhere today, or so I assumed. I went to the kitchen, made some food, and returned to my perch at the window, only to find the camper had disappeared. They were gone.

A hush fell over the darkening courtyard. A deer emerged from the forest, slowly poked its head through the fence and surveyed the hot tub. The still surface of the water formed a perfect mirror, filling me with a sudden desire to dive from my window straight.

I couldn't help but wonder when my life would finally rise and boil over. I was thirty-one and had just started my master's degree, but you couldn't do anything in the field of East Asian Studies without a PhD.

By the time I got my PhD, I'd be at least forty. Isn't it too late to get married and have kids? Plus, even if I did land a job in the U.S., Lao Xin would never be able to give up his chain of restaurants in China. Sure, he had come to America, but mainly to persuade me to return. He hadn't said those exact words, but it was pretty obvious that deep down, he hoped that when he boarded his flight he wouldn't be doing it alone.

Across from me lived a single girl who always left at night made up to the nines and didn't return until early morning. Where did she go every night? The bars? I'd lived in Eugene for three months now, but I still couldn't tell you where a single bar was. All I knew was home, school, and the road between. I eagerly waited for Lao Xin to return so we could explore the bars together.

He came back in January of 1998, but by then I had forgotten all about exploring bars. I wanted nothing but to hide away, just the two of us, in our little mountain retreat. Three months later, I was on my own again, and when he left, so went any desire I had to continue my studies. I couldn't take it anymore. I'd finish out the school year, but I was done.

My academic advisor Wendy Larson had recruited five students in 1997, one was an American, and the other four were from China. When I spoke to my fellow Chinese students about my decision to withdraw from UO, I didn't at all get the response I'd expected. On second thought, it was understandable. While changing major in 1986 was defiant, dropping out of UO seemed like I was throwing away everything I'd worked an entire year for. What was there to be impressed by?

Zhi Hua and her husband both received their PhDs in 1996. His was in chemistry, and he landed a job in Silicon Valley. At the same time, Zhi Hua found a tenure track position at a university in the South. After careful consideration of their prospective salaries, she turned down her offer and followed her husband to California.

Didn't people trade their careers for family every day? I wanted to give her a call. If anyone would understand me, it'd be her.

While Zhi Hua herself was adamant that I could call her anytime, her one-year-old son had very different ideas on the matter. Half the time she picked up the phone, all I could hear was a maelstrom of infantile wailing. She'd ask me to hold on a minute, then put the phone down, which gave me a front row seat to her coaxing and pleading. By the time he calmed down and she came back, I'd already have lost my nerve, and made up some mundane excuse for the call. However, one time I called it was as if he wasn't even there. After enough time had passed for it to seem natural, I finally blurted it out:

"I'm quitting school."

"Quitting?!" she repeated, unable to hide her astonishment.

"I wanna get married, but Lao Xin's never gonna give up his business."

"Yeah, I get that," she replied.

She only "got it," which meant she didn't agree with it.

She continued, "Even if you're not gonna do your PhD, I don't see why you can't stay just one more year to at least finish your master's."

"What's a master's gonna do?" I shot back. Besides, hadn't she herself thrown away a career for her husband even after finishing her PhD?

She went on, "OK, so let's say it's not going to do anything for you. Think of your advisor. She accepted you. She got you a scholarship. She put a lot of faith in you. If you throw it all away, it's not fair to her, or to any Chinese students that follow. She'll think we're all flakes who can't finish what we start."

She was right. I felt that pressure too. Recently, I'd been avoiding even catching a glance from Wendy. How could I look her in the eye and tell her I intended to leave the program? Eleven years ago, I proudly proclaimed straight to my computer engineering professors' faces that I had no interest in their field and was headed to the Chinese department. Back then, I was freeing myself. Barely a year ago, I'd written a grand personal statement professing my passion for Asian Studies and my burning desire to be a part of the University of Oregon family. Now, I was contradicting myself.

I felt ashamed. What wouldn't I have given to be able to sneak in the middle of the night and burn that statement before anyone could read it again?

However, with my return to Beijing looming at the end of the year, I began to see my school in an entirely different light. I realized I'd hardly even set foot on most of the campus. I made it my mission to make use of everything the school had to offer. For example, the swimming pool. One afternoon, I went after finishing my reading in the library. After swimming for an hour, I took the bus home, my hair still sopping wet. Instead of basking in the experience, I lamented that there was still so much I hadn't done. I hadn't really experienced what it was to be as a foreign student, or live any sort of American dream. And I was giving up already? Regret set in.

I've read Plato's *Republic*, but admittedly I've forgotten most of it. The one thing I can't forget is the Theory of Forms. I was simply transfixed by the image of us living our lives in a cave, seeing nothing more than the shadows of forms cast on the rocky wall before us. No matter how close we come, there will always be an imperfection that keeps us from realizing its ideal form.

As the bus took me further and further from school, sprawling green fields stretched out around me. I felt that somehow their beauty wasn't real. Maybe they were ideal fields, unreachable in their perfect beauty.

Chapter 20

The World of Ideal Forms

It turned out my decision to go back to China couldn't have been more right. I had a family now. I wasn't alone anymore. With Lao Xin's plentiful income, I was able to live the life of a full-time writer. Within a year, I'd written a full-length novel that was shortlisted for a literary award. In 1999, I signed on with the Beijing Writers' Association as a staff writer. I made the cover of *Youth Literature* the year after. Slowly but surely, my star was on the rise.

In 2002, Jiang Zemin introduced a socio-political theory called the "Three Represents" to redefine the Party. According to Jiang, the Party would no longer work to overthrow capitalist regimes using the might of the proletariat, nor would the ultimate goal of the Party be "to abolish private ownership, and confiscate all production materials owned by individuals." Instead, the Party's purpose would be to "represent the requirements for developing China's advanced productive forces, the orientation of China's advanced culture and the fundamental interests of the overwhelming majority of the Chinese people."

I couldn't care less about what the Party said, but to Lao Xin's father, it was like the word of god. Upon reading the statement, he called up Lao Xin and encouraged us to join the Party.

"Son, you're definitely a part of China's developing productive forces, and Wang Yuan represents China's advanced culture!"

We brushed off his enthusiasm, telling him that we had no interest in representing anything but ourselves, but secretly, we were a bit relieved. Lao Xin's father had been a Party member since the 1940s. He'd watched anxiously as his son amassed wealth, worrying about his business's legitimacy. According to China's Marxist principles, every cent that Lao Xin earned was illegal appropriation of his workers' labor, and could be confiscated any time. Now, we didn't need to worry anymore. Private ownership of businesses was not only recognized, but also considered "advanced" by the Party.

In the spring of 2002, rumors of fake vaccinations began to spread around the city. The government maintained that they had everything under control, but I took my daughter to the foreign services department at Beijing Union Hospital anyway. Their shots were imported and real. In the hospital's vast, bright waiting room I found an issue of *New Weekly*. Founded in 1996, the magazine focused on general news and city life. It was run by a staff of self-proclaimed "keen reporters and astute observers documenting the never-ending change of Chinese society."

The particular issue I'd found featured a piece entitled: "The Sudden Middle Class." Next to it appeared a colorful cartoon drawing of a three-person family with their dog, flying over a city in their brand-new car. It felt as if they were on a flying carpet whisking them away to an unknown paradise. The story read:

The term "middle class" is spreading like wildfire. The movement has begun, and the race is on. Everywhere you go, someone is asking: Have you made it yet?

According to the author, "making it" consisted of six things: A single-family house in the suburbs, imported French furniture, membership at a private club, frequent trips to restaurants with foreign chefs, religiously reading both the *Economic Observer* and *21st Century Business Herald*, and lastly, only giving birth to your children at

United Family Hospital.

I couldn't help but run the list against my own life. We did own a single-family house, though it sat empty in the suburbs north of the city. The major reason we hadn't moved there was that our nanny Rong didn't like it there. Our apartment on Yuquan Road was right next to the subway station, making it easy for her to get anywhere she pleased. I didn't really mind the distance because I could drive, but Rong didn't have that option. She only had one day off each week and liked to spend them enjoying all the city had to offer. She'd been working for me since my daughter's very first days, and with Lao Xin's restaurant empire growing by the day, my daughter, Rong and I were like our own little family, and I didn't want anyone in my family to be unhappy.

I wondered if I was a member of the middle class.

On a Sunday in October, 2002, Rong left the house first thing in the morning, made up to the nines. She said she was going to meet a cousin of hers who worked at a restaurant, before heading to Fragrance Hill to see the autumn leaves. She was always home by dinner, but at nine o'clock, she hadn't yet returned. Mobile phones were a luxury she couldn't afford at the time. Not knowing what else to do, I called the restaurant where her cousin worked, only to find she wasn't there either. Something was wrong.

I called the police to file a missing persons report, and was told I'd receive a call if anything came up. The following day, around 5pm, the phone rang. On the other end was a girl whose voice I didn't recognize. She told me that Rong and her cousin were being held in a detention center in the Changping district.

Back then, there was a set of laws in place called the Regulations for Detention and Repatriation of Urban Vagrants and Beggars. The law enabled city police to pick up homeless people off the street, detain them, then return them to wherever they'd come from. Most came from rural areas. The program had started off with the best intentions, but over time it transformed into something much more sinister. People were locked up and only let go after weeks of forced labor. It got to the point where it didn't matter if you were even homeless. Simply not looking like a Beijinger, or speaking with an accent was enough for officers to sentence you to a week's work before even deciding what to do with you.

I drove to Changping, winding through its serpentine streets, until I reached a large compound near a construction site. Its four towering walls were topped with wire fencing that sent them up even higher. Driving through the main gate, I passed a snarling, angry dog, then met a thin, squinting guard waiting for me. He looked not unlike the security guards at Peking University. I stated my business, and the names of the women I was there to pick up, expecting to be asked for any number of documents. The guard couldn't have cared less what form of ID I had in my purse, but was much more interested in how much money was nestled up beside it. According to him, the two women were both from Shandong province, and would be headed first thing in the morning. Train tickets had already purchased on their behalf. Even though they wouldn't be boarding the train, it was decided that I should pay for their tickets, in addition to their room and board for the last two days. All in all, it came to four hundred RMB to get them out. Way cheaper than I expected. A kidnapping at anyone else's hands would never have been so affordable.

I paid the fee, and collected Rong and her cousin, who were both silent the entire drive. I dropped her cousin back at work, before bringing Rong back home to my overjoyed daughter, who threw herself in the arms of her beloved "sister."

"Sister Rong, you look darker. Have you been in the sun?"

Rong bawled uncontrollably in the arms of her tiny admirer. It was the first sound she'd made since we'd exited the prison gates.

The whole tragic series of events had no small effect on Rong. She was a beautiful, well-dressed girl who never left the house with a hair out of place. She'd never been stopped by police before, which attributed to her assumption that she looked like a Beijing native.

But two days sifting sand in the glaring, hot sun had blackened her flawless skin. It took her at least two weeks to get her prized white skin tone back.

From that day on, she didn't dare go out on her days off. She couldn't even bring herself to take my daughter to the playground a hundred yards from our building.

In early 2003, we moved to the suburbs. Our gated community had nearly five hundred acres. Walking the perimeter took at least an hour. No cops would be around to pick up "homeless" people in our driveways. Finally, Rong could leave the house again. She was free to stroll by the lake, ride her bike to the neighborhood market, and take my daughter to the community play area. She even felt comfortable lounging by the lake reading a book on her days off.

We had just moved in, when the sudden death of Sun Zhigang shook the country to its core. Born in a village in Hubei province, Sun was fresh out of college and had set out for Guangdong in search of work. Unfortunately, he'd forgotten to bring his temporary residence permit with him. As a result, he'd been arrested and sent to one of the province's infamous detention centers. As smart as he was stubborn, he had a habit of defying orders, and was beaten to death as a show of force. His story was published in the *Southern Weekend*, a paper with a liberal stance and a massive audience.

In May of that year, three Doctors of Law: Yu Jiang, Teng Biao, and Xu Zhiyong, petitioned the National People's Congress to review the "Regulations for Detention and Repatriation of Urban Vagrants and Beggars." They claimed that the regulations infringed on citizens' personal freedoms, therefore violating the Chinese constitution and necessitating immediate amendment or all-out repeal. Soon after, He Weifang, Sheng Hong, Shen Kui, Xiao Han, and He Haibo wrote another petition. They approached Congress not as legal experts (though they were), but as citizens. The group demanded a special investigation into both the death of Sun Zhigang and the entire detention/repatriation system. By June, the "Regulations for

Detention and Repatriation of Urban Vagrants and Beggars" had become a thing of the past.

Rong was free, but I had no desire to move back to our apartment. I had gotten used to living in a single-family house. In the spring of 2003, SARS spread across the nation, putting everyone at risk. There had already been two confirmed cases in our building on Yuquan Road, which lead to a quarantine of the entire structure, including its inhabitants, for a full month. Sure, SARS didn't happen every day. It was probably a once-in-a-lifetime incident. But having one's neighbors further away in an area nearly devoid of cars meant fresh, clean air.

Another benefit living in a single-family home was avoiding the noise caused by neighbors renovating. Chinese people have a crazy enthusiasm for renovation. I guess it's one of the few things, if not the only thing, that they have complete control over. Every now and then, a neighbor rips up their home and remodels it. According to regulations, renovation work can only be performed from 8am to 6pm. For people with day jobs, it wasn't a big deal, but I stayed home all day. Each morning, I started up my computer just as the workers fired up their deafening drills and saws. In a detached house, I never heard a sound.

I love living in this quiet, suburban neighborhood. Rong, on the other hand, was less than pleased. She was young, and longed for the hustle and bustle of the city. She decided to leave.

Her replacement was a woman named Meng. She was only two years older than me, but already had a daughter in college. Meng was working to put her children through school, and couldn't care less where she did it. My daughter started kindergarten not long after Meng came. With no child to look after all day, Meng's job became exponentially easier.

I wasn't very close with our neighbors. None of us really went out of our way to socialize. It was the opposite of my grandmother's L-shaped fortress. Meng, on the other hand, had quite the circle of friends. She knew all the nannies and housekeepers in the neighborhood, and therefore had the inside scoop on families I didn't even know existed. One day as we ate, she regaled me with her newest discovery:

"Did you hear? Last night Mrs. Lin came home in the middle of the night, but forgot her house key. Her husband wouldn't get out of the bed to open the door for her, and she got so mad she smashed her car right into the garage. She took the whole door clean off!"

"I didn't hear a thing. I was sound asleep," I said.

Almost all the wives in the neighborhood were younger than their husbands. Mrs. Lin was the only woman who looked older, and stood out a bit because of it. Meng's story piqued my interest. The next time I passed the Lins' house, I couldn't help but slow down and stare. Their yard was the nicest in the neighborhood by far, bursting with fruit trees and flowers. As I peered into the shade of the trees, I saw Mrs. Lin peering back. When our eyes met, she emerged from the shade with a smile across her face. Embarrassment swept over me. I feigned interest in her yard, asking for some gardening tips for a fictional problem I'd been having. After answering me in painstaking detail, she added that she and her husband had known each other since middle school, and cultivated their love of horticulture when they were sent to labor together in the countryside during the Cultural Revolution.

"You guys were classmates?" I couldn't help but blurt out. "So you guys are the same age!"

"Yep. We were sent to the countryside together, came back to Beijing together, and started our business together. It's been thirty years now. I guess in this neighborhood, you don't really see many old-school couples like us, eh?"

"No. In fact, I didn't know any lived here," I replied in all honesty.

"Well, all relationships have their pros and cons. Old-school couples have their problems, and trophy wives have their fair share too."

"True, true," I nodded before retreating.

Trophy wife? I hated that term.

I wanted desperately to show that I wasn't a trophy wife. I had a career and brains, after all. The Beijing Writers' Association required its authors to meet at least twice a year. Once, they held a meeting at the city's Party Cadre School, which required an entry-exit permit from the guards at the gate. The conference lasted three days, and for those three days, I never parked my car in the garage. Instead, I backed into the driveway and parked there, so my Writers' Association badge would be visible through the windshield. I kept parking like this for at least two weeks after the conference ended.

A few days later, Meng approached me with a sullen look on her face:

"Everybody knows you're a writer now. They've all told their nannies and housekeepers to keep away from me."

My contract with the Beijing Writers' Association lasted three years. When it was coming to a close, a committee convened to debate my renewal. In 2000, I was a rising star. Three years later, that light had begun to dim. I stayed home and churned out novels based on my life in the 1990s. My first novel under contract had emotional impact, but lacked structure. My most recent novel was comparatively mature in terms of craft, but boring. Critics wondered if my career was over.

In the end, the committee decided to renew my contract, but I knew this was my last chance. If I couldn't produce good work in the next three years, I was done. I was under a lot of pressure, and stress can't be directly translated into inspiration.

In November ,2004, autumn's first winds came with the realization I was pregnant again. Not convinced by my own test, I went to the hospital for a test and sure enough, the test came up positive. On my drive home, I took a wrong turn into an interchange of seemingly endless spiral inclines, each more dizzying than the last. I took the first possible exit, and stopped the car on the side of the road. I sat in the driver's seat staring at the unfamiliar street. I had no idea where I was or where I was going.

China's one-child policy had been in place for about 40 years, but entering the 21st century, you could circumvent the rule by paying a fine. The idea of paying a fine was acceptable, but there was no way of predicting the amount. According to law, the fine was to comprise three to ten times the average per-capita disposable income of city residents. In 2003, that amount was estimated at twelve thousand RMB in Beijing. If I was charged the maximum of ten times that, it came to one hundred and twenty thousand. It wasn't a small number by any means, but was one I could bear. If the family planning office found out you had money, however, they would change the rule to three to ten times your family's annual income. I knew someone who had paid eighty thousand, and someone else that was out two million. Two million to bring a life into the world? It was unfair! Bringing a life into society should be seen as a contribution.

If I wanted to keep this child, my best option was to go to a foreign country. Thinking of moving abroad, my outlook suddenly brightened. This was a perfect chance to run away. My career had been bottlenecked for quite a while. I was running out of stories. Going to a foreign country would give me a much-needed break, and I could claim it was for the good of the family.

I'd made up my mind and immediately began looking around at options. My first choice was the United States, but I didn't know how to get there. EB1-A visas for aliens with extraordinary ability, and EB5 visas for investors were both available, but somehow I didn't know about them at the time. The most commonly known immigration programs were for Canada. I submitted my application, but due to an overwhelming number of applicants, it would take more than two years for it to be reviewed.

I received word of an investment immigration program in New Zealand, which awarded a business visa with unlimited entries after initial applications are approved. Visas in hand, applicants were required to wire a deposit of one million NZD to a New Zealand bank account before they could finally apply for conditional permanent residency. If, after two years, their money stayed in New Zealand, temporary status would be lifted, and permanent residency granted. My second child could be born in New Zealand while I was still on my business visa.

I applied, and less than a month later, passed the financial qualifications check. I got my business visa.

I flew to New Zealand in the spring of 2005, but New Zealand disappointed me. The biggest problem was that it had a very small population and a limited market. When I first arrived, I discovered New Zealand only had two supermarket chains: Food Town and Count Down, and about a month later, the two brands announced a merger. There were only three TV channels: New Zealand Channel One, New Zealand Channel Two, and New Zealand Channel Three. I bought a newspaper, and on the front page, I found news of the mysterious death of a couple of cows.

My immigration lawyer was from Hong Kong. He was friendly, but not exactly efficient. I'd been to his office twice, and he told me the same joke both times: "I have a client whose son liked gambling and lost over a million. He asked me to apply for an investment visa for his son, reasoning that the money his son lost could be deemed investment to the nation of New Zealand!" The first time, I wondered what he meant by the joke. The second time, I realized he was either lonely or bored. You'd never find this kind of lawyer in the States. You'd get charged for the time they spent telling you jokes.

However, New Zealand is a beautiful country. The entire coastline has a theatrical feel. At the ends of the smooth sand beaches, giant rock formations rise from the water. I wondered what mother nature's intention was in sculpting this corner of the world. Walking along the water's edge, I thought of Jane Campion's *The Piano*, and the way it depicted New Zealand's primal, windswept beaches. Finally visiting them myself, the film felt truthful in a new way.

Someone once told me that the Maori name for New Zealand is Aotearoa, meaning "land of the long white cloud." It all became clear. The magical feel of New Zealand's coasts comes from its spectacular clouds. Lenticular clouds hover above the horizon, linking mountain, sky, and sea. As wind blows through the mountain ranges, vertical oscillations form, as dry air becomes stratified with moisture. The result is unique clouds shaped into visible layers. One after another, eerie white discs rise from the peaks, taking on the shapes of spaceships or massive spinning tops. Sometimes they looked like avalanches tumbling down from the heavens. Other times, the clouds formed a great white whale breaching into the sky. Just as the clouds were shaped by topography, so too did the sea decide the color of the ghosts above. The South Pacific's near total absence of pollution produced clouds of a brilliant white like nowhere else in the world.

Looking up at those clouds, I thought again of Oregon. Eugene was drenched in rain for most of the year, and has dense foliage and deep forests not unlike New Zealand. I recalled feeling deeply lost on a bus, staring out the window over the vast fields. I had a strong feeling that even if Eugene wasn't ideal, it was much closer than New Zealand.

Around Christmas that year, my lawyer in Beijing sent word that Canada had finished its preliminary review of my application and had requested a physical exam. I decided to go to Canada. If I could settle in Vancouver, I could visit Eugene again. It was only about a seven hour drive.

One day, I watched a rerun of the Oscar's ceremony in 2004 when *The Lord of the Rings* swept the awards, winning nearly every major category. In his acceptance speech, Peter Jackson shouted "Go kiwi!" and those two simple words struck to the depths of my heart. Had I not lived in New Zealand, I likely would never have known that the kiwi was New Zealand's national bird or that New Zealanders called themselves kiwis.

My son was a kiwi. And thus, I would always have an attachment to this place. My determination to leave it for Canada came with no shortage of shame. I hadn't returned the kindness I'd been shown. However, I'd only been there a year, whereas I'd lived in China for almost forty. If I could turn my back on one country, why not another?

While preparing to leave, I went downtown to process some paperwork. New Zealand's roads twist and dip in a serpentine manner. I was always nervous going to downtown Auckland. Clusters of skyscrapers and narrow, one-way streets added difficulty to the rolling topography. This time, however, I never stopped to check my map.

I parked the car in a nearby lot and walked to my destination. As I was walking inside, a sense of meaninglessness swept over me like the tides on New Zealand's shores. It had taken me a full year to learn downtown Auckland, and it had all been a waste.

In March 2006, I returned to Beijing with my kiwi son in tow. We received our visas in September, and a month later, we were processing our landing paperwork at Vancouver International Airport. The Immigration Landing room is portioned off from the airport's main arrival hall by a large glass wall with a maple leaf on it. I watched our luggage circle the carousel while we waited for our interview. Eva was more interested in a drink from the vending machine at the far end of the room, but I didn't have a single coin of Canadian currency. To this day, every time I arrive at Vancouver International Airport, I can't help but take a moment to look at the Immigration Landing room. A native Canadian might not feel much seeing what was behind that glass wall, which never failed to stir my emotions. The same vending machine still stands at the far end of the room. It always makes me feel a little thirsty.

Before leaving for Canada, I'd taken on a job translating a book: *The Cinema of Martin Scorsese* by Lawrence Friedman. Other than *Taxi*

Driver, I hadn't watched any of the films, and usually only his most popular ones were available in video stores. I needed to find his more obscure films, like *Mean Streets.*

In 2007, Netflix offered all-you-could-watch DVDs by mail for only seven dollars a month. I signed up and set about renting the titles I needed. I was amazed. The internet really had the power to connect niche communities across the world. It's a huge blessing for artists and writers creating works that might not be as marketable. That day, I swore my loyalty to Netflix, and I've watched with delight as the company has grown.

Each morning, I'd drive Eva to school, brew a pot of coffee, and settle in for work. I set a pace of about two pages a day, but if those pages discussed films I hadn't seen, I'd lose hours watching them. Some included commentary, which meant even more time.

I rarely stayed at Eva's school for long. I had complete faith in Western education systems. But near the end of Eva's first year, her teacher, Mrs. Green, contacted me. She was concerned.

Eva had gone to kindergarten in New Zealand for six months. After we returned to Beijing, I did everything I could to keep her English up. I even entered her in a national English competition. She placed third in her age group and took home a gorgeous crystal trophy. It probably made her think her English was good enough as it was.

In Canada, ESL curriculum is divided into five levels. Eva tested into level 3. She couldn't understand why she, the third best English speaker among all of China's six-year-olds, had to go to a special class to learn English. In addition to the ESL students, the school had placed all of the school's special needs students in Mrs. Green's class, spreading her a bit thin. Twice a week, Eva was forced to leave her regular class and go to Mrs. Green's, alongside students who needed counseling for anger management, or had other behavioral issues. Eva didn't like getting grouped in with them and directed her frustration toward Mrs. Green.

One day, Mrs. Green instructed the class to use the word "wear" in a sentence. When called upon, Eva proclaimed, "Mrs. Green wears a nappy!"

When Mrs. Green asked what nappy meant, Eva explained that it was the word for diaper in New Zealand. Mrs. Green called and demanded I remove Eva from class immediately.

This wasn't the only incident. Mrs. Green felt that Eva's writing was messy, and asked her, "Why can't you write a bit neater?"

Eva replied, "'Cause I don't want to!"

I explained to her that it may have sounded like a question, but this was her way of telling you what to do. Eva didn't understand. Chinese teachers barked commands or even threats. *Write neater! I said neater! Keep writing like that and I'll chop your hand off!*

When Mrs. Green asked why she couldn't write neater, Eva thought she was starting a discussion, and that meant she could simply state she didn't want to.

I was worried about culture shock, but I didn't take the incident seriously. I believed Eva would eventually pick things up as time passed. When summer vacation came, I enrolled her in summer camps. The camps started every weekday at seven in the morning and went until six at night. It was way longer than a day at school. Ten weeks later, her English had vastly improved.

It was time for Eva to begin second grade. She was all smiles when I dropped her off, but she returned hanging her head. She'd been assigned to a combined first and second grade class. "It's common at smaller schools in Canada. It has nothing to do with how smart you are," I told her.

"You don't get it! Go see for yourself!" she yelled.

My translation schedule was hard enough to keep up with, but seeing Eva a step away from refusing to go to school, I had no choice.

The next day, I arrived just as Eva's class was scurrying off to PE. I immediately saw why Eva felt so dejected. She was taller than most kids her age, and as one of only two second graders in class, she stuck out like a sore thumb. It turned out the only other second grader in her class required a dedicated caregiver who never took an eye off him for a second, even when he went to the restroom. No wonder Eva felt crushed. All of Mrs. Green's other students had moved on to a dedicated second grade class.

I spoke with Eva's teacher, and found out she'd just come to the school that year. I asked her about the ESL class. She said she was only responsible for the second graders in the combined class. The rest of the second graders all went to Mrs. Green. The picture finally came into focus. Mrs. Green wanted nothing to do with Eva, and had dumped her on the first available victim.

I went back home and scolded Eva, "Do you believe me now? Mrs. Green may have sounded like she was asking, but this is her way of telling you what to do. That's just how Canadians make demands. If you don't obey, there are consequences. You were deceived by their false politeness!"

Eva screamed back, "I'm not going to school ever again!"

I left home and found a coffee shop where I sat and wrote a letter to her principal. I hated Mrs. Green. Why couldn't she have just yelled at Eva like a Chinese teacher?

If she'd yelled, Eva would have listened!

After a while, I calmed down. I thought of when we'd first arrived in Canada and I applied to volunteer at the school district. During a training session, a lecturer informed us that the majority of immigrants went through three adaptive stages. The first six months are the honeymoon phase, where excitement easily overshadows any adversity. People will laugh off most if not all of the difficulties they face during this period. After that, reality sets in, along with doubt over whether they'd made the right decision in coming here. During this phase, there's only one thing to do: hang in there.

It looked like I'd progressed to the phase where I just needed to persevere. I wiped away my tears and tore up the letter. It was pure conjecture, anyway. I had no evidence Mrs. Green had decided which class Eva was assigned to.

I went home, collected some of Eva's assignments, and compared them with earlier writing she'd done. The next day, I sought out the principal and laid out my evidence. I tried to prove that the work being assigned to Eva was far easier than the work she'd been assigned last year. It was unfair to hold her back.

A week later, the principal informed me Eva would be transferred to a combined second and third grade class. I was beside myself. A regular second grade class would've been fine, but my earlier assumption had to be true. Mrs. Green must have refused to have her whatsoever.

When I applied for Eva's transfer, I promised the school I'd be a model mother, which meant a commitment to communicating with Eva's teachers. These conversations revealed just how much of a problem Eva could really be. She had a knack for staying right on the edge. She never did anything serious enough to merit suspension, but did just enough that everyone was aware of her defiance. Teachers had to devote twice as much energy to her as anyone else. All I could do to pay back their time was step up and volunteer more. I attended every single school activity as penance for Eva's crimes.

One weekend, the school district organized a run in memory of Terry Fox: a Canadian athlete who'd attempted to run across Canada to raise money for cancer research, but had tragically succumbed to the disease before he could complete his journey. Our school was one of the smallest in the school district. The principal was worried that our contingent would pale in comparison to that of other schools, and urged one and all to come out. Eva and I arrived at Steveston Pier early in the morning and found our school's flag. Before long, we set out west along the coast. Some of the land around Steveston Pier is below sea level, and a dam holds back the water. Looking out to sea, it feels as if the ships are floating in mid-air.

About a mile in, Eva had had enough, leaving me to try and encourage her using every Chinese proverb I knew:

"Even nine miles is only halfway to ten."

"Genius is 1% inspiration and 99% perspiration!"

"Perseverance can carve stone!"

It didn't matter what I told her. She was done. As the school's flag disappeared into the distance, I gesticulated wildly in an attempt to encourage her, and failed to notice a bee which stung me right in the hand.

"To hang in there is to win...Ouch!"

My hand instantly started to swell as pain shot straight through my arm. Support staff immediately stepped out of the crowd and implored me to return to the starting line for medical care. Eva couldn't have been happier. A few years later, I overheard Eva explain karma to her little brother. "Karma is when Mom waved her hands around and shouted to me, 'To hang in there is to win...Ouch!'"

I'd gotten Canadian residency, but I still longed to return to America. Peace Arch border crossing was only a half hour drive from where I lived, and an hour past that was Seattle. Every possible weekend or holiday, I would jump in the car and head for the States feeling like a fish returning to water. Even the air felt fresher south of the border. I would often pull off at the first rest area to wander through the woods. "Ahh, that American air!" I'd exclaim. Every time, Eva rolled her eyes.

I felt like I'd known the State of Washington forever. It could've been that it reminded me so much of Oregon, with its sprawling, lush greenery.

Why was I so obsessed with Oregon? He may have lived in Vermont, but it was in Oregon that I encountered the crossroads Robert Frost described. When I gave up academia to marry Lao Xin, I thought I'd made the right choice. But in light of recent events, I realized I'd just taken the easier path. I know that being a wife and mother of two are not all I want out of life. But I'm a passive person. Given prosperity and security, I don't take the initiative to figure out who I really am. For people like me, the most suitable life is one of scarcity. I should have lived like Balzac, who only wrote to pay debts and inadvertently created masterpieces. If I had chosen the road less traveled, my life would have been full of uncertainty, through which I might've been forced to find that elusive self.

I had always wanted to re-visit Eugene. Though the drive was only seven hours from Vancouver, I wouldn't dare take on that drive alone with two children. Lao Xin visited just before Christmas. With him at the wheel, I could keep an eye on the kids.

We spent our first night in Seattle, then a few hours in downtown Portland the next day. GPS was available, but wasn't as popular as it is now. Lao Xin and I still relied on maps. Afraid of getting lost, we decided to stop at the first gas station we saw to pick up a map. However, after we pulled off the freeway, we realized that it was impossible for us to get lost. We were already on Franklin Blvd., Eugene's main street. In the distance, I could make out the red, beckoning glow of the "vacancy" sign in front of the Motel where we'd spent our first night in Eugene back in 1997. We headed straight for that sign as it shone through the misty Oregon night.

The next morning, Lao Xin hadn't slept well and wasn't going anywhere. I took the kids to the University of Oregon for a little walk down memory lane. I tried to recreate the feeling of being disoriented, but the days of drifting were gone without a trace. I had no idea how I ever felt lost in the first place. Everything was marked as clear as could be. When I was a student, campus was a vast labyrinth of trees and buildings. Ten minutes was just barely enough to make it from one class to another, factoring in my requisite cup of coffee. Today, I felt like I'd barely started walking when I reached the other end of campus.

We stopped to visit a classroom I remembered fondly, then our great adventure was suddenly complete. From there, I took the kids to see the apartment I'd lived in on the outskirts of the city. The building was on a street named Foxtail Drive. It was a short and perilously steep road. Lao Xin loved driving down it at breakneck speed when no one was around. He'd go so fast it felt like we were free-falling. It was terrifying.

"When we get to Foxtail, be careful kids. The road is really steep. Don't scream," I warned them, thinking for sure I'd hear screams from the backseat as I drove down it.

I found my old apartment, and took a picture to remember it by. On our way back to the hotel, Eva asked:

"When's Foxtail? Did we already pass it?"

I guess it wasn't all that scary, after all the steep mountain roads she'd ridden in New Zealand.

We got back to the motel to find Lao Xin exactly where we'd left him. We'd already done everything we'd planned to, and it was barely five o'clock. What were we supposed to do all night? Eva asked if I would buy her some Mario cards. They had them in Canada, but they were cheaper in the States and Oregon had no sales tax. We headed for the nearest shopping center. I was eager for one last chance to experience what I'd left behind.

As I pulled into the mall's parking lot, I noticed something wasn't right. Why were there barely any cars? Unable to shake the ominous feeling, I walked to the front doors, craning my neck for any sign of what was happening. The mall was closed.

At six o'clock? I couldn't believe it. I knew it was Sunday, but I was shocked nonetheless. It was so different from it was in my memory. In my mind, Eugene was positively boiling over with life, 24/7.

The next day, we headed home. I'd originally planned for us to stop and spend the night somewhere on the way back, but somehow we'd lost our sense of adventure. We drove for seven hours straight, all the way to the border.

The next Thanksgiving, I traveled to San Jose to visit Zhi Hua. I had high expectations and really looked forward to having a good talk, but when we were face to face, I found myself unable to say what I wanted to.

Canadian Thanksgiving is the second Monday in October. The weekends before are normal weekends for Americans, and Zhi Hua's children had extracurricular activities to go to. She asked her husband to take care of kids for the day and he agreed. He's a nice person and understood we were childhood friends. I watched Zhi Hua draw a map for him, explaining that the door to the dance school was behind the shopping mall. I could tell he'd never taken their daughter there before, so I suggested that Zhi Hua and I watch the kids.

Zhi Hua protested, "You never come to San Francisco. I have to show you around."

"I can take a group tour on Monday," I said.

While the kids were in class, we'd sneak off for a walk, to shop, or simply sit and chat. We had enough time, but I didn't know how to start the conversation. The atmosphere never felt right. How could I work into a conversation that I doubted the value of my marriage? How could I say that I wasn't completely myself in the role of a wife and mother? Zhi Hua was a talented girl back in school, but she was devoted to her family now.

A long day passed. After the children had gone upstairs, Zhi Hua and I stayed downstairs for a while. I still remember her final words that night, "Don't worry about the dishes. Just toss them in the dishwasher." Then she went upstairs too.

I sat alone on the living room sofa, tears streaming down my face.

Monday came and it was time for her to return to work. I hopped on a tour bus headed to San Francisco, but it took much longer than I expected. I missed my flight to Canada and had to take a red-eye back to Seattle.

I arrived at Sea-Tac at 1am. I rented a car, downed a cup of coffee, and hit the road. The endless stretches of rural land on either side of Interstate 5 were cloaked in pitch black. Once in a while, the flickering light of a home would appear off in the distance, or a gas station on the horizon, then darkness again.

There's a thirty-mile stretch of I-5 north of Burlington where it's just you and the mountains. It's like a void out of space and time, like something out of *Twin Peaks*. It's easy to picture agent Cooper recounting his day to Diane as he passes along this blank expanse of road. If he could talk his way through those winding hills, so could I. And as I drove, it occurred to me that I should try writing in English.

I'd been writing for almost twenty years at that point, but my best pieces were a couple of stories written in the 90s when I was jobless and hopeless. There's a saying in Chinese, "Poverty forms poetic excellence." I might not have the courage to give up my marriage, property and children to start over again, but I could force myself into the desert of language. Maybe writing in English would spark something fresh in me.

In May 2009, I resigned from my job at *Ming Pao* and enrolled at Vancouver Film School.

On the first day of school, the teacher asked us to name films we considered guilty pleasures. I knew the word "guilty," and I knew "pleasure," but a "guilty pleasure" was a totally foreign concept to me. Maybe it had something to do with crime film? One after another, my classmates rattled off the titles of movies I'd never heard of. When my turn came, I put forth Godard's *Breathless*, to a roomful of dumbfounded stares. Who would name *Breathless* a guilty pleasure? I was totally in the dark, but I could read their expressions. There was something wrong with my answer. After class, I searched online, and learned what a guilty pleasure really was. No wonder they'd looked at me like that.

I felt embarrassed, but wasn't that what I was looking for? Embarrassment, awkwardness, and misunderstanding? In short, I wanted to feel uncomfortable.

Our writing program had one class held in collaboration with the acting program. One week, we were doing an exercise in which a writing student would call out a word, and a troupe of actors would form a tableau based on that word. When my turn came, I couldn't think of a word to save my life, until an acting student asked, "Where are you from?"

"I'm originally from China, and I've lived in Richmond for three years," I replied.

As soon as they heard "China," whispers rippled through the troupe, who almost immediately announced they were ready.

Eight formed a line on one side of the stage while a solitary actor stood opposite them. The eight bore down hard against the actor standing alone. He stood his ground, unwilling to give way. His arms were outstretched, making him look like Jesus on the cross. He was the Tank Man.

My mind raced. My heart moved. Even they still remembered.

Chapter 21

The Ballad of Photo Studios

When I was living in Richmond, I went to Landsdowne Center more than any other mall in the city. It might only be the second largest mall in town, but it didn't take all day to find parking.

Next to the food court, there was a photo studio. The whole storefront was glass. Visible through it was a counter that took up the half the width of the store and a black curtain taking up the other half. I often saw an Asian man who looked about 60 sitting behind the counter. His demeanor reminded me a lot of the manager of the Canon repair shop near the Beijing Hotel, who donned immaculate white gloves before touching a camera.

The first time I'd gone there was in 2007. Eva's summer vacation was just around the corner and I wanted to take her to America, which meant both of us needed photos for our visa applications. It turned out that he spoke Mandarin and his last name was Lin.

"You have a Chinese passport?" he asked.

"I do."

"You haven't been in Canada long, have you?"

"Not really. Why?"

"If I were you, I'd wait until you've been here at least a year. You'll have a way better chance of getting approved."

"What's wrong with applying now?"

"You've only been here a few months. It makes you look impatient, like you might not come back."

His words were well-intentioned, and he wasn't wrong. American visa officers thought any foreigner had potential to overstay. If you hadn't been in Canada long enough, they might suspect that you had just used Canada as a stepping stone, but I wasn't a first-timer. I'd already been granted an F-1 visa in 1997 under less favorable circumstances. Back then, I was 31, single, broke, jobless...you name it. Ten years later, I had permanent residency in Canada and was married with two kids. I wasn't looking for another country to flee to.

I replied casually, "I'm just going to Seattle to buy some stuff at the outlets. They're insane if they think I'd stay illegally."

He shrugged, content to let it rest.

Soon, I had my ten-year, multiple-entry American visa in hand.

Not long after they arrived, my parents decided to spend Christmas in Las Vegas.

I couldn't have been any less excited to help my parents apply for American visas. I was working at *Ming Pao* and would have to take at least a half day off from work to take them to interviews. I'd tried every possible way of dissuading them, but my parents, especially my father, were stubborn as mules. He didn't care if he got rejected. "I'm seventy," he said. "If they turn me down, I just won't go to America for the rest of my life."

Therefore, off we went to Mr. Lin's.

Mr. Lin still remembered me and asked how I'd fared. "You end up getting your visa?"

"Yep."

He smiled, "Sounds like you guys have great luck."

He turned to my parents, "It'll be tougher for you, though. Chinese passports...no permanent Canadian residency...You'd be better off applying from China."

"See?" I was elated. "I told you many times. You just didn't listen. Mr. Lin has experience."

My father angrily grabbed me by the arm and insisted we go elsewhere. I didn't want to spend the time finding another studio. "Just forget about what he said. He's a photographer, not a visa officer."

But there was no changing my father's mind.

Mr. Lin shrugged as he watched us leave. He had no way of knowing he'd poked a hornet's nest.

My father ended up receiving a one-year, multiple-entry visa. He wanted nothing more than to return to Mr. Lin's shop and rub it in his face. "What do the Taiwanese know? Do they think they're better than us? China's in charge now!"

"How do you even know he's Taiwanese?"

"I knew it the second I saw him. He just has that look in his eye, like he just can't accept that us mainlanders have the upper hand."

Lin is one of the most common last names in Taiwan. Perhaps my father was right.

In 2009, I returned to Mr. Lin for a third time. Eva needed a photo to get her Chinese passport renewed. This time, I noticed a large frame on the counter full of sample photos for a variety of purposes. There were photos for Chinese, Hong Kong, and Taiwanese passports, Canadian Maple Cards, Chinese, American, and Canadian visas... It had never occurred to me before that different organizations required different photo sizes. What was the point? Why couldn't governments just come together and standardize their photo specifications?

Six months later, I returned for a photo to renew my son's New Zealand passport. I was glad to point out there wasn't a New Zealand photo in his collection, but Mr. Lin insisted he knew the requirements.

"It's easy to remember," he said confidently. "The dimensions for China and New Zealand are exactly the same."

Good to know.

I had a copy of the specifications on me, but his confidence won me over. I didn't even take them out of my bag.

One month later, my son's application was returned because the photo didn't meet the requirements. We'd gotten the size right, but overlooked that New Zealand required a white background while China allowed either white or light blue.

I rang Mr. Lin and explained the situation. "Can you edit it on your computer to save my son a trip?" I asked. He agreed.

An hour later, I arrived at Mr. Lin's studio. He was sitting behind the counter with a sullen expression on his face. Seeing me enter, he pushed a small envelope across the counter toward me. I could've picked it up and left, but I'd lost a bit of faith in his abilities. Borrowing a ruler, I double checked the dimensions before I headed home.

Checking his work in front of him was probably insulting. With a smile as real as a three-dollar bill, he remarked, "Your son's an easy one to find. That hair of his is a real rat's nest."

My son was never fond of haircuts. We always waited until his hair was unbearably long before I took him to get it cut. I shrugged and walked out.

Everyone has an ego.

One December, Landsdowne Center erected a giant Christmas tree in the indoor courtyard next to the food court. Lao Xin was coming just before Christmas and I'd planned for the whole family to take a picture under the tree. When he arrived, he suffered from severe jet lag, and went to bed around 7pm for days. Finally, he was able to stay awake in the evening and we excitedly went to Landsdowne.

There was a huge line in front of the tree when we arrived. We took our place in the end and waited patiently. I saw Mr. Lin walk out of his studio and look at the crowd with a sour expression. It was a slow season for identification photos. He might've been jealous of the crowd. When he laid eyes on us, a subtle sarcastic grin rippled across his face. I instantly realized there was something wrong, but I couldn't tell what. I was bad at "spot the difference" games. I asked

Lao Xin. He looked around and laughed heartily, "I think tonight is pet night with Santa." It was true. Everyone here was holding a dog or cat.

"Good thing we brought Cheng!" Eva never wasted a chance to tease her little brother.

I suggested we take a portrait at Mr. Lin's instead. It was rare that that we had the chance to get together for a portrait, and it would make Mr. Lin happy. Indeed, he was thrilled, and meticulously designed and composed the shot, all while keeping Cheng entertained. It was the best portrait our family ever took.

In May 2010, after having lived in Canada for 1,095 days, I'd fulfilled my residency requirement for citizenship. Once again, I went to Mr. Lin.

"Citizenship photos, please. Three people." I said, with exaggerated happiness in my voice.

Mr. Lin was stone-faced. It was just another work day for him. He had to have taken this photo thousands of times. But I wanted to share the joy with someone. Outside his shop was one of the mall's central walkways, overflowing with shop patrons. After three years living in Richmond, I couldn't throw a stone without hitting someone I knew, and immediately noticed one of Eva's classmates walking by with her mother.

I waved them, and they stopped to say hello. She didn't ask what we were there for, but I shouted, "We're here taking our citizenship photos!"

"Whoa! Congratulations!"

"Thanks!"

After they had walked away, Eva brought my mood crashing down: "You always talk too much! God!"

"What?" I had no idea what she meant. "What did I say?"

"Don't tell people we're taking citizenship photos."

"Why not?"

"I told my classmates I was born here."

I was stunned. I was going to give Eva a piece of my mind when Mr. Lin waved us behind the black curtain.

"It's normal," he whispered. I didn't quite get what he was saying. He shrugged and picked up his camera.

Once our applications were complete, I approached Eva about what she'd said.

"Why did you tell your friends you were born here?" I asked.

"Is that even a question? It's obviously better to be born here."

"I don't see the difference."

"If you're born here, you get a toonie every time your tooth falls out," she replied with a smirk.

Kids in Canada grow up believing in the tooth fairy. Eva hadn't heard about it until she could understand enough English. In the months before she found out, she'd lost two teeth and gotten nothing.

"How come the tooth fairy never comes to see me?" she whined.

Rather than admitting my knowledge had limits, I came up with a response: "She only does her tally once a year. You'll get your money next time."

A few months later, she lost another tooth, which she wrapped up with care and placed on her nightstand. When she awoke the next morning, she found her tooth exactly where she'd left it and no money in sight. She rushed into the kitchen, package in hand, demanding to know why the tooth fairy had failed to do her job again:

"It's been a year. How come she doesn't have all her numbers figured out yet?"

"Hey, you know how adults are. We're not as fast as you kids. Cut her a little slack," I replied.

Slumping into her chair, Eva pondered for a moment before asking, "Do you think this is discrimination?"

"What? No!" I exclaimed. I was so startled by the question and I spilled milk all over the counter. Pulling myself together, I assured her the tooth fairy had it under control. I guaranteed her she wouldn't forget.

"How can you be so sure?"

I lost my patience. "There's no such thing as the tooth fairy," I confessed. "It's just a story. It's your mother who forgot!"

And just like that, I'd ruined her innocence. Still, I preferred that to letting her think she was being discriminated against by Canadian fairies.

The next morning, Eva awoke to a shiny new loonie (a Canadian dollar coin) placed at her bedside.

"Did she come?" I asked, "or did your mother forget again?"

"I told you it was discrimination!" she said, with a sarcastic smile. "All my Canadian friends get a toonie. How come I only get a loonie?!"

She'd held this grudge for years, apparently. I assured her that coming from a different country didn't make her any less Canadian than her classmates who were born here, but having a mother learning Canadian culture from scratch might be a disadvantage. It finally occurred to me what Mr. Lin meant. He must have seen that kind of conversation all the time, or maybe he had experienced that same alienation.

"I'm proud that I've been able to choose where I live. I think I did a good thing bringing you to Canada," I told her.

"You just proved that being born in China isn't as good as being born here. Otherwise, why would you want to move in the first place?"

"I didn't like how the government ran the country." I said. "Besides, when I was young like you, government propaganda centered on how being born in communist China was the greatest privilege in the world. We were taught to love China unconditionally. When I got older, I realized what they were doing. I brought our family here because I wanted to show myself and the world I had a choice."

She contemplated, looking for a way to twist my words: "So,

you're saying you're a rebel?"

I was surprised. By explaining why we'd moved, I'd inadvertently figured myself out. Just like I'd transferred departments in college, I chose to leave China to rebel against the patriarchy.

"In a way, yes," I answered.

"Then so am I!" She shook my hand as if we'd just become allies.

I figured once we had our citizenship photos taken, we wouldn't have any more need for Mr. Lin. However, 2010 saw a massive influx of people taking the same final step I was. My application had been backlogged by the citizenship office, and a wait that normally took three to six months stretched into seventeen. During that gap, my Chinese passport and Maple Card both expired, requiring multiple visits to Mr. Lin. Each time I heard the click of Mr. Lin's camera, I thought it would be for the last time. But then another last time came.

On September 30, 2011, our citizenship application was finally approved. I was thrilled. Early that morning, we arrived at the Immigration, Refugees and Citizenship Canada offices on Expo Blvd. I was about to take my oath and finally become Canadian. The words that crossed my lips were like the signing of a contract. I swore to respect the laws of the land and the ways of the nation. I swore to be loyal to my new home and to the people who'd welcomed me as one of their own.

After the ceremony, Lao Xin announced he wanted our family to return to China. On the one hand, he needed me back in China to maintain his Canadian PR status; on the other, he didn't like spending so much time away from his children. Eva had spent six years in China, and regardless of her refusal to speak Chinese at home, could still get by. Cheng had left China at the age of three, and could barely speak a word of Chinese. Lao Xin once said he needed a translator just to talk to his son, and it wasn't a joke.

I had no strong desire to go back, but it did make sense. I wanted us to be together as a family. Plus, I never was able to stay in one place for very long.

I had a classmate named Susan. She was good friends with Zhi Hua too. Zhi Hua set out for America in 1990, while Susan headed for Canada the year after. Therefore, I had just one year to hang out with Susan frequently. As fate would have it, my life eventually became even more intertwined with Susan than Zhi Hua.

After I moved to Canada, she came to see me in Richmond and remarked, "Every place you live always feels temporary, like you're going to move again any day now."

Her words came as a shock. I never was one for decorating. I always got no more than the bare essentials at IKEA, which made my home feel more like a guest room in an extended stay hotel. Other people hung pictures, or planted gardens, but that was never me. I wasn't planning on moving anytime soon, but it was true that should the mood strike, I could be packed in an instant.

Before returning to China, I visited Mr. Lin's photo studio twice: one for Canadian passport photos, the other for photos for Chinese visas.

On December 6, 2011, I caught a red-eye to Beijing. Waiting in the foreigners' line at customs, I had truly become a "fake foreign devil." Still, I was amused to find that at least half the people in line were just as yellow as I was.

The next day, I drove to the local Public Security Bureau to report my arrival. Foreigners are obliged to report their address, should they stay anywhere other than designated hotels.

Chapter 22

Three Years of Broken Lotuses

W hen I first arrived back in China, our house was in a state
of disrepair from sitting unoccupied for years. When it came
time to paint, the contractor offered two prices: one for both materials
and labor, the other for just labor. A friend named Cao who managed
a large construction firm told me, "Always buy your own paint. If you
let them provide their own, they'll use the cheapest they can find and
charge you a huge markup."

I took her advice, but when it came to pay, my calculations and
the contractor's weren't even close. I checked and double-checked,
but a look at his ruler solved everything. The notches were far too
close together, making his measurements at least ten percent longer
than they should've been.

I told Cao about it, and she replied:

"I know it's frustrating, but don't blame him. Homeowners only
want the cheapest possible price, so contractors have no choice but to
quote so low they can't even turn a profit. They have to try and get it
back wherever they can."

I asked Cao if I should take the higher quote next time, but she
explained that higher prices wouldn't change the ruler back.

In 2001, historian Wu Si published a book called *Hidden Rules: The*

True Games in China's History. He theorized that China was governed by a series of unwritten rules, which he termed "hidden rules." Though not official, they were tacitly agreed upon by all. Even what I assumed would be a simple remodeling job came with hidden rules. From painting, to windows, to curtains, everything was an endless, maddening game I could never win. If you wanted any work to get done, you had to learn to play the game.

Why did everything have to be so unnecessarily complicated? Was it so wrong to expect an honest day's work for an honest day's pay? The answer lay in the fact that contractors would likely encountered a given homeowner once in their entire lives. Reputation had little place in the world of Chinese home renovation.

In fact, plenty of people in the Chinese business world are honest, but the trust they manage to build is rarely borne of a desire to do the right thing. They only choose to build trust when there is something to be gained. Good or bad, there are always ulterior motives.

Our gated community was built with a shared central heating system. Heating costs were strictly controlled by the city, which based pricing and fuel allotments on the average usage of Beijing residents. But most Beijing residents lived in apartment buildings. There was no way our property management company could heat a community of single houses on the same amount of gas. When they proposed raising heating fees to reflect the reality of the situation, most residents protested, leaving management with no choice but to turn everyone's heat down. As it started getting colder, residents lined up one after another to renegotiate. After the first round, some houses warmed up again, while others were hardly warmer than the air outside.

Only two groups of people got their heat back on: families of government officials or families of women who knew how to raise hell.

I went to register my own complaint, when in stormed an irate woman, Louis Vuitton bag in hand, who marched straight past the entire line and directly into the director's office. She threw his tea in his face and smashed his cup on the floor, screaming:

"It's sixty degrees in my house and you're sitting here drinking tea?! I'm telling you right now: if I don't wake up with my house at least seventy-five degrees tomorrow, I'm coming back and tearing your office apart with my bare hands!"

The director, tea dripping from his forehead, nodded in submission, and bowed as he saw her to the door.

Finally, it was my turn.

"Our house is too cold," I said.

"Put your name on this list," he replied flatly. "We'll send someone around in a few days. Make sure someone's home to let them in."

I wrote my name under the dozens already on the list.

Since our house was under sixty-four degrees, I had to keep electric heaters running nonstop in the rooms we actually inhabited. When I received notice that someone would be coming by the next day, I unplugged all the heaters, so they'd see just how cold the house really was. With all the heaters off, the house turned colder by the minute, eventually becoming unbearable. I attempted to keep writing, and I put on thick, padded clothing and gloves normally reserved for winter fieldwork.

Around noon, the warmest time of day, there came a knock at the door. The engineer took a look around, wrote a couple things in his notebook, then took his leave.

Another two days passed and nothing changed. I went back to speak with the director, and received another cool response:

"We checked it out. Your house is in the outer extremities of the heating network. All the houses out there are just cold. There's nothing we can do."

"That's impossible!"

"Don't believe me? Go to your neighbor Lei's house and see for yourself. Her house is cold too."

"I don't know Lei." I shot back. "Is she the one across from me with the two huge dogs? I'd like to see that house if you can arrange it for me." He pretended not to hear me and flipped through his book, eventually landing on the name of Qian. I was free to go see either the Leis or the Qians anytime I wanted, but I wasn't to bother the owner of the two ferocious dogs.

I didn't need him to tell me who had heat and who didn't. Even a blind man could see what they were up to. By no coincidence, the two families he told me to visit were like mine: simple businessmen and their wives who were devoid of the ability to make threats. There was no doubt that the management company was doling out heat only as they saw fit. The question was how they were even pulling it off. If five homes shared the same gas line, what high technology did they use to make two hot and three freezing? I've been puzzled about it to this day.

Of the hundreds of homes in our community, about half were freezing. In order to heat our houses, we needed additional gas lines installed. Sadly, the result of a resident vote indicated that most residents wanted things to stay as they were. Most of the people who wanted things to change spent a lot of time abroad, and while they participated in online discussions, they couldn't be there when it came to vote.

My son had trumpet lessons every Saturday at a music school hidden inside a cluster of high-rises. Parking spaces were always hard to find. On one such afternoon, we came out from class to find someone had parked directly behind me, blocking me in. All we could do was sit in our car and wait. About a half hour later, the car's owner sauntered over and drove off without even a hint of an apology.

All of a sudden, everyone who'd been sitting in their cars waiting for their kids stuck their heads out of their cars. Windows rolled down, and necks craned out as everyone tried to get a good view.

"What's everyone looking at?" Cheng asked.

"They're hoping for a fight," I explained. "Too bad for them."

If I'd been a lot younger, a lot stronger, and a hell of a lot braver, I would have smacked him into the ground. But as it was, I couldn't even summon two words to hurl at a person who'd trapped me in my car for half an hour. I could feel the crowd's disappointment as I let him drive away.

It was clear that I was somewhat of a misfit in China. Eva was too, but she wasn't quite aware of it, and that worried me. She took the subway to school, and nearly every day she'd come home with horror stories. Every day, it was pickpockets, people spitting on the floor, or people forcing the pregnant and elderly to stand.

I would always tell her, "Just mind your own business."

"What if I call the police?"

"By the time they got there, you'd be beaten to a pulp."

Eva loved nothing more than getting involved in other people's business. That, coupled with her fierce sense of justice was a disaster waiting to happen. I had no choice but to give her a last resort:

"Listen. If something does happen and you have to call the police, make sure you tell them that you're Canadian. In China, if something happens to a foreigner, the police will actually do something."

I'd finally referred to her as Canadian, just like she'd always wanted. I don't know if it was the right thing to tell her, but I'd tell her anything to keep her safe.

Once, she called me to say there'd been an accident. Her bus had collided with a car, but she wasn't hurt. It was the bus driver's fault but he refused to admit it. She happened to see the whole thing and wanted to stay on scene to give a statement. I was relieved she was okay and told her to head home as soon as she could. She didn't listen and hung up. A long while later, she came home dejected. It took more than half an hour for the police to arrive. As soon as an officer did, he yelled at Eva to get out of his way. She explained she was a witness, and the policeman said, "Who asked you to be a witness? Go home. You're only making more trouble."

I told her that Chinese police didn't use witness statements to solve cases. Surveillance cameras were watching every minute.

Whenever things like that happened, I always wondered whether I'd made the right decision in bringing my children back to China. The China I grew up in was being replaced by something very strange. Should I teach them tricks to survive in this society? I didn't want them to get used to living like this, but I didn't want them getting hurt either.

It seems to me that China's cultures of selfishness, materialism and injustice all stem from 1989, but not everyone out there would agree. As time passed, more and more Chinese thought that Deng Xiaoping did the right thing, crushing the uprising with an iron fist. "Look what happened to the Soviet Union," they'd remind me. "After the Soviet Union dissolved, every facet of the region fell into disrepair." "Look at Poland," they'd say. "Sure, the Poles won democracy, but at what cost? Their economy isn't any better off than it was before." When other socialist nations attempted to change, it was true that results had been less than positive. Maybe China didn't have democracy, but at least it had money. What more do we need?

I found myself embroiled in one such debate at some social event or another. Someone had brought up the story of Wang Dan—one of the leaders of the student uprising. He'd recently given a speech at a university in England on China's need for democracy. During his talk, a Chinese exchange student stood up and declared:

"Blah, blah, who cares? Save your breath. Thank god they smashed your so-called movement. Otherwise my dad's business wouldn't have been successful. He'd never have had the money to send me to England. I wouldn't be here right now."

Several in attendance nodded in agreement, while I posited a question, "Why couldn't China have developed its economy if the student democracy movement had won? Where was the logic?"

Someone said, "What's the point of arguing about this? The country is strong and the people are rich. All is good if the end is good."

But I don't think the end is good.

In February 2013, I tried submitting Lao Xin's application to renew his Maple Card. Five months later, we got a letter saying his photos didn't meet the requirements, and we would need to submit another photo. It was far better news than I expected. He only needed to submit a new photo.

I arranged a time with Lao Xin to get his picture taken, and that was that. After yet another four months, another letter came. This time, the size was correct, but they required the back of the picture to bear the official stamp of the photography studio, guaranteeing that the person in the picture was the applicant. There were only a number of studios in Beijing that could do this, and all of them were in Sanlitun, where foreign embassies were clustered. In other words, where Zhao's car was stopped and searched in 1989.

I told Lao Xin that he could simply go to Sanlitun to have his photo taken. He said he would but never did. It seemed that he needed me to arrange it for him and drive him there. He wouldn't waste his brainpower on such trivial things. We lived in Changping, a suburban area about 30 miles from Sanlitun. Since it was the most congested area in Beijing, it might take me two hours to get there, and another two to get back. It simply seemed daunting. Plus, it was my fault this time. I didn't read the instructions carefully enough. Sometimes, I was no better than an ostrich. I'd rather bury my head in the sand than deal with my problem. I never brought up Sanlitun again.

Around Christmas 2013, Lao Xin and I went to Hong Kong. We stayed in a hotel in the Mongkok district. From our window, I noticed a currency exchange shop across the street, and right next to that, a photo studio. The two shops were pretty much exactly the same size. If you've ever seen a Hong Kong currency exchange, you know how crammed they are. But my intuition told me that the Canadian immigration office would surely accept a photo from a Hong Kong studio, despite the size of the business.

After we'd exchanged some money, I dragged Lao Xin straight into next door. He was surprised, but complied. While his photo was being taken, I admired the large frame on the counter. It was just like the one Mr. Lin had, full of sample photos for a wide variety of purposes. Apparently, that photographer offered even more varieties than Mr. Lin did.

Ten minutes later, the owner stamped his official seal on the back of Lao Xin's freshly printed photos. It bore the shop's name, address, phone number, and, most importantly, the words, "I guarantee the true likeness of the person to this photo."

That stamp was the key to everything. This simple, slightly smeared blot of ink spoke volumes about the credibility of a Hong Kong business. In Hong Kong, you could go to any hole-in-the-wall studio, and Citizenship and Immigration Canada was more than happy to recognize the photo's legitimacy. In Beijing, you could only go to appointed places within walking distance from the embassy.

It worked. In April 2014, Lao Xin received a letter instructing him to appear on the 24th of that month at the Vancouver office of Citizenship and Immigration Canada to pick up his new Maple Card. This reason and that always got in the way, and it wasn't until October 20, 2014, that we finally found ourselves cruising over False Creek.

Living in China as a Canadian, I had a choice between two visas: a one-year dual-entry which allowed for a one-hundred eighty-day stay at a time, or a one-year multiple-entry, which was restricted to ninety days per visit. I'd chosen the former for my children. They could exit and re-enter China during school breaks. I got the latter for myself. Who knew when I'd need to head North America? What if one of my screenplays found a buyer, and I had to get to Hollywood to sign a deal?

The ability to come and go as I pleased was nice, but with only ninety days each visit, I found myself being forced to travel to some neighboring country or territory in order to reset the clock. I went anywhere they spoke Chinese. Hong Kong, Macau, Taiwan, Singapore, Malaysia...

I'd longed to go to Japan since I was young, but never once did I go, simply because of the language barrier. Thirty years ago, I might've been thrilled at the prospect of tackling a new language. I'd have memorized the entirety of *300 Key Japanese Phrases* in a month and set out the very next day, but now, I was intimidated. I'd studied English for almost thirty years, but still couldn't hold a conversation. Learning a second language was a never-ending frustration. I wasn't at all the brave resident of a global village I imagined I'd be.

My first book translated into English was released in May 2014, and Simon Fraser University invited me to lecture. It couldn't have come at a better time. My visa was just about up again. As soon as I'd set foot on Canadian soil, I headed straight for Landsdowne Mall and had my photo taken at Mr. Lin's studio. There was probably a photo studio at SFU, but a trip to Mr. Lin's studio would be a new installment to a story. I like stories.

"It's been a while," he said.

"Yeah, I moved back to Beijing."

"Wow," his eyes opened wide. "Does your daughter like it?"

"She's coping well."

"Good for you."

I was moody as I drove to SFU. Mr. Lin's questions had stirred up a number of things I hoped wouldn't surface again, but I only had myself to blame. Why did I go out of my way to see Mr. Lin? Wasn't this episode just what I was looking for?

After my lecture the next day, I headed for the new Chinese Visa Service Center in Vancouver. The new center was bright and spacious, nothing like their old, claustrophobic office above a Staples. There wasn't any need to line up down a back alley in the freezing cold anymore. You simply walked in, took a number, and took a seat. When your number was called, you went to the counter and handed in your paperwork.

I'd filled out all the necessary paperwork before I came, but while I was waiting, I noticed the forms had changed. I grabbed a copy of the new form, and mechanically copied everything from my old one until I reached the line for my occupation. I'd always written "housewife," but that day, I felt a new sense of self-worth. Maybe it was my new book, or I was simply on a high from that day's lecture, but I decided to put down "self-employed."

When my number was called, I handed my paperwork to a mild-mannered woman. She smiled as she pored over my forms. When she got to my occupation, she raised her head and asked, "What do you do for a living exactly? Are you a Painter? Writer? Designer?"

"I'm an author," I replied proudly.

She took on a much more imposing demeanor.

"Please write down which publications you've appeared in, and your pen name."

I had the feeling nothing good could come of this.

Stamping my forms and setting them in a separate pile, she informed me that the rush service I requested wasn't available, since authors' applications took longer to process.

I was leaving on Saturday, and it was already Wednesday. "How long does it usually take?" I asked, no shortage of worry in my voice.

"There's no set time limit," she replied. 'The staff at the service center isn't responsible for any actual decision-making. Our job is just to pass applications along to the consulate." Seeing how panicked I was, she tried to console me as best she could: "It's usually no more than two weeks."

"Two weeks? I'm leaving for China in three days."

She apologized and gave me the consulate's phone number. "Here. Give the consulate a call in a couple days if you don't hear from us."

I'd seen that number before. It was either busy, or wasn't answered at all. I knew exactly what was going to happen. My name would be checked against the China's list of dissident writers. I was positive my name wasn't on it, but simply being an author was enough to place me under additional scrutiny, which took time. They didn't care about my plane ticket. Why had I picked today of all days to get full of myself?

Heading back to my hotel, I immediately went to my blog and Weibo, and started deleting any content that could be remotely construed as critical of the Party.

On Friday, I got a call informing me I could pick up my visa. I was lucky to keep my original itinerary, but for as long as I lived, I'd never call myself an author at a Chinese visa office again.

As we crossed False Creek, I craned my neck to see the water under the bridge. The night before, while researching the route, I learned that False Creek was simply a saltwater inlet flowing backward from the Pacific. I continued my research until I encountered the story of the strayed gray whale.

In recent years, I'd noticed a change in myself. Before, when I revisited a place, it felt smaller. I felt myself taller, stronger and more mature. Now, when I revisited an old place, I felt a strange mix of joy and sadness. I felt joy because I recognized the familiar scenery, but I felt sad because I always picked up things that I'd missed before. The happiness was fleeting, but the sadness was overwhelming and lasted a while. Was it a sign I was getting old? How could I be getting old? I'd never grown up.

I remembered the morning of British Columbia Day in 2009. I'd always loved to listen to the radio while driving, but admittedly, I never paid attention to what was on. Around when I passed 12th street, a song came on that captured my full attention:

*Beautiful, beautiful, British Columbia...*It began.

The melody entranced me. Proud yet unassuming. This music

drew me in like no other had before. I cranked up the volume, and proceeded down an aural journey that I only understood half of the lyrics. There was only one line I was hundred percent sure of. Only one line. It circled around in my head:

Beautiful, beautiful, British Columbia...

Only when I got to school and saw campus was closed, did I realize that day was a holiday. I had to wait till the next day to ask my classmates what the song was. I fumbled through the one line I knew, but they all just shook their heads. "Can you sing more?" someone asked. "I could tell if you could sing more." I couldn't. By then, the melodies had already vanished into thin air. The whole song felt delusional to me, except that one line, lucidly spelled out, and trapped forever in my heart.

Beautiful, beautiful, British Columbia...

There's an old saying in China: "Lotus roots may break, but the fibers remain." When it came to my relationship with the country I was born in, it's just like that broken lotus root. During the three more years I lived there as a Canadian, I felt those fibers stretch so thin they were barely visible. They continued to stretch further and further until finally they snapped under the strain on October 20, 2014. The day, I accompanied Lao Xin to renew his Maple Card. Exiting those doors, I took stock of all that had happened in the years leading up to this moment. All my machinations, all my schemes and plans...I was tired of it.

I needed to get back to Canada, even if just for my children. Even if I was doomed to forever feel a lack of commitment to where I lived, I at least wanted Cheng and Eva to grow up in someplace where they could commit to. I wanted them to grow up to be real and true Canadians. I wanted them to live in a world where there wasn't a need for lies and schemes, where they wouldn't get ripped apart beyond repair.

Epilogue

God Bless China

In 2015, as I packed my bags for the umpteenth time that year, my thoughts again turned to America. Why didn't I just go there? I'd been starting over again and again, but I'd never managed to see my dream come true. What was I waiting for?

In June 2015, I arrived in California with the kids. After enrolling them in summer camps, I went to ask an immigration attorney about my options. He recommended an E2 visa, which allowed Canadians to invest a minimum of $150,000 in America. If all went well, I could get my visa before September, just in time to get Eva and Cheng into public schools.

Anyone in pursuit of an E2 visa first has to establish a company on American soil to serve as a vehicle for investment. When I'd entered the country at Los Angeles Airport, I'd stated to homeland security that the purpose of my trip was tourism. Because of that, registering a company would be a violation of immigration law. Even so, sometimes you gotta do what you gotta do.

Then came the matter of the investment itself. All our money was in a Canadian bank which allowed a maximum of five thousand dollars to be transferred online each day. It'd take over a month to get the investment across. I had to handle it in person, which meant risking leaving America again before I could finally put my application together and go to Canada to apply.

I booked a same-day round-trip ticket from LAX to YVR, leaving at seven in the morning. After my alarm shook me from oblivion at four, I set out in the pitch dark for the airport. Gliding silently through the stillness of the morning, my thoughts began to tumble over one another. I was worried that I'd be barred from returning to America.

They were sure to ask me the purpose of my trip. If I told them I was starting a company, it would only mean more questions. What if they looked at my record and asked why I was starting a company three weeks after entering as a tourist? Calling myself a tourist again wasn't a safe answer either. If I was a tourist, why would I go back to Vancouver in the middle of my vacation for six hours?

I drove on autopilot, lost in thought as the marble glow of dawn rose slowly over Long Beach. The sun's growing light melted together the dark details of the horizon, turning it all into one indistinguishable field. I heard a loud bang from nowhere, and a car came careening across the freeway from my left, and slid upside down in front of me. It felt like a slow motion shot out of an action movie. I instinctively swerved to the left to avoid it. Luckily no one was next to me. I was barely past the capsized car when I heard another impact. I didn't dare look back. My heart was beating out of my chest.

Still somewhere between dream and nightmare, I managed to arrive at LAX in one piece. I glided through check-in and security, then dropped myself on a seat beside the gate before retreating back into my universe of hypothetical troubles. If I was denied entry again, my children would be left to fend for themselves two thousand miles away. I'd have to buy them tickets online and guide them to the airport over the phone. Did they know where their passports were? Did I? Which drawer had I put them in? What if they forgot to lock the door? Who would water the flowers? I began to sink into despair.

It finally occurred to me that I'd barely managed to avoid a car accident. I should be thanking my lucky stars, not worrying about them potentially plotting against me. What was getting stuck in Canada compared to an actual matter of life and death? Why was I incapable of happiness? Gratitude? Of living in the moment?

I started to look back over my perpetual immigration. As soon as New Zealand counted me among its ranks, I started to dream of Canadian shores. Just after I'd taken my oath to the queen, I instantly wished I'd pledged allegiance to the flag of the US instead. Every place that had opened its arms to me had only been met with my indifference. I'd never stopped to appreciate what I had. I only lamented that there was still so much more out there. Let's say I got my E2 and could live in America. What far-flung corner of the earth would I start to pine for then? Would Earth even be enough?

The path to my E2 visa wasn't without its twists and turns, but in the end I finally held it in my own two hands. This time, I felt alarmed at how fickle I could be. I reminded myself over and over to be grateful for what I had, but I was who I was. Joy slipped through my fingers.

It was a cool October day in 2016 when I first noticed a free-floating black circle hovering in my right eye. Terrified, I stood completely still. My eyes darted from right to left to try and shake them off. Every time I looked directly at it, it would disappear. The moment I stopped trying, there it was, like it was teasing me. I called my eye doctor, whose soonest available opening was a week away. My terror must have been audible. The receptionist managed to squeeze me in that afternoon.

Many friends around my age had told me about eye floaters. I'd never had one before, much less the army that had suddenly invaded my field of vision.

My emergency turned out to be nothing of the sort. They may have appeared out of nowhere, but they were still just floaters. There was no cure, and they'd only get worse. All I could do to slow it down was put less strain on my eyes. In other words, spend less time on my computer and cell phone.

I was depressed. I stopped writing altogether and took to pacing back and forth through the house. I found ways of making even the simplest task take as long as possible. I could have taken the clean laundry upstairs in one go, but instead I divided it up into several trips just so it would take longer. One day, as I climbed the stairs and turned the corner, sadness overwhelmed me. I felt I was getting old before I'd grown up.

The pent-up grief within me suddenly broke out. My life had been wasted, and who was to blame? I decided on my grandmother. It was because I'd cut ties with her in such a hurtful way. The Chinese have a saying, "While your parents walk the earth, never disappear over the horizon." My grandmother was just about the only family I had, but she couldn't stand up to her fear of a despotic regime, and kicked me out. It was my disillusion with family bonds that exiled me.

I never really reconciled with my grandmother, and I regret not bidding her a proper farewell. She passed away three months after I left for Oregon in 1997. No matter what transpired between us, in the end she at least deserved a decent goodbye. It's no coincidence that every time I've faced a major decision in my life, her apartment appeared in my dreams. The dream is always the same. I walk out the front door just as the bus is coming, but as hard as I try, I can't ever catch it. I'm stuck running in slow motion. Every time, as the bus approaches Chang'an Street, I awake in a cold sweat.

My grandfather passed away in 1997 too. I like to think that if they had lived ten more years, I would have been able to help them in some way. I could have gotten them professional help. I imagined my grandfather's small victories with a speech therapist, while my grandmother tearfully grieved to a counselor about being dumped on someone's doorstep. Seeing it play out in my mind, my smile would rise to a chuckle, then a full-on laugh. But that wasn't real life. That only happens in movies.

Maybe we weren't so different, my grandmother and I. We're all prisoners of experience, but when time came to break out, I had at least one more tool than she had. When the time comes to write about my life, I'll have hundreds of thousands of words to say.

I couldn't wait for even another minute. I had to put my memories on paper. This would be the only difference I could make. I'd wanted to write this book for years, but I had been procrastinating. I always thought I had tomorrow.

After my grandmother burned the documents Lian had entrusted to me, I avoided him. I was afraid he'd ask for them back. I later heard that the newspaper he worked for had sent him to its Hong Kong branch. I was relieved. The next time we saw one another was well after 2000. Lian had been promoted to a leadership role at his news agency. When he went back to Beijing for business, he organized a reunion. I assumed he'd forgotten about the documents, or he assumed that I'd thrown them away in one of my many moves. I went to the reunion, and he didn't say a single word about the documents.

Years later, not long after New Year's 2017, I got a call from Lian. He'd become one of China's most successful movie producers. He told me he'd be visiting America with his family for Chinese New Year, and that they'd be stopping at Stanford. He asked if I wanted to get together there. Of course I wanted to. Zhi Hua taught at Stanford and I hadn't seen her in 10 years.

I booked a ticket from John Wayne Airport to San Jose. As I played with my phone in the departure hall, it suddenly occurred to me how funny it was: We three graduates from Peking University had to reunite in America. Then I thought of where my other friends had ended up: America, Canada, Australia, Europe...you name it. Almost everyone I knew in China who had made something of themselves had left the country.

From time to time, as I worked on this book, I pondered the aftermath of Tiananmen Protests. I believe they triggered the fall of Soviet-led communism throughout Europe in 1989, and at the time, it was widely believed that the Chinese Communist Party's fall was just around the corner. Still, the moment has yet to come. Instead, China's economy is thriving and its booming economy has strengthened the legitimacy of one-party rule. Modern political theory dictates that as a country's economy develops and its middle class grows, democracy develops alongside. But so far, that theory has proven invalid in China.

A question has come to me again and again: Why hasn't democracy happened in China despite its thriving economy? Waiting to board my plane, I had an epiphany. It must have something to do with people leaving the country. Leaving meant giving up on changing it entirely. All the political theory I'd read had left out emigration.

Fang Lizhi wrote in "China's Despair and China's Hope" (translated by Perry Link and published in the *New York Book Reviews*) that "as democratic consciousness spreads, it is bound to form pressure groups that will have ever greater power to weigh against the authority of the leadership." I also thought of Xiaoxia Gong's testimony at a US Senate meeting in June, 1990 when she claimed that "private entrepreneurs are the most ardent supporters of freedom and democracy."

It turned out we hadn't formed pressure groups, nor fought for freedom and democracy. After the Tiananmen Massacre, no one has the guts to protest anymore. Pressure groups will never emerge. Moreover, people will never be bound together by sympathy like they once were. The Chinese will always be a huge heap of loose sand. This is the most terrible consequence of the Tiananmen Massacre, and why we left China in the pursuit of happiness. But the more people leave China, the more hopeless China becomes. A familiar guilt swept over me. It had lived in the deepest recesses of my heart since 1989.

Toward the end of 2018, a scandal surrounding Meng Wanzhou, CFO of Huawei, established a new link between China, Canada and the United States. On December 1, 2018, Meng was detained by law enforcement on behalf of the United States as she was changing flights in Vancouver.

While Meng was facing extradition to the United States, China took retaliatory action. Two Canadians were arrested, including a former diplomat. One Canadian who had already been sentenced to 15 years on drug trafficking charges was hauled back to court for a retrial and has given the death penalty.

Since we moved to California in 2015, the three of us visited China at least once a year and stayed about ten days each time. We'd already bought plane tickets to visit Lao Xin in China over winter break. Because of the Meng Wanzhou incident, Eva was worried for our safety.

"Don't be afraid," I said jokingly. "Even if the Chinese government takes revenge on Canadians, they'll only target Caucasians. In the eyes of the Chinese government, only Caucasians are true foreigners."

Eva was furious and criticized me severely, "Isn't you who told me that coming from a different country didn't make me any less Canadian?"

She forced me to note my uncertainty of my identity. Although I'm proud to be Canadian, there's always a part of me that feels like a "fake foreign devil."

Since the start of the trade war between China and the United States, I've had a feeling that a time had come when Chinese people living in Western countries had to choose sides. In the past, I was content to break away from China in terms of citizenship alone, but now it seems this might not be enough.

Coming from China means that we need to do more simply because of the baggage on our backs. If we want to establish that Chinese people are not the same as China's fascist regime, we need to fight for China to become a country that accepts universal human values. Telling my truth of what happened 30 years ago is part of this effort.

As this story comes to a close, I am reminded of Michael Chang's words at the 1989 French Open.

God bless each and every one of you, especially China.

ACKNOWLEDGEMENTS

I'd first like to thank Brock Van Wey: a musician who has been living and working in China for over 15 years. He translated this book's Chinese songs, rhymes, and sayings to English as well as "L'Internationale" from French. His English interpretations of Cui Jian are the best I've ever known.

I'm grateful to Paul Christian, who has elevated my written English to new heights. Without his work, I couldn't let my writing face the light of day.

Many thanks to Tom Jenks, who suggested I edit out half of my original manuscript. The suggestion almost crushed me, but forced the book into a far better shape.

I'd also like to thank the photographer Yanguang He, who generously gave permission to reprint photos he took at the Tiananmen Square in 1989.

This memoir is deeply indebted to two books: *Standoff at Tiananmen* by Eddie Cheng, and Dingxin Zhao's *The Power of Tiananmen: State-Society Relations and the 1989 Beijing Student Movement*. Throughout writing this book, I turned to these countless times for dates and facts.

Last but not least, I'd like to give thanks to the people who fought the impossible fight depicted in this book. My gratitude is beyond words.

CPSIA information can be obtained
at www.ICGtesting.com
Printed in the USA
LVHW041949040719
623148LV00005B/69/P